Terrorism and
the Constitution

TERRORISM AND THE CONSTITUTION

SACRIFICING CIVIL LIBERTIES
IN THE NAME OF NATIONAL SECURITY

DAVID COLE

JAMES X. DEMPSEY

FOREWORD BY
CAROLE GOLDBERG

The New Press
New York

Originally published by The First Amendment Foundation, 2002
This edition published by The New Press, New York, 2002
Distributed by W. W. Norton & Company, Inc., New York

The authors gratefully thank Lynne M. Baum, Erin Corcoran, John J.
Donoghue, and Daniel Williams for invaluable research assistance.

ISBN 1-56584-782-2 (pbk.)
CIP data available.

The New Press was established in 1990 as a not-for-profit alternative
to the large, commercial publishing houses currently dominating the
book publishing industry. The New Press operates in the public interest
rather than for private gain, and is committed to publishing, in innovative
ways, works of educational, cultural, and community value that are often
deemed insufficiently profitable.

The New Press, 450 West 41st Street, 6th floor, New York, NY 10036
www.thenewpress.com

Printed in the United States of America

2 4 6 8 10 9 7 5 3 1

To Don Edwards,

for his lifetime commitment to the First Amendment, from his
leading role in the successful campaign to abolish the House
Unamerican Activities Committee to his still-unfulfilled effort to
enact a law prohibiting the FBI from undertaking investigations
infringing on the First Amendment. As longtime chairman
of the Civil and Constitutional Rights Subcommittee of the House
Judiciary Committee, Don Edwards cheerfully and tirelessly
pursued a principled and consistent oversight of the FBI.
His vision was simple and enduring: that domestic tranquility
can be secured without sacrificing the blessings of liberty.

Contents

Part I: Investigating First Amendment Activities: The FBI's Recent History

Part II: Control vs. Discretion: The Limits of Legal Restrictions on the FBI's Authority

Part III: The 1996 and 2001 Antiterrorism Acts: Curtailing Civil Liberties in the Name of Fighting Terrorism

PREFACE
TO THE SECOND EDITION

The terrorist attacks of September 11, 2001 marked a quantum leap in the deadliness and audacity of terror. They revealed a vulnerability that many in the United States had never before appreciated. And they have sparked a fundamental debate about the tension between liberty and security in the United States, and in particular about the capability of our government to keep us secure within the confines of due process, respect for freedoms of speech and association, and a system of government powers subject to checks and balances. This second edition, like the first, addresses these questions, and provides important historical perspective on the dangers that may lie ahead if we afford the government unchecked power at a time when we all understandably feel the need for more security.

The first edition of this book did not foresee the devastating scope of the attacks of September 11, but then neither did anyone else. However, in the first edition, we correctly predicted that there would be additional terrorist attacks against the United States and against U.S. interests abroad. We also correctly warned that the federal anti-terrorism effort was flawed and ill-suited to meet the terrorist threat. We repeat those warnings today and express our concern that the latest governmental reaction to terrorism is misguided not merely because it sacrifices civil liberties but also because it does so with little consideration of what went wrong in the days and months before September 11 and little regard to whether the changes will be effective. In a rerun of the approach that produced the ineffective 1996 Anti-Terrorism Act, we fear that policy-makers are latching onto approaches that will prove no more effective and just as regrettable from a civil liberties perspective.

By their very scale, the events of September 11 require all of us to reassess what is thinkable and unthinkable. The ensuing anthrax scare has made very real what previously appeared to be a relatively hypothetical threat of biological terrorism. And the fact that U.S. authorities failed to detect the September 11 attack in advance, despite its scope and scale, mandates comprehensive reconsideration of our intelligence capabilities and powers.

Nonetheless, the fundamental principles that ought to govern the response of a democratic society to terrorism remain the same — we should focus on perpetrators of crime, avoid indulging in guilt by association, maintain procedures designed to identify the guilty and exonerate the innocent, insist on legal limits on surveillance authorities, and bar political spying. The first edition foresaw and discussed all of these issues, and illustrated its points with specific historical examples. These issues are all the more pressing in the wake of September 11, and the history all the more important to keep in mind. If we are to learn from our mistakes, we must not lose sight of how we have gone astray in the past.

This second edition includes a new chapter, immediately before the Conclusion, that addresses the aftermath of the September 11 attacks, and focuses particularly on the anti-terrorism measures adopted in the wake of the attacks. Some of the new anti-terrorism powers given to government are justified. Some pose no threat to civil liberties. But many measures are unnecessary, unconstitutional, and may well prove counterproductive in the fight against terrorism.

We hope that our book offers some contribution to the ongoing struggle to preserve liberty while providing security.

David Cole
James X. Dempsey
Kit Gage

December 2001

FOREWORD
TO THE FIRST EDITION

Mounting a political campaign to curb investigative excesses of the FBI and other federal intelligence-gathering agencies is a steep, uphill battle. Powerful law enforcement institutions will vigorously resist any challenge to their control over dissenters; and they will claim that they must be free from constraints in order to protect the public from terrorists, militants, and other threatening elements.

Beginning in 1975, however, the National Committee Against Repressive Legislation (NCARL), with the help of law professors from across the nation, mounted a strong — and partly successful — effort to restrain federal investigative abuses that threaten First Amendment rights. The legacy of that political mobilization campaign is greater public awareness of the dangers of FBI overreaching, greater determination to protect unpopular groups from such treatment, and an effective coalition of concerned organizations. Jim Dempsey and David Cole have contributed to that legacy in the following forceful account of FBI assaults on First Amendment rights. My aim in this foreword is to highlight the contributions of those individuals and organizations who brought us to this point.

My story begins with the late Tom Emerson, who was Lines Professor of Law at Yale Law School, a distinguished scholar in the field of Constitutional Law, and longtime Advisor on Constitutional Law to NCARL. Professor Emerson had been a courageous defender of free speech during the anti-Communist hysteria of the 1950s, and that experience had taught him the importance of restraining government's investigative powers. The dangers of unchecked government power were underscored during the Watergate scandal, as the Senate's Church Committee exposed shameful patterns of FBI harassment of political enemies and government opponents. With the public expressing outrage over this conduct, Emerson and NCARL began in 1975 to issue calls for legislative controls on the FBI and other federal intelligence-gathering agencies. Remarkably, there has never been any federal statutory scheme that defines the scope and limits of FBI powers.

Four years later, the Justice Department developed and introduced, through Senator Edward Kennedy, a charter designed to supply a framework for both permissible and prohibited FBI activities. Professor Emerson, testifying on behalf of NCARL before the Senate Judiciary Committee, affirmed that "In a democratic society we must make certain that the mechanisms of law enforcement do not operate to suppress social change." Measured against this objective, the proposed FBI charter fell far short; and Professor Emerson demonstrated, in incisive detail, that the proposed charter allowed so many abuses to recur that it would be worse than nothing at all.

When the 1979 charter proposal eventually failed to be enacted, NCARL embarked on a more affirmative initiative, to gather support for alternate legislation reflecting the democratic principles that Professor Emerson had espoused in his testimony and in his scholarly writing. Those principles were:

- The FBI must be confined to the collection, analysis, and proper dissemination of information. It should not engage in disruptive action or covert action.

- In performing its function of gathering information, the FBI should be confined to the collection of information that has a direct and immediate relation to a violation of a federal criminal law.

- The improper practices of which the FBI has been guilty in the past should be carefully defined and specifically prohibited.

- The more intrusive techniques utilized by the FBI should be subject to judicial supervision through a warrant procedure.

- The collection of foreign intelligence within the borders of the U.S. and with respect to American citizens abroad should be subject to the same safeguards as the collection of domestic intelligence.

- Adequate controls to enforce legislation governing the FBI require measures which will provide accountability, internal oversight, and external oversight.

Drawing upon these principles, NCARL began its legislative initiative in earnest in 1985. For guidance in structuring the campaign, we turned to an earlier NCARL organizing success — the 1964 project to abolish the House Unamerican Activities Committee (HUAC). The foundation for that achievement had been a statement of principles by constitutional authorities that explained why HUAC's continued existence conflicted with fundamental American values. This statement had been circulated broadly among a variety of academic, labor, civil liberties, civil rights, and religious groups for endorsement. NCARL's Executive Director Frank Wilkinson, himself a victim of HUAC's inquiries, unearthed the letters, petitions, and statements that had been prepared in 1964 by civil liberties pioneers such as Alexander Mieklejohn and James Imbrie, and provided them to me and NCARL's two other Constitutional Law Advisors — Professor Emerson and Harvard's Vern Countryman, then Royal Professor of Law Emeritus. With the anti-HUAC model and Professor Emerson's testimony for guidance, we wrote a petition to Congress urging the enactment of an FBI charter. Without drafting the language of such a bill, we indicated the reasons why it should be enacted and the general form it should take. Our ultimate purpose was two-fold: to secure agreement, among leading individuals and organizations concerned about limits on the FBI, on a single, concrete program of action; and to garner increased public support for an FBI charter.

In November, 1987, we circulated this draft to a small number of recognized constitutional law authorities, seeking their feedback, suggested changes, and willingness to join a group of original signers. By March, 1988, we had thirteen original signers in addition to the three NCARL Advisors: Professors Anthony Amsterdam, C. Edwin Baker, Derrick Bell, Martha Field, Charles Lawrence, Howard Lesnick, Gerald Lopez, Martha Minow, Eleanor Holmes Norton, Christopher Schroeder, Steven Shiffrin, Aviam Soifer, and Clyde Summers. Soon thereafter, we assembled a list of 215 professors of public law across the United States, and the group of original signers solicited their endorsement of the petition campaign. An impressive group of 88 Constitutional Law scholars responded favorably to this appeal and provided their input. So in September, 1988, NCARL began circulating the petition, with these accompanying endorsements, to law professors across the nation and across all fields of legal study. By the end of this process, an astounding total of 590 law professors from 147 law schools, including deans from 20 of these law schools, joined in NCARL's petition. It was an impressive and unprecedented show of support from the legal academic community. [The petition and list of signing law professors are reprinted in the Appendix.]

The law professors' endorsement of an FBI charter gave NCARL's campaign tremendous momentum and credibility with other organizations. Soon thousands of other signers, from the Organization of American Historians, the writers' organization PEN, the American Library Association, unions, and civil rights and civil liberties organizations had been added to the petition. In all, more than 10,000 people affiliated themselves with this campaign.

Beginning in 1988, the impact of this political movement began to be felt in the Congress, as members Don Edwards (D-CA) and John Conyers (D-MI) introduced legislation known as the FBI First

Amendment Protection Act that incorporated many of the ideas advanced in the NCARL petition. In turn, the petition was used as a vehicle to mobilize local and regional support for the Edwards/Conyers bill and related legislation. Although more than 50 co-sponsors of this legislation eventually came forward, only one portion of the bill was enacted into law, and even that language was repealed shortly thereafter. It was a small and temporary legislative victory against overwhelming odds, and possible only because of the massive show of law professors' support, as well as the subsequent endorsements from so many others.

The success of a political organizing effort can be measured in several different ways. One obvious criterion is the achievement of a political goal, such as enactment of specific legislation. But other criteria also matter, such as the impact on public awareness, inspiring individuals to a politically active role, and establishment of organizational alliances. By these latter measures, the law professors' petition which NCARL orchestrated is a lasting accomplishment. As revelations of FBI abuses continue, the principles it stands for and the coalitions it built will become ever more important. *

Carole Goldberg
Professor of Law, University of California at Los Angeles
Constitutional Law Advisor, NCARL
Secretary, First Amendment Foundation

---

* *In 1997, NCARL helped found the National Coalition to Protect Political Freedom, 3321 12th Street NE., Washington, D.C. 20017, (202) 529-4225. NCARL'S longtime Washington representative and new Executive Director, Kit Gage, coordinates legal challenges against the provisions of the Antiterrorism Act on behalf of the coalition and played a key role in bringing this book to fruition.*

CHAPTER 1

INTRODUCTION

Terrorism presents a special challenge to a democratic society: how to prevent and punish ideologically-motivated violence without infringing on political freedoms and civil liberties.

Nothing presents that challenge more urgently and sharply than the terrorist attacks of September 11. There can be no doubt that terrorism is a serious problem. The United States and its citizens are the targets of dangerous groups and individuals at home and abroad. Government agencies must have the legal authorities and resources sufficient to prevent terrorism when possible and to prosecute it when it occurs. In responding to terrorism, however, we must adhere to the principles of political freedom, due process, and the protections of privacy that constitute the core of a free and democratic society.

The record of our nation's response to the threat of political violence is unfortunately one of repeated infringements on the First Amendment and other constitutional principles. As the Supreme Court itself has acknowledged, "History abundantly documents the tendency of Government — however benevolent and benign its motives — to view with suspicion those who most fervently dispute its policies."[1] This is by no means a problem unique to the United States, but unfortunately our constitutional commitment to political and religious freedom has not protected us from recurring official abuses. With confounding regularity, our government has, in the name of protecting national security, subverted the very rights and liberties "which make the defense of the Nation worthwhile."[2]

The Federal Bureau of Investigation, our nation's premier law enforcement agency, has the central role in fighting terrorism at home.[3] It brings to this task impressive resources, significant legal powers, and a jurisdiction that even extends overseas. In recent years, the Bureau has penetrated and prosecuted a bewildering array of organized criminal groups. It has pursued public corruption at all levels of local, state and federal government, while demonstrating a resistance to the kinds of corruption that have sometimes plagued police forces at the municipal level or in other countries. It has successfully investigated terrorist acts at home and abroad.

Yet this same FBI has throughout its history all too often violated First Amendment rights of freedom of speech and association. In the name of national security, it has undertaken the disruption and "neutralization" of peaceful protest. It has devoted resources to monitoring political activity rather than focusing on the investigation of criminal conduct. It has relied on sweeping theories of guilt by association rather than undertaking the harder but more productive work of identifying those individuals who are planning violent activity. It has resisted public accountability and limits on its discretion.

In the wake of the first bombing of the World Trade Center in 1993, and the bombing of the federal building in Oklahoma in 1995, Congress enacted the Antiterrorism Act of 1996,[4] one of the worst assaults on the Constitution in decades. It resurrected guilt by association as a principle of criminal and immigration law. It created a special court to use secret evidence to deport foreigners labeled as "terrorists." It made support for the peaceful humanitarian and political activities of selected foreign groups a crime. And it repealed a short-lived law forbidding the FBI from investigating First Amendment activities, opening the door once again to politically focused FBI investigations.

The 1996 Act never yielded any significant protection against terrorism, although it did lead to substantial incursions on constitutional rights. The Immigration and Naturalization Service took the Act as a green light to violate a fundamental principle of due process: that everyone has the right to confront his or her accusers. In dozens of cases after the 1996 Act passed, using procedures not directly authorized by the Act but sharing its hostility to fundamental due process, the government detained and sought to deport noncitizens (almost all of them Muslims) on the basis of secret evidence regarding their political affiliations with "terrorist organizations." After years of litigation, it became apparent that those the government sought to deport were not dangerous terrorists. In case after case, the INS was forced to release aliens when its charges against them were revealed to be nothing more than guilt by association. None of the 19 men who participated in the attacks of September 11 were among those, or had any connection with those, targeted by the government for deportation based on secret evidence. In addition, under the 1996 Act, the State Department published a politically selective list of "foreign terrorist organizations" to which it became a crime to give even humanitarian assistance of food and educational supplies, chilling political support but again yielding no impact on violent activity. Measures aimed at terrorism struck only the Constitution.

Civil liberties suffered a second blow in February 1999 when the Supreme Court ruled that immigrants selectively singled out for deportation in retaliation for their mere association with a "terrorist organization" have no right to challenge their deportations on First Amendment grounds.[5] The Court ruled both that Congress had cut off all access to courts for such claims in a 1996 immigration law, and that in any event aliens have no constitutional right to object to being targeted for deportation based on activities that would clearly be protected by the First

Amendment if engaged in by United States citizens. In effect, the Court put immigrants on notice that if they engage in political activity of which the government disapproves, they are vulnerable to selective retaliatory enforcement of the immigration laws.

And now, in the stunned aftermath of the September 11, 2001 atrocities, the nation is in deeper crisis than it has been in many decades. Once again, we are faced with undocumented claims that surrendering liberty will purchase security. Weekly, we see new measures proposed that run counter to fundamental constitutional principles: military tribunals, alien detentions, invasions of the attorney-client relationship, increased secrecy. And in the PATRIOT legislation adopted in October 2001, Congress expanded government surveillance powers, changed the domestic posture of the Central Intelligence Agency, and broadened the discretion of the executive branch to detain aliens indefinitely based on their associations and beliefs, rather than their acts.

The purpose of this book is to examine the civil liberties issues raised by government responses to terrorism, and to identify what is necessary to ensure that counterterrorism activities (especially of the FBI) are reliably consistent with the Constitution. The book seeks to place the terrorism problem in historical context by reviewing the FBI's persistent infringements on the First Amendment and its avoidance of meaningful controls on its discretion. Part I recounts several recent instances where FBI "counterterrorism" investigations consisted largely of monitoring First Amendment activity. These cases all arose after the reforms of the Watergate era, which were supposed to have reined in the FBI in response to earlier abuses. Part II outlines the legal framework that has permitted such intrusive investigations. Informed by this background, Part III examines the Antiterrorism Act of 1996, the PATRIOT Act of 2001, and emerging evidence of recent abuses. Finally, the conclusion proposes an alternative approach to fighting terrorism that is likely to be both more effective and more consistent with the Constitution than the path the government has taken.

FOUR STORIES

To understand the recurring nature of the government's misguided response to political threats, we start with four stories:

The Fifties: McCarthyism

In August 1952, Frank Wilkinson was testifying on behalf of the Los Angeles Housing Authority as an expert witness in an eminent domain hearing against slum property in the Chavez Ravine area.[6] The Housing Authority wanted to clear the slum to build public housing. Wilkinson had been on the Housing Authority staff for ten years, campaigning for the racial integration of public housing. His support for social justice had long since brought him to the attention of the FBI, which had secretly begun an investigation in an attempt to link him to the Communist Party. As Wilkinson finished his testimony at the condemnation hearing, he was asked on cross examination, "Mr. Wilkinson, will you now tell us of all the organizations, political or otherwise, with which you have associated?" In those times, the mere posing of the question carried an implied accusation that one was a Communist.

Wilkinson refused to answer the question, launching a public odyssey that included a trip to federal prison and a lifetime of defending the First Amendment. His insistence upon his constitutional rights made headlines the next day in the Los Angeles Times. The eminent domain court disqualified him as an expert and struck his testimony from the record. The Los Angeles City Council called upon the House Un-American Activities Committee to investigate the Housing Authority. The California Senate subpoenaed both Wilkinson and his wife, a high school teacher. When they refused to answer questions regarding their political affiliations, they were both fired from their jobs.

Wilkinson went on to organize community and legal efforts to defend the Constitution, helping to found what is today the National Committee Against Repressive Legislation (NCARL). The FBI continued to investigate, harass and disrupt his First Amendment activities. In July 1958, Congress subpoenaed Wilkinson and again asked about his political associations. He again refused to answer, invoking his First

Amendment rights. With Carl Braden, the civil rights activist, he was cited for contempt and convicted in federal court. He appealed all the way to the Supreme Court, where he lost by a vote of five to four.[7] In 1961, he served nine months in prison. When he came out, the FBI stepped up its neutralization campaign, as field offices were invited to interfere with his speaking engagements through "disruptive tactics." In all, Wilkinson was under surveillance for thirty-eight years. The FBI generated 130,000 pages of detailed reports on him and his friends at a cost of several million dollars. At the end of it all, the FBI concluded that Wilkinson and the group he founded to fight for the First Amendment had engaged in no illegal activities.

The Sixties and Seventies: COINTELPRO

On April 22, 1970, thousands of people gathered on Washington D.C.'s mall to celebrate the first Earth Day. Rallies in cities across the nation brought the total to twenty million Americans participating in what has been described as the "birth of the modern environmental movement."[8] The FBI was there. Headquarters had ordered agents in at least forty cities to spy on Earth Day events. Their reports identified groups and individuals associated with planning the event. They attempted "to link the environmental activists with organizations the bureau [had] already targeted for surveillance, infiltration, and disruption."[9] In Denver, the FBI's surveillance team recorded the remarks of Senator Gaylord Nelson. In Washington, D.C., agents carefully wrote down the slogans on signs carried by marchers and summarized each of the speeches, noting, for example, that Phil Ochs "made a few anti-war, anti-administration remarks."[10]

The Earth Day surveillance was part of a massive FBI program known as COINTELPRO, a set of secret investigations and disruptive actions against political activism across a wide range of issues. A special Senate committee chaired by Idaho Democrat Frank Church (the "Church Committee") in 1975 and 1976 found that the FBI had conducted a wide-ranging campaign of monitoring and disrupting political groups that were not engaged in illegal conduct.[11] At the peak of its efforts, the FBI was investigating all major protest movements, from civil rights activists to Vietnam war protesters to women's liberation advocates. Standard FBI methodology included bugging of homes and offices, wiretapping, break-ins, and informants. In addition, the FBI sought to spread misinformation, foment internal dissension, and even provoke illegal activity. The effort consumed tremendous resources and sowed distrust and fear among many seeking peaceful change in government policies, but it produced little evidence of criminal conduct.[12]

The Eighties: Central American activists

"Please call me about Nicaragua. This will be a friendly chat." A New York law student returning home one day in 1985 found that message written on an FBI business card left at her door. The student had never been to Nicaragua, but had recently attended a meeting about the Nicaraguan conflict at City University. As public opposition to U.S. intervention in Central America mounted in the early 1980s, many others also received visits from the FBI. Daisy Cubias, who worked with the Ecumenical Refugee Council in Milwaukee, was visited once at her job and twice at home by FBI agents who asked her about members of a coalition to which she belonged that opposed U.S. policy in Central America. A Santa Cruz man was called by the FBI after returning from a trip to Nicaragua; when the man declined to meet for an interview, the agent commented that he "sounded guilty." One FBI agent seeking to interview a Detroit woman explained, "We try to interview everyone who makes a trip to Nicaragua. We do it for positive intelligence gathering."[13]

FBI agents tried three times to contact Jill Clark, a member of the New Orleans chapter of the Committee in Solidarity with the People of El Salvador (CISPES). Questioned about the visits at a 1985 hearing, FBI Director William Webster defended the visits and testified, "We are not keeping track of the membership of CISPES as such."[14] Three years later, however, the Center for Constitutional Rights, a public interest legal organization in New York City, released thousands of pages of documents obtained under the Freedom of Information Act, showing that the

FBI had conducted a nationwide investigation of CISPES and other domestic groups whose only common feature was that they opposed American assistance to the military of El Salvador. The documents showed that, contrary to Webster's assurance, some FBI field offices in fact did undertake to identify CISPES members "as such." In the name of investigating "support for terrorism," agents monitored campus meetings, photographed peaceful rallies, checked license plate numbers in church parking lots, sent an informant into CISPES offices to copy or steal records, and questioned activists at home and at work. While the investigative efforts were nominally focused on CISPES, they ultimately collected information on the political activities of 1,330 groups opposed to U.S. policy in Central America.[15] Throughout, the FBI gave little attention to uncovering criminal conduct, and never found any evidence of terrorism or support of terrorism.

The Nineties: Palestinians and Muslims

Khader Musa Hamide immigrated to the United States in 1971. He earned a bachelor's degree in psychology and an MBA. He also became active in the Palestinian community. He distributed copies of a newspaper published by the Popular Front for the Liberation of Palestine (PFLP). The PFLP, the second-largest faction within the umbrella Palestine Liberation Organization, had engaged in violent activities in the Middle East, but it was also engaged in a wide range of lawful activities, including the provision of education, day care, health care and social security, as well as cultural activities, publications and political organizing. Hamide participated in demonstrations advocating Palestinian self-determination and helped organize large public dinners which featured political speeches, cultural performances, and humanitarian aid fundraising attended by hundreds of Palestinians and Arab-Americans.

In 1984, Hamide's activities brought him to the attention of the FBI. He and others in the Los Angeles area suspected of being PFLP members became the subject of an intensive FBI investigation. An undercover FBI agent moved into the apartment next door to Hamide for nine months. With the assistance of local police officers, the FBI documented in detail Hamide's participation in political demonstrations, his distribution of literature, and his speeches at public events. It painstakingly (but not very accurately) translated hundreds of pages of Arabic language newsletters. Yet the FBI made no attempt to follow the trail of the money allegedly collected by Hamide and the others to determine whether it supported lawful or violent activities. Once the FBI had characterized the PFLP as a terrorist organization, it did not matter to its investigation that Hamide and his friends were engaged in entirely lawful and peaceful protest activity.

After three years of investigation, the FBI found no evidence of criminal activity by Hamide or other alleged PFLP members in Los Angeles. But rather than close its investigation and move on, the FBI asked the Immigration and Naturalization Service (INS) to deport Hamide and several others in order to "disrupt" their political activities and hamper the PFLP. In 1987, shortly after Hamide applied for U.S. citizenship, FBI and INS agents arrested him and his Kenyan-born wife and six others and sought to deport them immediately. The government, invoking long-unused provisions of the McCarran-Walter Act, charged them with being deportable for being associated with a group that advocated "world communism." In a chilling preview of what was to come in other cases, the INS sought to detain the "Los Angeles Eight" on the basis of secret evidence, but an immigration judge refused to go along, and released them. Federal courts blocked the deportations, characterizing the government's case as based on "guilt by association," but the Justice Department appealed to the Supreme Court, which ruled that aliens can be singled out for deportation based on their legal, political activities.[16]

THE LIMITS OF POST-WATERGATE REFORMS

These stories span nearly five decades, revealing a troubling pattern of FBI surveillance and "disruption" of legitimate political activity. After the Church Committee in 1975 and 1976 documented the FBI's illegal and harassing tactics, public and Congressional outrage spawned a series of reforms intended to prevent political spying and harassment. The reforms were significant, but, as the CISPES and LA 8 cases illustrate, the changes were by no means as deep or as permanent as many had believed. While FBI officials tried to dismiss the CISPES case as an aberration, they refused to admit any overreaching in the LA 8 case, and the Supreme Court effectively endorsed the government's tactics. It is clear that a focus on political activity and reliance on guilt by association have been enduring elements of the FBI's approach to its national security and counterterrorism missions.

The FBI, the Justice Department to which it reports, and the government as a whole still have not accepted or implemented a concept of "intelligence" that fully respects political freedoms. Consequently, through the 1980s and 1990s, the FBI continued to undertake investigations that, while lacking the extreme tactics of COINTELPRO, shared the philosophy and approach of the counterintelligence investigations condemned by the Church Committee. Arab-American community leaders, Palestinian students, Amnesty International members, and environmental activists were among the subjects of FBI counterintelligence or antiterrorism investigations in the last two decades whose focus on political activity recalled the abuses of the past.

The adoption of the Antiterrorism Act of 1996 showed how little had been learned from the abuses of the past and how alluring remained the concept of unrestrained intelligence investigations focused on political ideology. The Act's explicit criminalization of support for peaceful activity effectively authorized FBI surveillance and infiltration of political, religious and ethnic groups engaged in peaceful humanitarian and political work. Its repeal of a prohibition against using First Amendment activities as the sole basis for an investigation further encouraged politically motivated investigations. Its reintroduction of guilt by association into the immigration laws allowed the exclusion and deportation of immigrants and foreign visitors not for what they have done but for the causes and groups with which they have associated. And the endorsement of secret evidence in immigration proceedings against alleged "terrorists" denied the most fundamental of rights — the right to defend oneself by confronting one's accusers.

The 1996 Act's provisions, it must be concluded, have had little direct impact, either positive or negative, on the fight against terrorism. The support for terrorism provisions have thus far resulted in only three prosecutions. The "Alien Terrorist Removal Court" was never used — in part because the Justice Department claimed authority outside the Act for using secret evidence in deportation proceedings with even fewer due process protections. The government carried out a number of successful prosecutions of terrorists, including of members of the al Qaeda network, but did so without relying on the 1996 Act authorities And the FBI continued to resist outside checks on its discretion, instead adopting a "new" strategy that emphasized intelligence gathering and sought ever increasing mountains of data about legal activity.

CHILLING EFFECT ON THE FIRST AMENDMENT

In the past, the Bureau intentionally used investigations to intimidate. An FBI memorandum in September 1970 urged questioning members of one group in order to "enhance the paranoia in these circles and ... further serve to get the point across that there is an FBI agent behind every mailbox." [17] When confronted with charges of political harassment today, the FBI responds that its *intent* is not to intimidate. Viewed objectively, however, widespread FBI monitoring and questioning of people regarding their political activities has an inescapable chilling effect. For protest groups already at odds with the government, or for minority ethnic or religious groups, such attention inevitably inhibits and reduces the level of political activities in which the group's members feel free to engage. Word travels fast that the FBI has been to visit somebody and has asked about the group's activities, membership, or funding.

The government's case against the LA 8, for example, had a devastating chilling effect on the activities of Palestinians throughout the United States. And when the FBI began interviewing Arab-Americans during the Gulf War in 1991, many were afraid to speak out, both because of concern that neighbors and co-workers would assume that there was a reason for the FBI visit and for fear of being subjected to racial harassment. In Orange County, California, after two interviews in 1991, the homes of Arab-Americans were hit with bottles, possibly as an outgrowth of the FBI's questioning of neighbors.[18] And the Gulf War interviews of Arabs were mild compared to the targeting of Arabs and Muslims in the wake of the terrorist attacks of September 11. These tactics simultaneously silence the community targeted and build suspicion of law enforcement. As Casey Casem, a Los Angeles radio host and prominent Arab-American said, "When Arab-Americans become suspect, then Arab-Americans tend to want to carry a low profile and not speak out on issues they believe strongly in. The interviews are thus impeding our First Amendment rights."[19]

Such feelings, of course, are not unique to Arab-Americans. They are an inevitable consequence of law enforcement questioning that follows lines of politics, ethnicity or religion. Yale Law School professor and First Amendment scholar Thomas Emerson described the impact of government surveillance on what he called "the dynamics of the system of freedom of expression:"

> Suspicions that government infiltrators are reporting the discussions at meetings dampen the spontaneity or destroy the harmony of a political gathering. Thus many people will hesitate to attend a meeting where the police are taking down license numbers or engage in a demonstration where they are being photographed.[20]

This chilling effect, amplified by agents' attempts to neutralize or disrupt those loosely defined as national security threats, has a corroding effect on the political and social integration necessary to the maintenance of security in a democratic society. To promote security, we need to avoid engendering the sense that dissenters are excluded from society. This alone is a powerful reason to adopt a model of intelligence that does not define threats in terms of politics and to develop counterterrorism strategies that do not devolve into the monitoring of suspect groups or communities.

POLITICAL MONITORING VERSUS CRIMINAL LAW ENFORCEMENT

For much of its modern history, our nation has grappled, often unsuccessfully, with the question of how to separate the few who resort to violence from the many who criticize the government and work peacefully to change the dominant political culture. In the 1950s, this challenge was posed by the threat of Communism. Today's challenge is terrorism.

What are the means to prevent attacks like those of September 11, and to promptly identify, arrest and convict the perpetrators of such acts, without casting a net that sweeps in peaceful dissent? If a fundamentalist religious group or a militia group is preaching the propriety of violence or advocating support for terrorism, when should the FBI be permitted to investigate, and how long and intensively should it continue investigating? If a person or group is involved in violent activity, should the FBI identify and monitor others who share the same ideology? If a group is raising money and sending it to a politically active foreign group, should the FBI be permitted to investigate? Should the government be able to prohibit all support for a group that engages in both violent and peaceful activities? These questions are central to the fight against terrorism.

The FBI's predominant approach, followed throughout its history, has been to designate certain ideologies or groups as suspect, to attempt to identify their adherents, members, supporters or associates, and then to monitor the activities of all those identified. This "guilt by association" intelligence model presumes that all those who share a particular ideology or political position must be monitored on the chance that they will slip into criminal activity in order to achieve their political objectives. It blurs the distinction between "support" for a cause and participation in violence. Thus, even if an investigation begins with an allegation of violent conduct, it often expands to include many who share the same ideology, without any evidence linking them to the crime. At its worst, this approach has led to investigations aimed mainly at disrupting, discrediting and neutralizing "targets" instead of developing evidence of criminal conduct that can be presented in a court of law.

A better approach recognizes the critical distinction between criminal conduct and political activity. This approach accepts angry criticism of government as healthy to a democratic society and constitutionally protected. It requires the government to have suspicion of personal involvement in past, ongoing or planned criminal conduct before it investigates a group or an individual; if there is no evidence of criminal conduct, persons and groups should be left alone, regardless of their beliefs or the actions of those with whom they associate. The goal of this criminal model is not to draw the widest possible picture of an enterprise, but to narrow the scope of inquiry. Rather than viewing advocacy and violence as part of a continuum, the approach tries to draw a distinction between the two.

Professor Emerson described the choice as follows:

> The problem is not the government's power to investigate a crime that has been or is about to be committed, ... since, in such cases, any impact upon the right of an individual to freedom of expression has never been considered to be of constitutional dimensions. ... Rather, the issue arises where the collection of data is not related, or only remotely related, to law enforcement and is principally designed to inform the government about the political beliefs, attitudes or activities of individuals or organizations in the community. It must be conceded that the distinction involved is often difficult to draw; it is, however, fundamental to the constitutional issue.[21]

Adherence to a criminal standard does not mean that the FBI must remain deaf to statements calling for violent activity, nor, as some have irresponsibly said, does it require the FBI to wait until a bomb goes off before it can act.[22] While a person cannot be prosecuted under the Constitution for saying that federal buildings should be blown up, law enforcement agencies may constitutionally investigate to determine if a person making such statements plans to act on them, for conspiracy to blow up federal buildings is a crime. What the First Amendment demands — and what the FBI has too often forgotten — is that an investigation must be narrowly limited to determining whether violent activity is in fact being planned. The government should not extend its attention to an individual without reason to suspect — apart from ideology — that he shares in the criminal plans or activity. And if evidence is not soon developed that a suspected group is in fact engaging in or planning violent activity, the government should withdraw its attention, until and unless new evidence provides reason to suspect that the group or individual is planning acts of violence.

THE CONSTITUTION AND
AN EFFECTIVE COUNTERTERRORISM STRATEGY

This focus on criminal conduct, critics claim, is too narrow. In order to maintain security, government officials and terrorism experts tell us, we must surrender some of our liberty.[23] But in the past, we have sacrificed liberty without benefit to security. There is no necessary contradiction between a robust application of constitutional rights and an effective counterterrorism strategy. To the contrary, an antiterrorism policy that cuts corners constitutionally is likely to be ineffective.

Terrorist acts are criminal regardless of ideology and are best handled by strategies that are as divorced from ideology as possible. Much of the FBI's efforts, however, and much of the 1996 Antiterrorism Act and the immigration provisions of the 2001 PATRIOT Act focus not on acts of violence but on the political or religious ideology that motivates them. This approach is inevitably imprecise and inefficient. First, for practical reasons alone, the FBI cannot monitor all adherents of certain religions or ideologies on the chance that they may engage in terrorism sometime in the future. Our nation harbors too many diverse religions, ideologies and nationalities for the government to monitor effectively. Second, the ideological approach encourages stereotyping that not only stigmatizes the innocent but may lull security services into ignoring genuine threats that do not fit an ideological or ethnic pattern. The ideological approach is bound to be static, while the "face of terrorism" can change rapidly: Muslim fundamentalist one day, white separatist the next, anti-technology loner the next. The Oklahoma City bombing demonstrated the frightful destructiveness of a person of little ideology and no apparent affiliation.

Third, politically focused investigations are likely to be counter-productive and may actually contribute to violence. Political freedom is a society's safety valve, allowing the passionately critical a nonviolent way to express their dissatisfaction with the status quo. Dissent is the mechanism for initiating social change. Shutting off this safety valve only encourages those who have no desire to see the process of peaceful change work. Further, if entire groups are identified as enemies, the cohesiveness of the group may harden against society, substantially diminishing the likelihood that law enforcement agencies will find coop-erative witnesses. If the FBI treats an entire nationality or group as sus-pect, members of that nationality or group will in turn treat the FBI as suspect, making even legitimate investigation much more difficult.

In 1991, Frank Wilkinson and the National Committee Against Repressive Legislation launched a campaign calling for legislation to complete the process of reforming the FBI. At the heart of the campaign was a petition calling for legislation —

> limiting FBI investigations to situations where there are specific and articulable facts giving reason to believe that the person has com-mitted, is committing, or is about to commit a specific act that vio-lates federal criminal law, and also limiting such investigations to obtaining evidence of criminal activity ...

Despite the support of over 500 legal scholars across the country, the proposal has never been adopted. As a result, there is no such statutory limitation on the FBI. The principle that the FBI should confine itself to collecting evidence of crimes and potential crimes should be a central premise of our national antiterrorism strategy, yet it is nowhere reflect-ed in our statute books. If it had been, we might have avoided some of the abuses we detail here. In the wake of the events of September 11, the need for reform is more, not less, urgent than ever.

PART I

INVESTIGATING FIRST AMENDMENT ACTIVITIES:

THE FBI's RECENT HISTORY

CHAPTER 2

THE FBI's INVESTIGATION OF CENTRAL AMERICAN ACTIVISTS, 1981 - 1985

"...it is imperative at this time to formulate some plan of attack against CISPES and specifically, against individuals,... who defiantly display their contempt for the U.S. government by making speeches and propagandizing their cause while asking for political asylum.

"New Orleans is of the opinion that Department of Justice and State should be consulted to explore the possibility of deporting these individuals ...." *Teletype message to FBI Headquarters from New Orleans field office, November 1983.*[1]

OPENING THE INVESTIGATION

In 1981, the Justice Department ordered the FBI to determine whether the Committee in Solidarity with the People of El Salvador

(CISPES) was an agent of a foreign power, that is, whether it was controlled or directed from abroad and thus required to register and disclose information about its finances under the Foreign Agents Registration Act (FARA). CISPES was a U.S.-based organization, composed largely of U.S. citizens, many of them college students. It opposed U.S. aid to the military of El Salvador and openly supported the aims of the Frente Democratica Revolucionario (FDR), the political organization for the rebel groups in El Salvador.[2] The organization acknowledged that it had contact with FDR leaders, and that it had provided funding for humanitarian activities in El Salvador. After a brief investigation, the FBI advised the Justice Department that there was no substantiation for the concern that CISPES was a foreign agent. Rather, the FBI told the Justice Department, CISPES appeared to be an independent, domestic group engaged wholly in lawful, nonviolent political activities.[3]

Nonetheless, in March 1983, the FBI opened an international terrorism investigation of CISPES. It did so on the basis of allegations that CISPES was controlled by the Salvadoran rebel organization, the Farabundo Marti National Liberation Front (FMLN), and was channeling funds to it, and that a CISPES chapter was planning terrorist attacks in the U.S.

Most of these new allegations came from Frank Varelli, an immigrant with family ties to El Salvador's security apparatus who moved to the U.S. in 1980 and took upon himself the mission of exposing a Communist underground that he believed was at work here.[4] By the time the FBI opened the counterterrorism investigation in 1983, Varelli had long been providing information to the FBI about CISPES and other Central American groups. Varelli came under the supervision of an FBI agent who gave him free rein to infiltrate the CISPES chapter in Dallas.[5]

Varelli's specific allegation that CISPES was planning terrorist attacks related only to the Dallas chapter of CISPES. Nonetheless, when FBI headquarters approved the Dallas field office's opening of a full investigation against CISPES, it also directed 10 other field offices to examine local CISPES activities.[6] From the outset, the investigation had a dual focus: "establishing the extent of CISPES support of terrorism in El

Salvador, and the potential of committing terrorist operations in the United States."[7]

The initial phase of the investigation failed to turn up any evidence that CISPES was planning terrorist attacks in the U.S. The FBI's San Diego office recommended on October 7, 1983 that the investigation be closed: "Information to date indicates that the organization is involved with information campaigns, fund raising functions, and promotion of peaceful demonstrations against United States policy in El Salvador."[8]

EXPANDING THE INVESTIGATION NATIONWIDE

Nonetheless, on October 28, 1983, FBI headquarters officials ordered the investigation to be expanded to all field offices nationwide. In doing so, headquarters instructed its field offices "to determine location, leadership, and activities of CISPES chapters in your respective territories through sources, investigation, and surveillances," and "not to investigate the exercise of First Amendment rights."[9] These were inherently contradictory instructions, for aside from the unsubstantiated allegations by Varelli that the Dallas chapter was planning violence, all the evidence available to the Bureau indicated that CISPES was involved exclusively in activities protected by the First Amendment. Faced with this contradiction, field offices proceeded to collect and report information on a wide range of First Amendment activities.

For more than two years, the FBI conducted surveillance of a nationwide political organization on a scale not seen since the 1960s. Agents took thousands of photographs at peaceful demonstrations, monitored rallies on college campuses, attended a mass at a university, spied on church groups and labor union locals, sent an informant to numerous meetings, rummaged through trash, collected mailing lists, took phone numbers off posters opposing intervention in Central America, recorded license plate numbers of vehicles parked outside public meetings, and obtained long distance billing records from telephone companies to trace patterns of association of activists. By the time it was over, the FBI had gathered and added to its files information on the political activities of approximately 2,376 individuals and 1,330 groups.[10]

The CISPES case generated 178 "spin-off" investigations of other groups and individuals. Congressional investigators later found that in four of the cases involving other groups, the investigations were apparently "based solely on [the groups'] ideological similarity to or association with CISPES." Three other groups were targeted because the FBI believed them to be CISPES chapters, even though the groups had their own names and no connection with CISPES other than a shared ideological perspective. The FBI opened a case on another group, the Birmingham Committee in Solidarity with Central America ("BCSCA"), without any clear reason at all; when the investigation failed to establish any connection between CISPES and BCSCA, the Birmingham FBI office nonetheless received headquarters' approval to obtain BCSCA's telephone toll records upon the field office's bald assertion that BCSCA was identical to CISPES. Spin-off investigations of individuals were initiated on the basis of attendance at the showing of a CISPES-sponsored film, the appearance of names on lists of participants at CISPES conferences, and similar associations. In one case, the FBI investigated a university professor on the basis of a question he posed on an exam and a speaker he had invited to class.[11]

While the investigation was still in progress, FBI Director Webster denied to Rep. Don Edwards' House Judiciary oversight subcommittee that the FBI was keeping track of CISPES members per se.[12] Years later, the Center for Constitutional Rights obtained FBI reports disclosing that a number of FBI field offices did in fact try to identify all CISPES members in their area. For example, the Phoenix office reported to headquarters in October 1983 (the memo was addressed to Webster, although it is unlikely he ever saw it), "the case will remain open to further identify the local members of CISPES."[13]

Overall, the CISPES investigation and spin-offs generated a broadly comprehensive picture of grassroots opposition to United States policy in El Salvador. Neither the CISPES investigation nor any of its spin-offs, however, produced any reliable information of planned violence or other illegal activity, and no charges were ever brought against any individual or group.

GUILT BY ASSOCIATION

"In Dallas' opinion, the key word is solidarity. All of these groups
M-19 CO, FALN, FMLN, etc, are connected, extent depending on the
groups themselves. In regards to CISPES, one must remember that
80 [%] of their membership are Anglo middle class individuals, many
very well educated, the same profile as WUO [Weather
Underground Organization] members in the 1960's." *Memorandum
from the FBI's Dallas field office to Headquarters, January 1984.*[14]

The CISPES investigation was driven by the concept of guilt by
association. The first application of the concept came in the opening of
the case: the FMLN was a terrorist organization; CISPES "supported" the
FMLN; therefore, reasoned the FBI, CISPES was to be treated as a terrorist organization. The second application of guilt by association occurred
when the Dallas field office's investigation was extended to other CIS-
PES chapters and ultimately nationwide. The Dallas FBI office had allegations that the CISPES chapter *in Dallas* was planning terrorist attacks,
yet the FBI opened an investigation on all CISPES chapters nationwide,
solely on the basis of their shared ideology and political goals. Guilt by
association also led the FBI to open spin-off investigations of groups
associated with CISPES. And finally, the FBI turned to guilt by association
when it sought to justify the CISPES investigation by reference to CIS-
PES' associations with other, more radical groups.

By April 1994, the FBI had compiled a list of groups "either in support of CISPES or connected with CISPES in some fashion." The list
included Oxfam America, the Southern Christian Leadership Coalition,
the ACLU, the U.S. Catholic Conference, and Amnesty International.[15]
Guilt by association was stretched to the breaking point when the FBI
suggested a link between CISPES and two bombings in Washington: Even
as it acknowledged that the bombings were "probably not perpetrated or
directed by" CISPES, the FBI bootstrapped its case against CISPES by noting that one bombing took place at "about the same time" a CISPES rally
was held in Washington and that responsibility for the other was claimed
by another group espousing positions "similar to those of CISPES."[16]

As an intelligence concept, guilt by association justifies ever-expanding investigations: each association widens the circle of suspects and justifies still further investigations of the new suspects' associations. The purpose of the investigation becomes establishing the broadest possible network. By contrast, domestic criminal investigations may be opened only upon suspicion of specific, individualized criminal conduct. When an investigation is limited by this criminal standard, investigators seek to determine who is engaged in planning or carrying out violent activities, and guilt by association is inapplicable. But under the FBI's foreign counterintelligence and international terrorism investigations, the criminal standard does not apply: the FBI does not believe it is limited to investigating violent conduct. The CISPES investigation, as an international terrorism investigation, was governed by the counterintelligence guidelines and was not subject to the criminal standard, even though it took place in the U.S. and focused mainly on U.S. citizens.[17]

MONITORING FIRST AMENDMENT ACTIVITIES

The CISPES investigation involved close monitoring of core political activity. The FBI collected detailed information on a planned march on Washington to demonstrate against U.S. involvement in Central America and passed it on to the Department of Justice Criminal Division, the Defense Intelligence Agency, the Secret Service and the Secretary of State, even as the Bureau noted, "All reports indicate plans for a peaceful march." The reporting included the numbers of buses that were expected from various cities, the times of their departure, and the cost of the trip per individual.[18] One FBI report on CISPES described in detail a campaign by a coalition in San Francisco in support of a local ballot initiative. The FBI report pointed out that the mayor, the local archbishop, and "all local congress people" also supported the initiative.[19] The Louisville office reported that CISPES distributed literature to the public "urging U.S. citizens to write their respective congressmen to express their concerns over increasing U.S. involvement in El Salvador." The Mobile office reported on a two-hour radio program in which a CISPES supporter described the group's political positions. The Pittsburgh office quoted at length from a newspaper article entitled, "Churches and the Peace Movement."[20] An agent in Wichita removed a flyer captioned "Stop U.S. Intervention in Central America and the Caribbean" from a bulletin board in the Liberal Arts Building at Wichita State, and sent a copy to Headquarters.[21]

One of the most striking aspects of the CISPES investigation is the amount of confusion that existed within the FBI about what investigation was and was not permissible under the First Amendment. It is not that FBI officials were unaware of the First Amendment implications of the investigation. Indeed, it is clear from internal FBI memos that many agents and supervisory officials involved in the case were anxious to adhere to First Amendment limits. They just did not know what those limits were or how they could be reconciled with the investigation's stated objective of identifying CISPES chapters, leaders and activities.

One telling example came from the Cincinnati field office. Its investigation of the local CISPES chapter turned up contacts with an order of Catholic nuns. The field office cabled headquarters, asking for "guidelines regarding investigations of captioned matter, *vis-à-vis* religious organizations-specifically the Roman Catholic Church."[22] The field office knew there was something wrong with investigating an order of Catholic nuns, but that is where the guilt by association concept of intelligence monitoring had led it.

In July 1984, FBI Headquarters sent a ten page memorandum to all involved offices "to reiterate . . . guidelines and instructions for these investigations." The headquarters instructions noted that "some offices have reported information recently regarding political statements and political lobbying." Headquarters explicitly directed that "Political activities or political lobbying . . . are not, repeat not, targets of this investigation and should not be monitored." [23]

The directive had no impact. Two weeks after receiving it, the Denver office sent Headquarters a memorandum stating that, "in spite of attempts by the Bureau to clarify guidelines and goals for this investigation, the field is still not sure of how much seemingly legitimate political activity can be monitored."[24] The same week, the Chicago field office sent Headquarters a progress report describing CISPES as a group that "organizes campaigns to pressure legislators to vote against covert and overt intervention in Central America."[25] The following month, the Cleveland FBI office filed a report on an upcoming public conference on U.S. military involvement in Central America, sponsored by the United Steel Workers Union, the United Auto Workers, the National Education Association, and the United Church of Christ Commission for Racial Justice. The report listed who the speakers would be and what topics they would be addressing, including "The 1984 Elections" and "Winning the Labor Movement to Non-Intervention."[26] The memorandum concluded that "Cleveland plans to follow the progress of the conference."[27]

Monitoring of political activity persisted until the very end of the investigation. On June 4, 1985, weeks before the investigation was closed, the Houston field office submitted to headquarters 104 photographs of "a march conducted in Houston, Texas, on April 20, 1985 by the Texas April Mobilization for Peace, Justice, and Jobs."[28]

What allowed the CISPES investigation to veer out of control was not the lack of headquarters' attention to the First Amendment. It was something more fundamental, something inherent in the nature of intelligence investigations and in the use of guilt by association as an investigative guide. COINTELPRO's monitoring mentality has persisted within the FBI. Instead of narrowly focusing its efforts on confirming or denying the specific allegations that CISPES was planning violent acts, this "intelligence" inquiry expanded into an unlimited effort to identify all possible CISPES chapters, activities, and associations. While the FBI Headquarters advised field offices not to monitor First Amendment activities, other memoranda directed agents to identify CISPES members and activities. Since CISPES chapters by and large only engaged in the planning and staging of meetings and demonstrations, agents in the field were understandably confused. Some quietly ignored the case — there was remarkably little reporting from the New York field office, for example. Others did as they were told and unreflectively reported every meeting and poster.

"SUPPORT FOR TERRORISM" —
A NEW, UNDEFINED BASIS FOR INVESTIGATION

When the CISPES investigation was opened, there was no specific statutory prohibition against providing support to a terrorist organization. Aiding and abetting others in criminal conduct was, of course, illegal, as was engaging in a criminal conspiracy, but there was no legislation specifically defining "support for terrorism," or authorizing officials to designate certain groups as terrorist. In 1984, after the CISPES investigation had been opened, the Reagan Administration proposed legislation to make "support for terrorism" a crime.[29] (The Reagan legislation was strikingly similar to the legislation later proposed by the Clinton Administration and adopted in the 1996 Antiterrorism Act.) The Reagan legislation was strongly criticized as inconsistent with the First Amendment, and it was not enacted, but the FBI was undeterred by the lack of statutory authority. It carried on its investigation of CISPES' alleged "support for terrorism," using the broad discretion granted it under an executive order on intelligence activities and guidelines issued by Attorney General William French Smith that were ironically supposed to limit counterintelligence investigations.

The field offices and headquarters never specified what "support for terrorism" meant, but nobody seemed to have thought it was limited to conduct that supported others in planning or carrying out violent attacks. In the absence of a requirement to focus the investigation on illegal or violent activity, the headquarters directives on the First Amendment could not effectively prevent the monitoring of political activity. With only the guidance of broad concepts like "support for terrorism" or "foreign direction or control," agents investigated whatever activities CISPES engaged in: meetings, rallies, and grassroots organizing.

The problem was compounded by the FBI's use of the words "leftist" and "terrorist" seemingly interchangeably. A March 4, 1985 Dallas memorandum stated, "This investigation was based on reliable asset information that CISPES provides international support to the leftist movement in El Salvador." In another memo, the Dallas office reported, "Source advised the following organizations are active in El Salvadoran leftist activities: Houston Human Rights League, Catholic Charities Refugee Halfway House, Holy Ghost Catholic Church, . . . Nuclear Weapons Freeze campaign . . . ."[30]

The interchangeable use of "leftist" and "terrorist" has deeper significance. The central theme of FBI political investigations from the Bureau's inception through the middle 1980s was the threat of a worldwide Communist takeover. The investigation of Martin Luther King, for example, was nominally begun on the grounds that Communists were among his close advisors. Even the attempted deportation of the "LA 8" in 1987, discussed in the next chapter, was based on their alleged membership in a group that supported Communism. As the Soviet Union collapsed, however, Communism ceased to be a guiding principle for FBI counterintelligence investigations. Terrorism emerged as the new threat to which government officials pointed when claiming that a surrender of liberty was necessary to purchase security. The CISPES case was part of this transition from "Communism" to "terrorism" as the continuing justification for the special legislative authority and broad national security powers that the FBI had grown accustomed to during the Cold War.

WAS CISPES AN ABERRATION?

In 1988, FBI Director William Sessions testified that the CISPES case was an "aberration." Yet between January 1982 and June 1988, the FBI opened 19,500 international terrorism cases, many on subjects *not* suspected of being directly involved in terrorist activity, according to a General Accounting Office (GAO) study.[31] Of 158 cases that the GAO examined in detail, forty-four percent contained no allegation that the target was involved in criminal behavior or was even a member of a terrorist group; the only justification for the investigation was a suspicion of the subject's undefined association with or link to a terrorist group.[32] As in the CISPES spin-offs, the link to a terrorist group that provided the basis for opening the investigation was sometimes very tenuous — the subject attended a meeting or had a contact with a group or an individual.[33] In one case, the FBI opened an investigation on a group simply because it was named in a brochure distributed by another group already under surveillance.The FBI monitored meetings, demonstrations, religious services, or other First Amendment activities in eleven percent of the 19,500 international terrorism cases. This means that at least 2,000 separate investigations were undertaken between 1982 and 1988 where the FBI monitored First Amendment activities.[34]

Moreover, in reviewing actual case files in seventy investigations that were based only on the subject's suspected association with or link to a terrorist group, the GAO found the FBI inspecting First Amendment activities seventy-four percent of the time. Thus, in cases opened without a criminal predicate, the FBI was most likely to monitor First Amendment activities.

In addition to CISPES and its spin-offs, other FBI investigations in the 1980s also focused on Central American solidarity groups and foreign policy critics. The Bureau maintained a file captioned "Salvadoran Leftist Activities in the U.S.," which collected information on sanctuary activities and demonstrations. It had files titled "Nicaragua Proposed Demonstrations in the U.S." in eighteen cities. It opened an investigation of the Latin America Support Committee after the CISPES case was closed.[35] It continued to collect information on demonstrations protesting U.S. involvement in Central America under another case file entitled "Nicaraguan Terrorist Matters." In 1986, a year after the CISPES case was closed, the FBI Chicago field office reported on peaceful demonstrations held by the Pledge of Resistance, a domestic group opposed to U.S. foreign policy, as part of the "Nicaraguan Terrorist Matters" file.[36] And through at least 1987, the FBI conducted a domestic security/terrorism investigation of the Pledge of Resistance.

OVERSIGHT AND CONTROL

The CISPES case reveals both the potential value and the very real limitations of the current system of accountability and control. The Office of Intelligence Policy and Review (OIPR) is the Justice Department's internal watchdog for intelligence and international terrorism matters. Yet it allowed the investigation to go on for 27 months, and only ordered the case closed on June 18, 1985, seven days after Rep. Don Edwards' subcommittee questioned FBI officials about the nature of the Bureau's investigations into CISPES and other Central American-related groups. When Edwards tried then and again in 1986 and 1987 to learn more about the FBI's investigation, FBI officials responded with only fragmentary answers. It was not until January 1988 that the full scope of the investigation was brought to public attention, two and a half years after the investigation was closed, and only as a result of a Freedom of Information Act request filed by a public interest group, the Center for Constitutional Rights (CCR).

At a hearing in 1988, Rep. Edwards described the difficulties his subcommittee experienced in trying to conduct oversight of the CISPES investigation:

> [T]he subcommittee began asking questions about CISPES in 1985, and it has taken us over three years to get the full story. The Director [of the FBI] states now that CISPES generated 180 spin-off cases. In August 1986, we asked how many spin-offs there were, and the FBI said it didn't understand the question. We first asked to see the CISPES file in 1987. We got access to the file after the case hit the front page of the New York Times in February 1988. In April 1985, Director Webster testified that the FBI was not interested in the members of CISPES per se. Now that proves to be not so. Another FBI official strongly denied in February 1987 that the FBI was passing information to the National Guard in Salvador through Varelli. It now appears pretty clear he did. The FBI assured us it was not investigating the sanctuary movement. It is now clear the FBI surveilled sanctuary churches and investigated some sanctuary activities.[37]

In 1988, after the full outlines of the story were revealed by CCR, the Congressional intelligence committees conducted full investigations, including a review of many documents that had not been released to CCR. Edwards also insisted that the staff of his subcommittee be permitted to review the FBI's classified file. The FBI itself produced a critical internal report, and the FBI director testified publicly that the investigation had been misguided. But the intelligence committees, in their separate investigations, declared that they had found no systemic flaws meriting legislative remedy. The FBI claimed to have improved its internal procedures, and the Department of Justice amended the Attorney General guidelines to provide additional guidance for investigations involving domestic groups composed primarily of U.S. citizens. Edwards introduced H.R. 50, the FBI First Amendment Protection Act, to prohibit the FBI from opening investigations on the basis of First Amendment activities. After six years, he finally succeeded in including in the 1994 crime bill a provision prohibiting the FBI from opening or maintaining investigations of "support for terrorism" solely on the basis of First Amendment activities. But two years later, that limitation was repealed in the Antiterrorism Act, meaning that no lasting statutory reform came of the CISPES fiasco.

IMPLICATIONS FOR THE FUTURE

In retrospect, the CISPES investigation of "support for terrorism" can be seen as one of the testbeds for the principles embodied in the Antiterrorism Act of 1996 and the PATRIOT Act of 2001. It is noteworthy, therefore, that when all the facts were revealed in 1988, the FBI was criticized for interpreting "support for terrorism" to include peaceful political and humanitarian activities. The FBI admitted that the CISPES investigation had been overbroad, had improperly focused on First Amendment activities, and had been a waste of resources. It appeared to have learned a lesson.

But soon, rumblings began again that the FBI's hands had been tied. Officials and former agents complained that criticism of the CISPES investigation had had a chilling effect within the Bureau, that agents recalling the CISPES experience had become over-cautious. Following the 1993 World Trade Center bombing, officials grew bolder in these complaints, paving the way for enactment of the 1996 Antiterrorism Act, which repealed the Edwards amendment and adopted a "support for terrorism" provision that essentially legalized the FBI's approach in the CISPES investigation, by making it a federal crime to support the legal activities of designated foreign terrorist groups.

CHAPTER 3

THE INVESTIGATION AND ATTEMPTED DEPORTATION OF THE LOS ANGELES 8

"This document hopes to identify key PFLP people in Southern California sufficiently enough so that law enforcement agencies capable of *disrupting the PFLP's activities* through legal action can do so." *FBI report, "Popular Front for the Liberation of Palestine (PFLP) Los Angeles Area" (1986) (emphasis added).*[1]

On January 26, 1987, FBI and INS agents in Los Angeles arrested six Palestinians and a Kenyan. Suggesting that it had broken up a terrorist cell, the government held the seven immigrants in maximum security, charged them with being affiliated with the Popular Front for the Liberation of Palestine (PFLP), and sought to deport them under the 1952 McCarran-Walter Act for being associated with a group that advocated the "doctrines of world communism." One week later, the INS arrested another Palestinian on the same charges, making eight "respondents" in all. The government's sensationalized allegations of terrorism and its use of the much-criticized McCarran-Walter Act received national attention, and the detainees were soon dubbed the "LA 8."[2]

In less than a month, however, an immigration judge ordered the eight released from custody because the government was unwilling to present publicly any evidence to support its claim that they should be detained as threats to national security while their deportation cases worked their way through the system. In the fifteen years since the arrests, the case has taken many twists and turns, including an evidentiary hearing lasting six weeks over the course of two and one half years, four trips to the appeals court, and review by the Supreme Court.[3] It produced landmark court rulings upholding the First Amendment rights of noncitizens and rejecting the government's attempts to target political activity, only to see them reversed in a devastating decision by the Supreme Court. Other rulings limiting the discretion of the government to use secret evidence in the name of national security still stand. Through it all, the government has never shown or even alleged that the LA 8 were engaged in any terrorist activity or supported any unlawful activities of the PFLP. They have never been charged with a crime, or under any of the deportation provisions addressing actual criminal conduct or conduct threatening national security.

Instead, at the FBI's urging, the government by its own admission targeted the eight for engaging in lawful activity — activity clearly protected under the First Amendment for U.S. citizens — that the government contends supports something else, first "world communism" and later "terrorism." The case highlights the government's persistent tendency to rely on guilt by association as a substitute for investigations focused on establishing individual involvement in violent activity. Like the CISPES investigation, the case provides a window into the FBI's counterterrorism program, revealing another instance in which the FBI's preoccupation with political activity, in particular with statements critical of the U.S. government and its foreign allies, overwhelmed any investigative interest in uncovering evidence of violent crimes.

TARGETING AND "DISRUPTING" POLITICAL ACTIVITIES

Over the past fifteen years, as the Justice Department has repeatedly changed its legal theories for deportation of the eight, the one constant has been the government's motive to deport them for their alleged political affiliations and activities. The INS initially charged all eight under provisions of the McCarthy-era McCarran-Walter Act that made it a deportable offense to be affiliated with a group that advocated the "doctrines of world communism." Then-FBI Director William Webster admitted to Congress two months after the arrests of the eight that they "had not been found to have engaged themselves in terrorist activity."[4] Webster admitted, "If these individuals had been United States citizens, there would not have been a basis for their arrest." Nonetheless, Webster asserted, the investigation was properly grounded under the Attorney General guidelines governing international terrorism investigations.

When the LA 8 challenged the constitutionality of the initial "world communism" charges under the McCarran-Walter Act, the INS dropped those charges, filed new charges, and announced at a press conference that the change was merely tactical and that the INS continued to seek the deportation of all eight because "[i]t is our belief that they are members of [the PFLP]."[5]

The INS charged six aliens with technical visa violations, such as taking too few credits on a student visa. The other two, Khader Hamide and Michel Shehadeh, were permanent residents, and therefore were not subject to deportation for visa violations. They have faced only association-based charges throughout the case. After the INS dropped the charge that they were associated with a group that advocated "world communism," it charged that they were associated with a group that advocated destruction of property, and then with a group that advocated attacks on government officials. (In all instances, it was the same group, the PFLP). In 1989, the federal district court declared these ideological provisions unconstitutional, but the government appealed. In 1990, Congress repealed these McCarran-Walter Act provisions, but the INS simply added new charges, now charging Hamide and Shehadeh with providing material support to a "terrorist organization." Significantly, the INS did *not* allege that Hamide and Shehadeh provided material support to any terrorist *activity*, also a deportable offense, but instead argued that they could be deported solely for providing material support to a "terrorist organization," even though the organization engages in a wide range of lawful activities and they are alleged to have supported only its lawful ends.

As the case progressed, it became clear that the INS was seeking to deport the LA 8 precisely because the FBI disapproved of their political activities. Lacking any evidence that they had been involved in criminal conduct, the FBI turned to the INS. The language with which the FBI described its goal was the very language of COINTELPRO, the FBI's discredited domestic political harassment program of the 1960s and 1970s, the FBI said that its purpose was "to identify key PFLP people in Southern California so that law enforcement agencies capable of *disrupting* the PFLP's activities through legal action can do so."[6] The FBI specifically urged the INS to deport Hamide because he is "intelligent, aggressive, dedicated, and shows great leadership ability," and therefore "[b]y removing Hamide through criminal or deportation proceedings the PFLP will be severely hampered in Southern California."

The INS adopted the FBI's COINTELPRO objectives. A senior INS official wrote that the INS's long-term goal was to "seek eventual deportation of [PFLP] members sufficient to disrupt their activities in this District."[7] The INS District Director admitted that all eight "were singled out for deportation because of their alleged political affiliations with the [PFLP]." He stated that "there was no ground" for deporting Hamide and Shehadeh "other than their political affiliations and activities," and that "the reason our office devoted such resources and took such steps to deport these individuals is because of their alleged affiliation with the PFLP." He stated that the INS did so "at the behest of the FBI, which concluded after investigating plaintiffs that it had no basis for prosecuting plaintiffs criminally, and urged the INS to seek their deportation."[8]

ALIEN BORDER CONTROL COMMITTEE

The government's efforts against the LA 8 did not arise in a vacuum. In November 1986, just two months prior to instituting deportation proceedings against the LA 8, the Justice Department was considering internally a document entitled "Alien Terrorists and Undesirables: A Contingency Plan." The document was circulated by the Alien Border Control Committee, a secret inter-agency task force organized in 1986 to develop, among other things, plans for the "expulsion from the United States of alien activists who are not in conformity with their immigration status." The "contingency plan" proposed building a detention camp in a remote area of Louisiana to hold "alien undesirables" pending deportation. It listed the estimated number of students from Arab countries staying in the U.S. with expired visas, and identified certain countries, all Arab, as being likely origins of terrorist aliens. [9]

Among other tasks, the Alien Border Control Committee sought to develop plans and procedures for deporting aliens critical of U.S. policies. Committee memos indicate that it wanted to "speed up" the removal of "alien activists who are not in conformity with their immigration status." The Committee was specifically looking for ways to use secret evidence: "Where criminal prosecution is not practicable for an alien actually engaged in the support of terrorism within the United States, procedures should be developed, utilizing current authorities, if possible, to expeditiously deport such aliens while protecting classified information and the methods by which such information is obtained." [10]

Whether or not the Alien Border Control Committee had any direct connection with the LA 8 case, the documents show that the Justice Department was at the time the case began consciously looking for ways to use the immigration laws to disrupt political activities of persons engaged in no criminal conduct.

MONITORING FIRST AMENDMENT ACTIVITIES

The deportation proceedings against the LA 8 were preceded by a three-year FBI investigation that again underscores the dangers of political spying. In 1986, FBI agents wrote a 1300-page report on PFLP "support activities" in Los Angeles.[11] The report consisted entirely of accounts of lawful, peaceful, and nonviolent political activity. Over 300 pages of the report are devoted to tracking the distribution of PFLP magazines and other literature with an intensity usually reserved for shipments of illegal drugs. Agents intercepted the magazines on arrival at the Los Angeles airport, weighed the boxes, conducted surveillance on the men who picked them up, and reported on meetings of suspected "distributors" of the literature. Agents also wrote detailed accounts of numerous political demonstrations and dinners, and extensive accounts of political speeches, placards, and leaflets.

The FBI was preoccupied with the "anti-U.S." and "anti-Israel" statements of the LA 8. Agents wrote that the eight were "anti-peace, anti-United States peace settlement, anti-Jordanian peace settlement, and anti-Israel." Agents repeatedly noted that individuals made statements or carried placards at demonstrations that were "anti-US, anti-Israel, anti-Jordan." One FBI memo accused Ayman Obeid of carrying an anti-American slogan at a demonstration protesting Israel's invasion of Lebanon, and stated that his "protesting against US foreign policy with the PFLP, which advocates the overthrow of the US government, is assumed to be against his visa status." Another memo charged that Bashar Amer was "devoted to the PFLP and not the US." The report described articles written by Hamide as "anti-REAGAN and anti-MABARAK." It concluded that PFLP members "hate the US."

In later defending its actions in court, the government pointed to three dinner dances held for the Palestinian-American community in Southern California. These events, called "haflis," were a routine part of Palestinian-American political and cultural life across the nation, and were the principal mechanism for raising money for humanitarian aid for Palestinians in the Middle East.[12] According to the FBI itself, each of these events was widely advertised, open to the public, and attended by crowds as large as 1,000.

Judge Stephen V. Wilson, the federal district court judge who reviewed the government's case, found no evidence that any fundraising at these open public events was intended to support illegal activity.[13] To the contrary, Judge Wilson concluded, FBI agents had ignored evidence available to them showing that the events were legitimate fund-raisers for legitimate charitable organizations. "[T]he government's own evidence shows that at the St. Nicholas event in February 1985, the fundraising was expressly for the benefit of US OMEN," a U.S.-based, IRS-certified charitable organization. And while the government "ha[d] no evidence of what actually transpired at the San Bernardino VFW dinner in June 1985" (because the agents did not go inside), the FBI had received information that the "fundraising would be represented to the audience as for the benefit of 'the mothers and orphans of Palestinians in the Middle East.'"

Judge Wilson found that the PFLP engaged in a broad range of lawful activities, including the provision of "education, day care, health care, and social security, as well as cultural activities, publications, and political organizing." He concluded that in the government's 10,000 page submission "there is no evidence in the record that could have led a reasonable person to believe that any of the plaintiffs had the specific intent to further the PFLP's unlawful aims."

As the case against the eight progressed, the government's theories became more radical. Ultimately, in the words of Judge Wilson, the government argued that when it is acting in the name of national security, it "can do pretty much what it wants to do." Judge Wilson rejected this contention as "utterly without a basis in law," and "quite disturbing to hear from the government as a justification for its conduct in a case where the plaintiffs have made a preliminary showing that the government in effect treated them as if it could do whatever it wanted."

ADVANCES — AND A MAJOR SETBACK — ON FIRST AMENDMENT GROUNDS

Two months after the arrests, the LA 8, joined by numerous Arab, Irish, and other immigrants' rights and peace organizations, filed suit in federal court against the Attorney General and the INS, charging that the

McCarran-Walter Act's ideological deportation provisions were unconstitutional under the First Amendment, and that the eight had been selectively targeted for deportation based on constitutionally protected political activity. On January 26, 1989, two years after the initial arrests, Judge Wilson ruled that aliens living here have the same First Amendment rights as citizens, and that the McCarran-Walter Act provisions were unconstitutional. [14] In an attempt to evade the district court's ruling, the INS filed new charges against Hamide and Shehadeh, characterizing the PFLP as a group that advocated the assault of government officials. Wilson, a Reagan appointee, ruled that these new charges were unconstitutional for the same reasons that the earlier charges were — they punished individuals solely for their association with a group that advocates disfavored ideas. After Congress repealed the McCarran-Walter Act in 1990 and enacted a new law making it a deportable offense to "engage in terrorist activity," the INS substituted new charges against Hamide and Shehadeh under the new law. It did not charge them with actually engaging in or supporting any terrorist acts, however. Rather, it charged them only with providing material support to the PFLP, a "terrorist organization," and argued that such support, even for lawful ends, was a deportable offense.

In January 1994, the district court ruled that the LA 8 had been selectively targeted for deportation based on their First Amendment activities while similarly situated members and supporters of the Nicaraguan Contras, Afghanistan Mujahedin, and anti-Castro Cuban groups had not been deported. On that basis, the court blocked the deportation proceedings. In November 1995, the U.S. Court of Appeals for the Ninth Circuit affirmed, squarely rejecting the government's argument that immigrants are not entitled to the same First Amendment protections as U.S. citizens. The court stated:

> [T]he values underlying the First Amendment require the full applicability of First Amendment rights to the deportation setting. . . .
> Because we are a nation founded by immigrants, this underlying principle is especially relevant to our attitude toward current immigrants who are part of our community. . . . Aliens, who often

have different cultures and languages, have been subjected to intolerant and harassing conduct in our past, particularly in times of crisis. [Citing Alien Enemies Act of 1798 and Palmer Raids of 1919-20.] It is thus especially appropriate that the First Amendment principle of tolerance for different voices restrain our decisions to expel a participant in that community from our midst. [15]

After the Ninth Circuit decision, the INS submitted 10,000 pages of evidence to the court — much of it FBI surveillance of the eight — and argued that this evidence showed that it was justified in targeting the respondents for deportation. Judge Wilson reviewed all of the evidence, and ruled that all of the activities revealed therein — distributing newspapers, participating in demonstrations, and organizing humanitarian aid fund-raisers — were protected by the First Amendment. (Later, Judge Wilson found that the government had withheld from plaintiffs still more documents demonstrating that defendants targeted plaintiffs for their membership and association with the PFLP. The district court characterized the withheld documents as "smoking guns.") The government appealed again, arguing that no one — citizen or noncitizen — has a First Amendment right to support the lawful activities of a foreign "terrorist organization."

In October 1996, the INS moved to dismiss the respondents' federal case against it, arguing that a "court-stripping" provision in the 1996 Illegal Immigration Reform and Immigrant Responsibility Act deprived the federal district court of jurisdiction to hear the eight immigrants' constitutional challenge to its actions. Judge Wilson denied the INS's motion to dismiss, ruling that the eight were constitutionally entitled to immediate federal district court review of their First Amendment selective prosecution claims. The Court of Appeals unanimously affirmed. [16]

Despite its many defeats in the courts, the Justice Department continued to press for deportation of the LA 8. In June 1998, the Supreme Court granted the Justice Department's request to review the case. The Court indicated that it would address only a jurisdictional question — whether the federal courts retained jurisdiction to hear the LA 8's claim in the wake of 1996 changes in the immigration law. The Court expressly rejected the government's request that it review the central First Amendment rulings of the federal trial court and the Ninth Circuit appeals court.

In a stunning reversal, however, the Supreme Court in February 1999 ruled that Congress had stripped the federal courts of all power to review challenges to selective enforcement of the immigration laws. [17] Despite the fact that it had denied review of the First Amendment rulings, the Court then went on to rule that aliens lack any constitutional right to object to their deportations on the ground that they were singled out for membership in an organization that engages in terrorism. The First Amendment, the Court had previously held, plainly protects the right to join groups that engage in violence, so long as one does not specifically intend to participate in or abet such violence. The Communist Party was such a group, according to Congress, yet as discussed below in Chapter 7, the Supreme Court repeatedly held that association with the Communist Party could not be punished absent specific intent to further its illegal ends. Yet despite the fact that the activity the LA 8 were accused of would be clearly protected by the First Amendment if engaged in by U.S. citizens, the Court held that they had no right to object to being singled out for deportation for such activity. The decision denied all immigrants the freedom to engage in political activity, for they must fear that the INS will target them for deportation in retaliation for such activity.[18]

OTHER FBI INVESTIGATIONS IN THE ARAB AND ARAB-AMERICAN COMMUNITIES

The FBI's investigation of the LA 8 was not unique. Arabs and Arab-Americans have long been a particular focus of FBI intelligence gathering.

The Gulf War visits

In January 1991, as the U.S. and its allies prepared to go to war with Iraq over its occupation of Kuwait, native Texan David Najjaab received a phone call from an FBI agent who said he was concerned about Najjaab's safety. Najjaab, an advertising photographer and co-chairman of the Arab American Institute, a bipartisan organization that encourages participation in American politics, met the FBI agent at a Denny's restaurant. The agent started the interview by saying that he was concerned about hate crimes against Arab-Americans. But he then began asking for names of the Arab American Institute's members, and asked Najjaab whether he was familiar with any dissident student groups. The agent said the FBI was trying "to get a handle on the Arab-American community." He asked Najjaab, "Do you know anyone planning to blow up a federal building?"

Najjaab's unsettling encounter was part of a nationwide effort by the FBI to question Arab-Americans and Arab nationals about terrorism.[19] Some of those interviewed were born in the U.S. Some were naturalized citizens. Others were permanent residents. Many were politically active or active in Arab-American organizations. Many were apparently selected solely on the basis of their prominence in local communities. The interviews occurred at people's workplaces and homes.

As part of the effort, agents showed up at the office of a San Gabriel Valley surgeon, a U.S. citizen who had been in the United States for 23 years. As the doctor's patients looked on, the agents showed their badges to the receptionist and asked to speak to the doctor. Other agents questioned customers and owners of Arab-American-operated stores and restaurants in Brooklyn, and interviewed dozens of New York City Arab-Americans in their homes.[20] The agents posed a detailed series of questions about leaders in the Arab-American community, their views on terrorism, and their knowledge of specific people. Some of those interviewed were asked questions about their support for the U.S.-allied war effort against Saddam Hussein, or about their views on Israel and U.S. policy in the Persian Gulf. In Arkansas, the state police participated in the interviews. In Los Angeles, the LAPD anti-terrorist squad participated.[21]

There was some evidence that the interviews were part of a longer term effort. In January 1991, the Arkansas state police director said that his troopers had been questioning Arabs for two to three months at the request of federal agencies. New York Newsday reported on January 29, 1991, that FBI agents had been interviewing Palestinian-Americans in the New York City area for the past four months, inquiring about travel plans, contacts with known Arab-American leaders, and those leaders' professional and non-professional activities. FBI spokesperson Joseph Valiquette said that the interviews being conducted in the New York City area were "part of long-term, ongoing investigations."[22] The head of the Arab Community Center in Youngstown, Ohio said that he first heard from the FBI a year before the January 1991 visits.[23] Col. Tommy Goodwin, director of the Arkansas state police, when questioned about visits his troopers conducted with the FBI, candidly admitted, "They're profiling people constantly. I guess stereotyping people. It's something I would say they do unconsciously."[24]

Despite bitter protests, the FBI continued its interviews after the Gulf War ended.[25] As of March 1991, the ACLU, the Center for Constitutional Rights and the American-Arab Anti-Discrimination Committee were reporting that the FBI was continuing to question pro-Palestinian activists and Palestinian-Americans.[26]

GUPS — Union of Palestinian Students

The breadth of the FBI's surveillance of Arab communities is revealed in a box of documents that Hearst newspaper reporter Dan Freedman received in 1995.[27] The documents, a response to a long-forgotten Freedom of Information Act request Freedman had filed in 1989, revealed that for ten years, from 1979 to 1989, the FBI had conducted a nationwide investigation of the General Union of Palestinian Students (GUPS), a student organization loosely committed to Palestinian identity and self-determination. The specific reason for starting the investigation was unclear from the censored material provided to Freedman, but the documents made it clear that the case was not an investigation of criminal conduct. This was another intelligence monitoring case. At the beginning of the investigation, the Detroit field office set forth "two investigative objectives: (1) Ascertain the formation of new GUPS sub-chapters throughout the US, and (2) Determine the identity and where-abouts of GUPS leaders." It was the group's political ideology that attract-ed the FBI's attention. FBI memos show that agents clearly understood that the purpose of the organization was to "provid[e] assistance to Palestinian students in their education and settlement in the United States and to report, explain, correct and spread the Palestinian cause to all people."

Agents surveilled a wide range of legitimate First Amendment activities. They trailed GUPS members. They tracked the formation of new GUPS chapters around the country and expanded the investigation to include groups with "any interest in PLO issues." Agents staked out a symposium at the University of Michigan on "Peace in the Middle East;" shot rolls of film at GUPS national conventions (at a June 1986 conven-tion in Houston with 200 attendees, FBI agents took 256 photos) and later attempted to obtain information on those in attendance; collected fliers, literature, and articles written in student newspapers on GUPS events; reported the chants from peaceful rallies ("Reagan, Reagan, you should know, we support the PLO"); gathered biographical data on speakers at GUPS events; and surveilled places where GUPS meetings and retreats took place and recorded the license plate numbers of cars in the parking lot.

The FBI field office in Charlottesville, North Carolina attempted to intimidate GUPS chapters at various universities in the area. Agents interviewed numerous members of GUPS. A memo explained that, based on the large number of interviews conducted, those members not personally contacted were made aware of the FBI's "interest" in the orga-nization. Others were propositioned by the FBI to serve as informants on GUPS activities, and the agents noted where GUPS members refused to do so.

The GUPS case further illustrates the limitation of the oversight mechanisms. The Congressional committees never objected to the investigation. Indeed, it is not clear that anyone in Congress ever even knew of the investigation's existence. If the Intelligence Committees posed any questions about the case privately, they had no impact. None of the monitoring and infiltration techniques used in the case required court approval. The Office of Intelligence Policy and Review (OIPR) in the Justice Department, which received periodic reports on the case, let it proceed *for five years* before pointing out that the FBI's summaries did not specify any facts showing that GUPS was involved in international terrorism. The FBI responded, "FBIHQ is confident that such information is available but perhaps was not properly articulated [in the report to OIPR]." Headquarters promised to submit a supplemental report. OIPR allowed the case to continue for another five years, until 1989.

Chapter 4

Intelligence Investigations from Amnesty International to Earth First!

The FBI investigations in the 1980s against activists in the Central American solidarity movement and persons of Arab descent were not isolated incidents. The FBI's tendency to focus on political activity and guilt by association infected its investigations across a broad spectrum, involving not only activities with a foreign nexus but also purely domestic ones.

Amnesty International

In 1987, Harold Pickering was at work at the Phoenix, Arizona Fire Station No. 11 when he received a phone call from an FBI agent. The caller said he wanted to talk to Pickering about something important, but he would not say what it was over the phone. Pickering agreed to meet the caller at his home. Pickering later testified to Rep. Don Edwards' Judiciary oversight subcommittee:

> On April 1st, the agents came to my house. Some of the guys at work thought that since they had decided to come over on April 1st, that this might be an April Fool's prank by a couple of firefighters. I suggested this to the agents when they came to the door and they presented their badges. They came in after I invited them and they asked if I had sent or received any communication from the Soviet Union.[1]

Only then did Pickering realize that the FBI's interest had been prompted by letters he had written for Amnesty International to the Soviet embassy urging release of prisoners of conscience held behind the soon-to-crumble Iron Curtain.

From 1987 to 1989, the FBI interviewed more than two dozen Amnesty members who had written to Soviet or East Bloc embassies on behalf of political prisoners. Those interviewed included school teachers, doctors, business professionals, housewives, and students.[2]

The interviews lasted from a few minutes to an hour. In several cases, as with Harold Pickering, FBI agents telephoned or visited people at work. Many of those interviewed found the agents polite, but many also sensed an implication of wrongdoing. FBI agents generally conducted the interviews by asking open-ended questions and avoided disclosing how the contact came to the Bureau's attention. Instead, the Amnesty members faced vague questions such as, "Have you been in contact with any Soviets lately?"

Many of those interviewed expressed both confusion and anger that the FBI would scrutinize their human rights work. Several said that they worried about adverse effects on their employment. In one case, the FBI agent had characterized his interview as an "educational visit." In other cases, the interviewees felt that they were being lectured by the FBI agents or warned that their efforts could be exploited by the Soviets. In all cases, the visit or interview resulted in an FBI file on the Amnesty member.[3]

As part of the same effort, the FBI interviewed children doing school projects, grammar school teachers, and citizens unaffiliated with any group. One man in Ohio wrote to tell Congressman Edwards that for many years he had been writing to foreign embassies in Washington, usually to voice his opinion about what he considered to be unfair, repressive, or disagreeable policies of foreign governments. In October 1988, an FBI agent visited him at his workplace to inquire about the general purpose of such letters and to discover the type of work in which the subject was involved.

A sixth grade elementary school student, Todd Patterson, wrote letters to 169 foreign countries in 1983 requesting information for a school project. This prompted an unannounced visit by the FBI to Todd's home in Newark in late 1983. An FBI agent questioned Todd's parents, and later the boy himself, about the school project and the international correspondence received in response to Todd's letters. After these interviews, the FBI created a file on Todd. While the FBI maintained that it conducted no further investigations after 1983, FBI documents indicate that it continued to monitor Todd's activities as late as December 1985.[4]

In May 1989, a school librarian, Phyllis Grady, returned home to Haverstown, Pennsylvania from a weekend trip to find a handwritten note from an FBI agent left at her front door requesting a meeting. Grady had been active in Amnesty International since 1984. She often sent letters to foreign governments on behalf of prisoners of conscience and forwarded copies of the letters to the respective embassies in Washington, DC. At the meeting, the FBI agent told Grady that her name was on a "list" at the Yugoslavian Embassy. The agent asked if Grady had been recruited to spy for Yugoslavia. The agent also indicated that her phone might be tapped.[5]

The FBI argued that it was not "investigating" Amnesty International or the other letter writers. Rather, the FBI said that it was monitoring the Soviet embassy and Soviet diplomats and that, as a part of that effort, it sought to interview persons who had contact with the embassy or its officials. But the tactics of the FBI put the Amnesty International members and others in the position of having to justify to the FBI facially innocent contacts with certain foreign persons or entities. And as a result, the chilling effect on these citizens was the same as if they were being investigated: they were still being asked to explain why they were engaged in a First Amendment activity.

THE "LIBRARY AWARENESS" PROGRAM

In 1985, the FBI launched a program of visits to public and university libraries, where agents sought to interview librarians, asking for information regarding the readers of unclassified technical and scientific journals.[6] In New York City, the visits were part of a systematic program designed to "develop counterintelligence awareness" among librarians at technical and scientific libraries. FBI agents visited other libraries around the country whenever they believed that a foreign national they suspected of being an intelligence officer may have used the library. FBI agents asked librarians to be wary of "foreigners" or persons with "East European or Russian-sounding names." Library staff were requested to report to the FBI any "suspicious activity." According to the FBI, suspicious activity included speaking a foreign language or requesting books on "underground tunneling, military installations, or technological breakthroughs."[7]

The FBI sought access to a broad range of information from library records. FBI agents asked to view library databases and search checkout records, to monitor the reading interests of those with Eastern European or Russian names, and to scrutinize books checked out through interlibrary loans. Disclosing this type of information is a violation of state library confidentiality laws in most states.

When the visits were brought to light by objecting librarians, the FBI at first tried to minimize the scope of its investigation, claiming that the "Library Awareness" program was confined to a few specialized libraries in New York, and later that it was a "very, very limited" probe of libraries in three U.S. cities. In fact, FBI agents approached libraries across the country, including university libraries in Los Angeles, California; Madison, Wisconsin; College Park, Maryland; Buffalo, New York; Houston, Texas; Arlington, Virginia; and Cincinnati, Ohio; and a public library in Broward County, Florida. An FBI agent approached one librarian at his home, and on at least one other occasion, the FBI put a wiretap on a library phone and installed hidden cameras to spy on the activities of library patrons.

The FBI underestimated librarians' attachment to the First Amendment and the privacy rights of library users. The librarians took their case to the press and to Congress, demanding that the Library Awareness program be stopped. The FBI defended the program, claiming that it had been created in response to proof that Soviet intelligence services were using American scientific and technical libraries, and that KGB agents had stolen hundreds of thousands of items of microfiche from such libraries as a means of keeping pace with American technological advances. However, the Association of Research Libraries testified at Congressional hearings that it had received no reports of widespread theft of microfiche from American research libraries. As a result of the librarians' protests and the widespread press coverage and editorial criticism, the FBI largely stopped asking librarians for their assistance, although it did not stop trying to identify certain foreigners' use of libraries.

MONITORING ASSOCIATION: LANCE LINDBLOM

In the FBI's view, virtually any association with a suspect foreign national, no matter how seemingly innocent, can trigger an FBI inquiry. Once the FBI has looked into an association, even if the contact was in fact innocent, a file is kept for potential future reference. And once a counterintelligence or international terrorism file is created, it can be kept secret indefinitely, thus shielding FBI counterintelligence practices from the public scrutiny to which criminal proceedings are subject.

Sometime in the mid-1980s, Lance Lindblom — a U.S. citizen — came to the attention of the FBI's counterintelligence division. At the time, he was the president of a major philanthropic foundation, and in that capacity he met regularly with foreign leaders and political dissidents. Apparently, one of those foreigners was of interest to the FBI, and therefore the FBI scrutinized Lindblom. The effort was short-lived. Lindblom checked out to the FBI's satisfaction. But the inquiry generated a small file. Some time later, when Lindblom filed an FOIA request, the FBI admitted it had a file on him, but refused to disclose its full contents or to say what had triggered its interest in Lindblom. It also refused to expunge the record, even though it admitted that the file consisted of reporting on Lindblom's associational activities and contained no evidence of illegal activity on Lindblom's part. The FBI claimed that it was entitled to retain a file on innocent First Amendment activity because it might be useful someday. The federal appeals court in the District of Columbia agreed.[8]

MONITORING ACT-UP DEMONSTRATIONS

The FBI's monitoring of First Amendment activities is not limited to foreign nationals or groups with foreign ties. The AIDS Coalition to Unleash Power (ACT-UP) was highly visible in the late 1980s and early 1990s, using dramatic rhetoric and unconventional protests to call attention to the AIDS epidemic in the United States, promote greater funding for AIDS research, and advocate equal treatment of those affected by the disease. In one typical demonstration, more than 1,500 AIDS activists descended upon President George Bush's home in Kennebunkport, Maine in September 1991, marching to within a quarter-mile of his estate and chanting "Shame!" At the beginning of the march, they held up a piñata shaped and painted in the likeness of Bush, and then proceeded to hit it with golf clubs until it broke, releasing scores of condoms. The end of the march was marked by a "die-in," during which demonstrators lay down in the street to dramatize the death toll among AIDS victims. The boisterous but nonviolent protest continued for four hours, in the presence of the Kennebunkport police force, score of state troopers, and Portland officers.[9]

This kind of angry advocacy brought ACT-UP to the attention of the FBI, which began collecting information on the group as early as February 1988. The minimal information released under the Freedom of

Information Act shows that the FBI used informers to collect information on the group and its members throughout the nation.[10] At least 16 FBI field offices were involved.

How long the group, which advocated and practiced only nonviolence, was watched by the FBI, or for what purpose, remains unclear.[11] At one point, the FBI apparently feared that the group's members were engaged in a plot to carry out kidnappings, assaults, and assassinations during a June 1989 AIDS conference in Montreal. But the collection of information began prior to this allegation, and when nothing violent occurred in Montreal, the investigation continued for many years, until at least October 1993. As is often the case in counterintelligence investigations, the FBI exchanged information about ACT-UP with local police, often to tip them off to planned demonstrations.[12]

In 1995, after the Center for Constitutional Rights released documents it had obtained under FOIA from the FBI's ACT-UP file, FBI Director Louis Freeh quickly promised to undertake a "complete review" of the case. Two weeks later, Freeh sent a memo to all 56 field offices, similar to the several memos sent during the CISPES investigation, reminding agents that activity protected by the First Amendment cannot serve as the basis for an investigation. The head of the FBI's New York field office, where half of the ACT-UP documents were found, said his office never targeted ACT-UP because "[t]hey don't even come close to the guidelines on opening up a criminal investigation."[13]

MONITORING OTHER DEMONSTRATIONS

In the 1980s, the FBI regularly collected information about protest demonstrations by a wide range of groups across the ideological spectrum. The Senate Intelligence Committee found that the FBI had a practice of "passively receiving and disseminating information on political protest demonstrations:"

> This appears to be a fairly routine practice, especially with information from local law enforcement agencies and other established FBI liaison contacts in both government and private sector institutions.

The line between passive receipt and informal solicitation is hard to define and may not necessarily be reflected in FBI files. More importantly, an undetermined but substantial amount of information about protest demonstrations by a wide range of groups across the ideological spectrum is acquired, maintained and disseminated by the FBI. Many, if not most of the demonstrations reported on posed no threat to the public safety, but the information is perpetuated in the files of the FBI and other agencies.[14]

The FBI collected some of this information under specific investigations, as in the CISPES case. It obtained other information under a general case classification for investigations concerning civil disobedience and demonstrations.

EARTH FIRST!

The summer of 1990 was supposed to be "Redwood Summer" in northern California. The militant environmental group Earth First! planned to blockade roads and engage in other civil disobedience in an effort to halt logging in 30,000 acres of virgin redwood. Earth First! had been associated with such tactics as the "spiking" of trees with steel rods that would cause chainsaws to snap, endangering loggers, but before the summer of 1990 the group had disavowed such measures. The protests planned for 1990, in which college students were to come to northern California and stay with local activists, were patterned after the Mississippi Summers of the civil rights movement. All volunteer workers were required to pledge their commitment to nonviolence.

Just before noon on May 24, 1990, Earth First! organizers Judi Bari and Darryl Cherney were driving in downtown Oakland when an explosion tore through Bari's Subaru station wagon. Local police who rushed to the scene were joined soon by FBI agents, including members of the FBI counterterrorism squad. Bari suffered a fractured pelvis and was rushed to the hospital in critical condition. Cherney received minor injuries. They and their colleagues in Earth First! assumed that the bombing was meant to interfere with their work organizing Redwood Summer. They expected the FBI to focus its attention on anti-environmentalists who had increasingly targeted Earth First! and Bari for criticism and threats.

But when Cherney was released from the hospital soon after the bombing, he was taken into police custody, and by the end of that first day, police indicated that they would charge Cherney and Bari themselves with transporting explosives. The following day, Bari was placed under arrest in her hospital bed. The authorities said that they believed that Bari and Cherney had made the bomb themselves and that it had accidentally exploded while they were carrying it to an unknown target.[15] Police and FBI agents searched houses in Oakland where Bari and Cherney had stayed and questioned their friends.

Over the next two months, the local police and the FBI continued to assert that Cherney and Bari were responsible for the bombing, claiming that nails seized in a search of Bari's house were found by the FBI lab to match the nails in the bomb. Even when a letter signed by "the Lord's Avenger" was received taking credit for the bombing, investigators continued to focus on Bari and Cherney, suggesting that the letter may have been composed on a typewriter found in Bari's house.

Finally, on July 18, the Alameda County district attorney's office announced that it would not file criminal charges against Bari and Cherney. Police and FBI officials promised to continue their investigation, but there were never any subsequent arrests or charges in the case.

Only years later did information emerge proving what Bari had long suspected: that before the bombing, the FBI had been investigating Bari and Cherney as suspected terrorists, and that immediately upon hearing of the bombing the FBI had concluded that its suspicions were confirmed.[16] Indeed, so sure was the FBI that Bari and Cherney were terrorists, based on their association with Earth First!, that the FBI failed to pursue other avenues of investigation until it was too late. Sheila O'Donnell, who investigated the case for Greenpeace U.S.A., concluded, "With the FBI, I think they had Earth First! terrorists dancing like sugarplums in their head. I don't know that they ever for a moment asked, 'Are these people victims?' . . . . If you come to the scene of a crime with your own theory of who's responsible and you refuse to turn that around, you build a house of cards that will come crashing down around you."[17]

The first FBI agent who responded to the scene of the bombing was Timothy McKinley. As soon as he had determined the identity of the victims, McKinley contacted the FBI office in San Francisco, which, according to the report McKinley dictated the next day, advised him that Bari and Cherney "were the subjects of an FBI investigation in the terrorist field." McKinley conveyed this information to local police. The physical damage to the car itself, which indicated that the bomb had been hidden under the seat, was ignored. Instead, the FBI and the police reported that the bomb must have been placed on the floor behind the driver's seat, where Bari and Cherney would have seen it. Oakland Police Sergeant Mike Sitterud wrote an entry in his police log thirty minutes after the bomb went off, stating "Earth First! leaders suspected of Santa Cruz power pole sabotage, linked to federal case of attempted destruction of nuclear power plant lines in Arizona." (The latter was a reference to an FBI undercover investigation that had led to the arrest of Earth First! founder David Foreman in 1989.)

At 7:50 on the night of the bombing, the FBI agent in charge of the terrorist investigation unit in San Francisco met with Oakland police and told them that Bari and Cherney "qualified as terrorists and that there was an FBI investigation going on other incidents where these individuals were suspects." According to Oakland police officers later questioned under oath by Bari's lawyers, the FBI agent said that Bari and Cherney were involved in organizing demonstrations in the redwood region, and that Cherney had been arrested for climbing the Golden Gate Bridge to unfurl a banner with an environmental slogan. The FBI official also drew a connection between Bari and a bomb planted at a sawmill in Cloverdale, California. And the FBI told police that Bari and Cherney were prime suspects in the sabotage of power lines in Santa Cruz earlier that year, a charge that was never substantiated.

All in all, the FBI already had a substantial dossier on Bari and Earth First!, making no distinction between violent acts and nonviolent acts of civil disobedience, and linking Earth First! to incidents for which it had not taken credit, where the only connection was the presence of logging or other environmental issues.

Author David Helvarg found that, "[a]ccording to files released under the Freedom of Information Act, the FBI's interest in Earth First! goes back . . . almost to the founding of the group in 1980."[18] In 1987, the Phoenix office of the FBI opened a domestic terrorism investigation, which came to involve FBI offices in California, Montana, and New Mexico. The investigation focused on Earth First! co-founder Dave Foreman. An FBI undercover agent befriended Earth First! members and participated in the planning of an effort to knock down a power line. Problems with the nature of the investigation were revealed by a tape the agent had inadvertently made of himself telling other agents, "This [Dave Foreman] isn't really the guy we need to pop, I mean in terms of an actual perpetrator. This is the guy we need to pop to send a message. And that's all we're really doing . . . ."[19] Evidence like this deflated the government's charge that it had broken up a dangerous terrorist group. Foreman and five others pled guilty to reduced charges. The case served as a window into Earth First! chapters nationwide. In the course of the investigation, the FBI wiretapped more than sixty people in communication with Foreman, including Judi Bari.[20]

The bombing of Judi Bari served as further reason for the FBI to look at the group. Even after the police had ruled out Bari and Cherney as suspects, the FBI obtained the telephone toll records of Earth First! activists in northern California and compiled a list of 634 out-of-town phone calls they had made. The San Francisco FBI office then sent the numbers to field offices throughout the country, asking for the name, address, physical descriptions, employment, criminal records, and other information, based only on their having received a phone call from Earth First! Helvarg reports, "More recently, the FBI has been identifying (and misidentifying) Earth First! spin-off groups to industry and other law enforcement agencies, creating problems for local environmental activists."[21]

The FBI never found out who made the bomb that wounded

Bari, and may never have really tried. A civil lawsuit against the law enforcement agencies on behalf of Cherney and Bari's estate was still pending in 1999.[22]   But the Bureau's efforts included a widespread investigation of environmental activism in northern California. [23]

CONCLUSION

The problems identified in Part I persisted in the face of attempted reforms of the FBI. After the Church Committee documented the FBI's COINTELPRO program and related abuses, the Justice Department for the first time subjected the FBI to guidelines that purported to limit its investigations of political activities. While these reforms did curtail the FBI's activities to some extent, the FBI retained a substantial degree of uncontrolled discretion, especially in situations where the issue or group in question had a foreign component, bringing it under more lenient foreign counterintelligence guidelines. The political monitoring approach characteristic of counterintelligence investigations continued to influence the FBI's response to terrorism. The FBI's wide-ranging investigations of Central American activists in the early 1980s revealed that the changes had not been as fundamental as many had believed. Again, after public (and internal) criticism of the CISPES probe, the Bureau claimed that it would institute new controls to prevent such investigations from recurring.[24] But the investigations of Palestinian and Islamic groups in the late 1980s and 1990s showed that again the reforms had failed to address underlying problems.[25]

Part II

Control vs. Discretion:
The Limits of Legal Restrictions on the FBI's Authority

CHAPTER 5

MECHANISMS FOR CONTROL OF THE FBI

No single constitutional provision, statute, or oversight body can, in isolation, effectively control a police and counterintelligence agency like the FBI. What is needed is a system of interlocking constraints, based on principles essential to a free and democratic society:

- Government powers should be limited constitutionally.

- The functions and authorities of agencies should be specified in binding laws adopted publicly by the legislature.

- Crimes should be narrowly defined, and citizens and noncitizens alike should be subject to arrest, detention or punishment only under standards of fundamental fairness ("due process"), including the opportunity to know and challenge the evidence against them.

- Executive agencies should be subject to control and oversight by the legislature and by an independent judiciary committed to the protection of individual rights.

- Members of the society should have an enforceable right of access to information about the policies and practices of the government.

- Agencies and officials should be accountable to individuals harmed by their overreaching.

- The rights of association and freedom of expression should be protected, including the right to engage in peaceful opposition to government policies and to support the peaceful activities of causes and groups, foreign and domestic, that the government opposes.

LEGAL CONTROLS/LEGAL DISCRETION

The legal system that has evolved to control the FBI incorporates all these protections. The First Amendment to the Constitution protects the freedoms of speech and association, the Fourth Amendment protects privacy against unreasonable searches and seizures, and the Fifth Amendment guarantees due process. Statutes define the offenses within the FBI's criminal investigative jurisdiction.[1] Other statutes limit the use of some intrusive techniques, requiring, for example, the approval of a judge before the government can conduct a wiretap or plant a bugging device.[2] Guidelines promulgated by the Attorney General set standards for the initiation and conduct of all investigations and regulate such investigative techniques as the use of informants and undercover operations. Annual Congressional statutes that authorize and appropriate funds for the FBI sometimes place conditions on the expenditure of those funds, and Congressional oversight committees can inquire into the propriety of FBI activities. The Freedom of Information Act (FOIA) creates in principle an enforceable right of access to government records.[3] The courts have jurisdiction over suits against the Bureau and individual agents for violations of constitutional, statutory and common law rights.[4]

Each of these controls, however, is limited in practice, leaving the

FBI substantial leeway to intrude on legitimate political activities. No statute or "charter" comprehensively delimits the functions and authority of the FBI: its broad "counterintelligence" mission, for example, stems only from a succession of vaguely worded presidential orders. The federal criminal code includes statutes that, if interpreted broadly, would criminalize militant rhetoric against the government.[5] Judges rarely deny requests for wiretapping.[6] Attorney General guidelines leave the FBI wide discretion, can be easily rewritten or reinterpreted, and in any event are not enforceable in court. Guidelines on counterintelligence investigations are largely classified and therefore are not even available for public scrutiny. Congressional oversight is inconsistent, often driven by partisan disputes rather than principle, and easily stymied by Executive Branch resistance. Indeed, the Congressional oversight committees just as often serve as defenders and promoters of the agencies they are supposed to be controlling. The FOIA has exceptions sharply limiting citizen access to law enforcement and national security records, and the judiciary too often has been reluctant to exercise its intended role in reviewing Executive Branch decisions to withhold information.[7] And the courts have erected almost insurmountable barriers to citizens' lawsuits challenging intrusive government investigations or other abuses of power.[8]

THE CONTEXT FOR THE 1996 AND 2001 ANTITERRORISM LEGISLATION

The powers under the 1996 and 2001 antiterrorism statutes were granted to an agency that, despite periodic efforts to control it, continues to enjoy considerable discretion and immunity from control. This Part summarizes the legal history of the FBI's investigative powers. It will show that the legal reforms adopted over the years to control FBI investigations were incomplete and ultimately ineffective, as the recurring FBI infringements on First Amendment rights recounted in Part I demonstrate.

This is not to suggest that the FBI today is no different than it was under J. Edgar Hoover. As far as we know, the systematic violations of law that characterized COINTELPRO are not being repeated today. There has been no proof, for example, that the FBI continues to engage in illegal break-ins or warrantless wiretaps. Nor is there evidence that the FBI is using the worst "dirty tricks" of COINTELPRO, such as sending anonymous derogatory letters to employers and family members, circulating phony pamphlets and fliers, or fomenting internal dissent and encouraging violence to disrupt activist organizations. (Then again, there are no broad protest movements today of the kind that prompted the FBI to break the law in pursuit of its vision of the national interest.) Our concern is not so much with illegal FBI conduct, but rather with how much the FBI can do *legally* to intrude on political freedoms. The laws as written and interpreted grant broad latitude to investigate political activity and interfere with First Amendment rights.

THE ABSENCE OF STATUTORY LIMITS

The FBI has no legislative charter. As Attorney General Griffin Bell testified in 1978, "Despite its long history, the Bureau has received very little statutory guidance."[9] Efforts to enact a statute delimiting the FBI's authority foundered in the final year of the Carter Administration. Today only a smattering of miscellaneous statutes define the FBI's powers and duties.[10] One authorizes the FBI to detect and prosecute offenses against the United States, to assist in the protection of the President, and to investigate "official matters" under the control of the Department of Justice and the Department of State.[11] Another authorizes the Attorney General to collect crime records and exchange them with federal, state, and local agencies.[12] A third authorizes the FBI to train state and local law enforcement officers.[13] A fourth permits FBI agents to carry firearms, serve warrants, and make arrests.[14] Another limits the FBI Director to a single ten-year term, a provision intended to prevent the rise of another J. Edgar Hoover (who held office for 48 years) but at the same time to insulate the FBI Director from the normal cycle of Presidential appointments.[15]

The substantive criminal laws might provide some limits on FBI investigations, but the FBI has found authority in a number of broad criminal statutes to conduct wide-ranging investigations encompassing political activities.[16] In the past, the FBI conducted investigations of lawful political activity under the Smith Act and the Voorhis Act, which facially punish speech and advocacy.[17] The seditious conspiracy statute[18] makes it a crime to conspire to overthrow the government of the United States, and continues to be used to investigate persons and groups who have no chance of overthrowing the U.S. government. In June 1983, the FBI arrested four alleged members of a Puerto Rican nationalist group in Chicago and charged them with seditious conspiracy. Their convictions were upheld by the federal court of appeals.[19] Later in the 1980s, the statute was used to investigate and arrest white supremacists and "left-wing" radicals; in both cases, juries refused to convict, but the investigations and prosecutions substantially disrupted the activities of the individuals and organizations involved. Most recently, the seditious conspiracy statute was used to obtain the conviction of Sheik Omar Abdel Rahman for his connection with a group plotting to bomb the Holland and Lincoln Tunnels in New York City, even though the government acknowledged that the Sheik was not directly involved in the planning. Recently, the government has relied on money laundering statutes and other authorities to investigate humanitarian fundraising for disfavored foreign organizations.[20]

Likewise, the federal laws criminalizing espionage[21] could provide some guidance for the FBI's counterintelligence investigations, but the Bureau has long claimed the authority to investigate the lawful activities of domestic groups that oppose United States foreign policy or that "support" certain foreign governments or factions, even where there is no suspicion of criminal conduct.[22] On this basis, even at the end of the Cold War, the FBI examined lawful contacts between citizens of the United States and those of certain foreign nations, as illustrated by the Library Awareness program and the visits to Amnesty International members discussed in Part I. The search for foreign influence on lawful political activity was also the basis for the FBI's investigation of the nuclear freeze movement, where the Bureau claimed to be seeking to determine whether anti-nuclear activists were acting under the direction and control of the Soviet Union, even though no specific criminal violation was suspected. This same rationale also justified the investigation of CISPES for "supporting" the FMLN of El Salvador. Most recently, it has served as the basis for wide-ranging inquiries into the activities of Arab-Americans and Muslims.

In the absence of meaningful statutory limits, efforts to control the FBI have for the most part come from within the agency or the Executive Branch. As the next chapters illustrate, these internal efforts have proven woefully inadequate.

CHAPTER 6

SEVENTY-FIVE YEARS OF REFORM AND RETRENCHMENT

Harlan Fiske Stone, Attorney General in the 1920s, launched the first effort to control the FBI's investigation of political activity.[1] Stone was reacting in part to the domestic intelligence programs established during World War I, when the Bureau of Investigation (as the FBI was then called) investigated thousands of individuals for "un-American activities." The investigations continued even after the war ended, culminating in the notorious Palmer Raids of 1920, in which some 10,000 persons were arrested on suspicion of being "anarchist" or "revolutionary" immigrants subject to deportation.[2] Describing the Bureau's activities before he took office as "lawless, maintaining many activities which were without any authority in federal statutes,"[3] Stone pledged to limit the FBI to investigating only such conduct as was made criminal by federal law. "The Bureau of Investigation," Stone announced, "is not concerned with political or other opinions of individuals." Upon appointing

J. Edgar Hoover as acting director of the Bureau of Investigation, Stone directed that the activities of the Bureau were to be "limited strictly to investigations of violations of the law."[4]

The constraints imposed by Stone were never embodied in legislation (setting an unfortunate pattern for subsequent efforts to reform the FBI) and proved short-lived. Beginning in the mid-thirties, the FBI reinstituted and expanded its domestic intelligence activities. President Franklin D. Roosevelt, in a series of oblique orders, directed the FBI to collect intelligence about "subversive activities" and "potential crimes."[5] In the exercise of this jurisdiction, the FBI went beyond investigating crimes to searching for suspected foreign involvement in a wide swath of American life. In 1976, the special Senate committee known as the Church Committee wrote an extensive history of the FBI. Referring to the Roosevelt order, it concluded: "By using words like 'subversion' — a term which was never defined — and by permitting the investigation of 'potential' crimes, and matters 'not within the specific provisions of prevailing statutes,' the foundation was laid for excessive intelligence gathering about Americans."[6] Under the Roosevelt executive orders, the FBI once again began to investigate law-abiding domestic groups and individuals. By 1938, the FBI was investigating alleged subversive infiltration of the maritime, coal, steel and automobile industries, educational institutions, labor unions, youth groups, political organizations, and Roosevelt's partisan critics.[7]

The FBI's intelligence programs did not cease with the end of the Second World War. "Instead," the Church Committee found, "they set a pattern for decades to come."[8] Executive directives by Presidents Truman and Eisenhower continued to direct the FBI to investigate "subversive activity," without defining what that might be.[9] "Congressional deference to the executive branch, the broad scope of investigations, the growth of the FBI's power, and the substantial immunity of the Bureau from effective outside supervision became increasingly significant features of domestic intelligence in the United States."[10] By 1960, the FBI had opened approximately 432,000 files at headquarters on individuals and groups in the "subversive" category.

COINTELPRO — TO "DISRUPT"AND "NEUTRALIZE"

The legal regime established under Presidents Roosevelt, Truman and Eisenhower set the stage for the worst abuses in the FBI's history, and eventually led to more comprehensive efforts at reform. Boosted by enactment of the anti-Communist Internal Security Act of 1950, the FBI undertook an intensive campaign aimed at suspected Communists, working in tandem with Senator Joseph McCarthy and the House Unamerican Activities Committee (HUAC). HUAC, the Senate Internal Security Subcommittee, and state-level "little HUACs" depended heavily on the FBI for information. The committees were obsessed with membership, drawing up lists of names and constructing links among organizations. Targets of the committee were confronted with information from informers, but had no opportunity to cross-examine their accusers and no access to evidence in the possession of the FBI that would assist their defense. Those who refused to testify by invoking the Fifth Amendment often lost their jobs and were ostracized from their communities. Those who refused to testify by invoking their First Amendment rights of expression and association — Frank Wilkinson was one — were punished with prison sentences for contempt of Congress.

In 1956, the FBI brought many of its domestic spying operations under the formal designation of "COINTELPRO" (COunterINTELligence PROgrams). Their express goal was to "disrupt," "discredit" and "neutralize" domestic protest groups. As the Church Committee later explained, "The origins of COINTELPRO [were] rooted in the Bureau's jurisdiction to investigate hostile foreign intelligence activities on American soil."[11] With the opening in 1961 of a COINTELPRO program against the Socialist Workers Party, a purely domestic group, the effort lost any pretense of being directed against foreign-controlled groups. Programs against the Ku Klux Klan, civil rights groups, and the "New Left" followed. Over the course of fifteen years between 1956 and 1971, in the words of the Church Committee, "the Bureau conducted a sophisticated vigilante operation aimed squarely at preventing the exercise of First Amendment rights of speech and association, on the theory that preventing the growth of dangerous groups and the propagation of dangerous ideas would protect the national security and deter violence."[12]

The FBI's long campaign of investigation and harassment against Frank Wilkinson exemplifies the wasteful and anti-democratic nature of the Bureau's Cold War political surveillance. The FBI began investigating Wilkinson as soon as he became interested in social reform in the 1940s. When Wilkinson was fired from the Los Angeles Housing authority, he dedicated his time to organizing public support to abolish HUAC. Even before the first meeting of the National Committee to Abolish HUAC * was held, it was smeared by accusations in the press that several of its organizers were Communist. The FBI devoted huge resources to following Wilkinson around the country. It disrupted his public speaking engagements by arranging for hecklers and by causing the cancellation of hall rentals. It planted false accusations in the press. It shared its files on Wilkinson not only with HUAC, but also with private groups, such as the American Legion. It disseminated anonymous "poison pen letters," tapped phones, broke into offices and examined bank records. The FBI even stood silent and waited after learning of an assassination plot against Wilkinson.

Wilkinson's trial for contempt of Congress illustrates, in a lesson still relevant today, the danger inherent in denying the right of cross-examination and denying defendants access to exculpatory information the government has about them. Wilkinson's conviction was based primarily on the testimony of a sole informant, Anita Bell Schneider, whom Wilkinson had met only once. At the trial and in the Supreme Court's decision, she was described as a "creditable witness." Over 25 years later, as a result of a long and hard-fought lawsuit, Wilkinson obtained previously secret documents from his FBI file. Among them was one showing that, before his trial, the FBI had concluded that Schneider "exhibited emotional instability," and that it was "not considered advisable" to use

---

* *The National Committee to Abolish HUAC is now the National Committee Against Repressive Legislation (NCARL). Its educational affiliate is the First Amendment Foundation, publisher of this book.*

her as a witness. The government failed to disclose this evidence to Wilkinson or his lawyers at the time of his criminal trial or appeals.[13]

The investigation of the Socialist Workers Party was another typical COINTELPRO operation. From 1961 to 1976, the FBI used 1300 informants in the investigation, who supplied the Bureau with detailed reports on SWP debates and activities, as well as at least 12,600 pilfered SWP documents. FBI agents themselves conducted 204 illegal break-ins ("black bag jobs") against the SWP, removing or copying an additional 9864 documents. The FBI conducted 20,000 days of telephone wiretaps and maintained bugs in SWP offices for the equivalent of 12,000 days. It conducted aggressive interviews of SWP members and their relatives, neighbors and employers, which an FBI memorandum at the time said were intended to "enhance the paranoia" of members. The explicit purpose of the investigation was the disruption of the SWP. The FBI sought to create hostility and racial discord within the organization, to frustrate its efforts to form alliances with other groups, and to cause certain members to lose their jobs. [14] The investigation was doggedly pursued even though none of the 1300 informants ever reported a single instance of planned or actual espionage, violence, terrorism, or other illegal activities, and even though the investigation did not result in a single arrest for any federal violation. In fact, informants routinely reported that the SWP was a peaceful organization.

COINTELPRO also involved extensive surveillance of anti-Vietnam War demonstrations and campus protests, broad informant reporting, break-ins, warrantless wiretaps, infiltration of nonviolent civil rights groups and legal organizations supporting them, and efforts to get teachers fired, to prevent targets from speaking, to block the distribution of newsletters, and to disrupt peaceful demonstrations and meetings. Among the FBI's targets was Dr. Martin Luther King. The techniques to achieve these goals "ranged from the trivial (mailing reprints of *Reader's Digest* articles to college administrators) to the degrading (sending anonymous poison-pen letters intended to break up marriages) and the dangerous (encouraging gang warfare and falsely leading the members of a group to believe that one of their own was a police informer)."[15]

Throughout COINTELPRO, the FBI undertook activities knowing they were illegal or without legal support. In an extreme case, the FBI encouraged the violent raid by Chicago police that resulted in the killings of two Black Panthers, Fred Hampton and Mark Clark.[16]

POST-COINTELPRO REFORMS AND THEIR LIMITATIONS

Public and Congressional outrage over the abuses of COINTELPRO prompted efforts to reform FBI operations, particularly as they affected political spying. Measures specific to the FBI were accompanied by reforms directed at the entire national security apparatus. The Congressional budget process was reformed to give Congress annual opportunities to use the purse strings to control executive agencies. Congressional oversight of the FBI and the foreign intelligence agencies was established. The Senate created the Select Committee on Intelligence in 1976 and the House established its counterpart in 1977.[17] President Ford issued a public Executive Order on intelligence activities, replacing the secret directives, orders and statements on which Hoover had based his domestic intelligence operations. Congress strengthened the Freedom of Information Act, with the intent of ensuring more effective judicial review and making information about the national security programs of the government more accessible. In the Pentagon Papers case, the Supreme Court ruled that the press could not be stopped from publishing classified national security information.[18] The Supreme Court also ruled that U.S. citizens could not be wiretapped in the name of national security without a court order,[19] and Congress responded by enacting the Foreign Intelligence Surveillance Act (FISA), requiring a court order for electronic surveillance undertaken in the name of national security.[20] Attorney General Edward Levi adopted guidelines spelling out publicly for the first time the standards for opening and conducting domestic security investigations.[21] And the Justice Department successfully prosecuted two FBI officials who had ordered black bag jobs in the course of COINTELPRO investigations.[22]

Some of these reforms had a lasting impact. Even before the Attorney General guidelines were adopted, there was a sharp decline in the number of FBI domestic security investigations, and the guidelines reinforced and institutionalized the trend. The revised FOIA resulted in the public disclosure of substantial information.[23] The Congressional committees established reporting requirements on the use of intrusive techniques such as undercover operations.

The reforms, however, were incomplete. Part of the problem lies in the continuing secrecy that precludes public accountability. For example, while the FBI budget is largely public, the specific funding for the Bureau's counterintelligence and counterterrorism programs is obscured in more general categories. Nor are the budgets for the CIA, the National Security Agency, or the other foreign intelligence agencies subjected to public scrutiny and debate; while the total aggregate budget for foreign intelligence has recently been made public after a FOIA lawsuit, all further details remain secret. The guidelines limiting counterintelligence and international terrorism investigations also are classified secret in large part.

Another reform that was never undertaken, contrary to the recommendations of the Church Committee, was the adoption of "charter" legislation to define the FBI's powers and responsibilities. Consequently, the main source of the FBI's counterintelligence authority is still an executive directive without judicially enforceable standards.[24] The FBI continues to claim authority to investigate legal activities of United States citizens.[25]

Moreover, some of the reforms have been reversed. President Ronald Reagan, soon after taking office, pardoned the two FBI agents convicted for their role in illegal COINTELPRO burglaries. President Reagan's Justice Department rewrote the Attorney General domestic security guidelines to expand authority for collecting information on political activities.[26] He issued a new Executive Order 12333 on intelligence activities, which was scarcely less ambiguous than the directives issued by Roosevelt (the concept of "subversive activities" was supplanted by "international terrorist activities," a term similarly left undefined).[27] The Reagan Administration interpreted the FOIA narrowly, especially as it applied to the FBI and the intelligence agencies, and the courts in many cases deferred to Executive Branch decisions to withhold documents. In 1984, Congress amended the FOIA to exempt whole categories of CIA files from review, and in 1986, it amended the FOIA again to codify the Reagan Administration's restrictive reading of the law.[28]

Still other reforms were not as far-reaching as expected. Thus, while national security wiretaps are no longer conducted illegally, the secretive court set up under the Foreign Intelligence Surveillance Act of 1978 to review government requests for wiretapping authority in national security cases has never denied a single one of the thousands of requests for electronic surveillance presented to it since its creation,[29] and since 1994 this same court has had authority to issue warrants for clandestine physical searches.[30] Some argue that the mere existence of the court has constrained the use of these techniques, even if the court's orders have not done so directly, but the evidence is inconsistent with this theory: the number of wiretaps in counterintelligence and international terrorism cases has risen steadily, from 546 in 1989 to 839 in 1996. Similarly, under the 1968 law governing wiretaps in criminal cases, including domestic terrorism cases, there has been a similar expansion in wiretap activity, from 673 in 1987 to 1186 in 1997. The number of federal wiretaps in criminal cases increased 141% from 1987 to 1997.

Congressional oversight also has proven to be limited, and the little oversight that has been conducted has not led to significant reform. For example, the well-publicized inquiry by the House Judiciary and Government Reform Committees into the fatal law enforcement assaults on the Branch Davidian compound in Waco, Texas in 1993 produced no legislative or administrative reforms of FBI practices. After a 51-day siege by the FBI's Hostage Rescue Team, an FBI assault on the compound ended in the building's burning to the ground, killing over 80 people, including 22 children. The Committee hearings lacked a reform agenda and were riven by partisanship. A more substantive and non-partisan Senate inquiry into the killing of the wife of white separatist Randy Weaver in Ruby Ridge, Idaho also failed to produce any legislative reforms. Congressional inquiries into allegations of misconduct in the FBI laboratory and in the handling of FBI files for White House background checks also yielded no legislative reforms.[31]

ATTORNEY GENERAL GUIDELINES ON DOMESTIC SECURITY INVESTIGATIONS

The one step forward, one step back character of FBI reform can be seen in the evolution of the Attorney General "guidelines" on domestic security/terrorism investigations. Domestic security investigations are those directed at homegrown groups, like the KKK and the Weather Underground, which operate only in the United States and have no foreign allegiance or support. Attorney General Edward Levi first issued public guidelines for FBI domestic security investigations in 1976.[32]

The Levi guidelines required suspicion of criminal conduct before a domestic security investigation was opened. This "criminal standard" remains in place today and currently provides:

> A domestic security/terrorism investigation may be initiated when the facts or circumstances reasonably indicate that two or more persons are engaged in an enterprise for the purpose of furthering political or social goals wholly or in part through activities that involve force or violence and a violation of the criminal laws of the United States.

This "reasonable indication" standard is substantially lower than the standard of probable cause required by the Fourth Amendment for searches and seizures and for arrests and indictments. It does, however, require specific facts or circumstances indicating a past, current, or impending violation before a full investigation may be conducted.

The guidelines also authorized a "preliminary inquiry" on a group or individual on a much lower threshold — whenever there was an "allegation or information indicating the possibility of criminal activity." Even for a preliminary inquiry, however, the guidelines required a criminal nexus. And the guidelines specifically required consideration of "the danger to privacy and free expression posed by an investigation."

Guidelines, however, are easily changed. After Ronald Reagan took office, his Attorney General, William French Smith, relaxed the guidelines.[33] The criminal standard was preserved, but the guidelines were rewritten to make it clear that the FBI could open an investigation based on mere advocacy of crime. Smith's changes remain in effect today. The guidelines now state, "When, however, statements advocate criminal activity or indicate an apparent intent to engage in crime, particularly crimes of violence, an investigation under these guidelines may be warranted."

Data provided to Rep. Don Edwards when he was chairman of the FBI oversight subcommittee of the House Judiciary Committee shows that the Smith changes resulted in investigations triggered by mere rhetoric. The FBI throughout the 1980s and early 1990s engaged in approximately two dozen full domestic terrorism investigations per year under the Smith guidelines. Through the early 1990s, nearly two-thirds of these investigations were opened on the basis of statements by members of the target group, before a crime had been committed. In many of those cases, the group never subsequently engaged in violence nor engaged in any criminal conduct.

While the Smith guidelines preserved the earlier caution against infringing on First Amendment rights, they also made it clear that such infringements were not prohibited. Thus, for example, the guidelines authorize the use of informants to infiltrate a group "in a manner that may influence the exercise of rights protected by the First Amendment," so long as approval is obtained from FBI Headquarters.

The Smith guidelines also applied two expansive concepts to domestic security investigations: the "enterprise" concept perfected in organized crime investigations, and the concept of "intelligence" investigations. The guidelines contain a lengthy passage explaining the significance of these concepts:

> An intelligence investigation of an ongoing criminal enterprise must
> determine the size and composition of the group involved, its
> geographic dimensions, its past acts and intended criminal goals,
> and its capacity for harm. While a standard criminal investigation
> terminates with the decision to prosecute or not to prosecute, the
> investigation of a criminal enterprise does not necessarily end, even
> though one or more of the participants may have been prosecuted.
>
> In addition, the organization provides a life and continuity of
> operation that are not normally found in a regular criminal activity.
> As a consequence, these investigations may continue for several
> years. Furthermore, as Justice Powell noted, the focus of such inves-
> tigations "May be less precise than that directed against more con-
> ventional types of crime." . . . It often requires the fitting together of
> bits and pieces of information[,] many meaningless by themselves[,]
> to determine whether a pattern of criminal activity exists. For this
> reason, the investigation is broader and less discriminate than usual....

The guidelines go on to warn that an "investigation of organizational activity . . . may present special problems particularly where it
deals with politically motivated acts." The guidelines urge that "special
care must be exercised in sorting out protected activities from those
which may lead to violence or serious disruption of society." But even
this warning is ambiguous, allowing investigation of activities that "*may*
lead to . . . serious disruption of society." That standard would easily
encompass investigations of both the civil rights and the anti-Vietnam
War movements.

Another significant goal of the Smith revisions was to make it
clear that the FBI could collect public material (pamphlets, fliers, newspaper clippings, reports of interest groups), including material on the
exercise of First Amendment rights. [34] Soon after it revised the guidelines, the Justice Department issued an opinion concluding that the FBI
may collect publicly available information if an individual or group
meets the standard for either a full investigation or a preliminary inquiry.
Thus, on the strength of only an "allegation or information indicating the
possibility of criminal activity," the FBI may conduct a preliminary

inquiry consisting entirely of the collection of publicly available information reflecting the exercise of First Amendment rights. This interpretation opens the door to monitoring investigations in which the FBI uses informants and local police sources to maintain a name-indexed dossier of public statements and other open political activities of domestic groups.[35]

THE FREEH REINTERPRETATION

The Justice Department further relaxed the domestic security guidelines following the Oklahoma City bombing. The modification was accomplished by an interpretative memorandum from the Department of Justice, the language of which was negotiated by FBI Director Louis Freeh. The memorandum reminded agents that the standard of "reasonable indication" for opening a full domestic terrorism investigation is "substantially lower than probable cause." It stated that a full investigation would be justified if three factors exist: (1) statements threatening or advocating the use of violence; (2) "apparent" ability to carry out the violence; and (3) a potential federal crime. The memorandum went on to emphasize that a preliminary investigation could be opened if the FBI received "partial information" or an allegation suggesting the existence of some, but not all, of the listed factors. "Thus, a preliminary inquiry ... would be appropriate if either the statement itself or other information suggests an ability or intent to carry out violence."

Most significantly, the memorandum stressed "that any lawful investigative technique may be used in a preliminary inquiry, with only three narrow exceptions: mail covers, mail openings, and nonconsensual electronic surveillance. ... Indeed, with appropriate approval, a preliminary inquiry may include the development and operation of new sources or informants, or even 'the planting of undercover agents in the [suspected] organization.'"

Freeh testified that the purpose of the reinterpretation was to give the FBI "a lot more confidence to conduct and begin investigations, where in the past we were clearly not encouraged and, indeed, in some ways persuaded not to conduct some of these investigations."[36] Following the reinterpretation, the number of open domestic security investigations rose from approximately 100 in 1995 to more than 800 in 1997.[37]

FOREIGN COUNTERINTELLIGENCE GUIDELINES

Separate Attorney General guidelines govern the FBI's counterintelligence and international terrorism investigations. The FBI defines international terrorism as terrorism inside or outside the U.S. carried out by a group with ties outside the U.S.[38] The intelligence guidelines permit the investigation of Americans and others in the U.S. who are not suspected of breaking the law, but are engaged only in political activities. Unlike the domestic terrorism guidelines, large portions of the foreign intelligence guidelines are classified. But enough of the definitions section is unclassified to appreciate their political focus. The guidelines authorize the FBI to investigate "intelligence activities," which are defined to include "any activity" undertaken for or on behalf of a foreign power "to affect political or governmental processes" in the United States. A foreign power is defined to include a foreign government or any of its components, a faction of a foreign nation, a foreign-based political organization, and a group engaged in international terrorism or preparatory activities.[39] Amnesty International, the Palestinian Liberation Organization, the African National Congress, the Irish Republican Army, and opposition political parties abroad are all foreign powers under this definition, and any activities undertaken in the United States for or on their behalf, even wholly nonviolent political activity, may spark a counterintelligence investigation.

Many U.S. residents have connections of kinship, ethnicity or religion with conflicts around the globe. Our government asserts a role in many of these conflicts, sometimes supporting one side or the other in ways that do not enjoy unanimous support of the U.S. population. Unavoidably, therefore, some residents will find themselves at odds with the U.S. government's position. Such individuals often establish ties of support with foreign causes that the U.S. government opposes. In recent decades, for example, many Americans identified with and engaged in political activities to support the Irish Republican Army, the FMLN in El Salvador, and the African National Congress.

These activities are protected by the Constitution. The Supreme Court has held that the First Amendment protects membership in or affiliation with an organization having both legal and illegal aims, unless the individual specifically intends to further the group's illegal aims.[40] The guidelines state that no United States person (defined as a citizen or permanent resident alien) may be considered an agent of a foreign power "solely upon the basis of activities protected by the first amendment." But the FBI has interpreted its guidelines as authorizing the investigation of individuals who are members of or who support a foreign organization that engages in both legal political and illegal terrorist activities. As the CISPES and LA 8 cases demonstrate, once a group is deemed terrorist, the FBI does not carefully distinguish among the activities of its members or supporters. The FBI operates on the assumption that it can investigate membership, recruitment, and fundraising, regardless of whether the individuals investigated participate in or support the organization's illegal activity.[41]

The guidelines' definition of international terrorist is limited to one who knowingly "aids or abets" any "individual or group that knowingly engages in international terrorism or activities in preparation therefore." "International terrorism" is in turn defined as activities that "involve violent acts or acts dangerous to human life that are a violation of the criminal laws of the United States or that would be a criminal violation if committed within the jurisdiction of the United States." As the CISPES case showed, however, the FBI has stretched these concepts to cover a broad category of "support" activities for groups designated as terrorist, whether or not the support actually amounted to "aiding or abetting" violent acts. The term "support for terrorism" — the focus of the CISPES investigation — does not appear in the unclassified definitions section of the guidelines.

Even after the FBI conceded that the CISPES investigation had spun out of control, it continued to defend the practice of investigating "support for terrorism" without distinguishing between support for legal and illegal activities of a foreign group. In his testimony about the CISPES case, FBI Director William S. Sessions elided that distinction:

> The original focus and intent of the CISPES investigation were to determine the extent of monetary and other support by CISPES for terrorist movements and activities in El Salvador; ... to identify those individuals who knowingly supported terrorist groups in El Salvador through efforts in the United States; and to determine the extent of any control over, or influence on, CISPES by the FDR or FMLN. *This focus was proper* ....[42]

Movements and groups that can be labeled terrorist are often engaged in both legal and illegal activities. The IRA had Sinn Fein, a legal arm engaged in legitimate political activity. The African National Congress engaged in both violent "terrorist" acts and nonviolent anti-apartheid activity. And according to Israeli security services, Hamas, one of the world's most notorious "terrorist groups," devotes ninety-five percent of its resources to nonviolent social services. [43] The focus of an FBI investigation of a terrorist group should be to determine the nature and extent of support for the group's *illegal* activities. But as Sessions' statement illustrates, the FBI deems it appropriate to investigate support for the legal activities of groups labeled "terrorist" by the U.S. government, without any direct connection to illegal acts.

In the wake of the CISPES investigation, the Attorney General's guidelines on international terrorism were revised, but it appears that the changes did not address the question of what type of support may be investigated. To the contrary, as far as one can determine from the unclassified excerpts made available, the guidelines still fail to distinguish between support for legal activities and support for illegal activities of a foreign group. A memorandum to all field offices accompanying the guideline changes states:

Paragraph (b) provides that when the FBI investigates a group that is substantially composed of United States (U.S.) persons under the FCIG [Foreign Counter-Intelligence Guidelines] on the basis that the group is acting for or on behalf of a foreign power, *the investigation shall be limited to activities of the group relating to that foreign power.*

Paragraph (b), in conjunction with paragraph (a), sets limits on investigations of groups substantially composed of U.S. persons that are believed to be acting for or on behalf of foreign powers. An investigation of such a group should be directed toward determining the veracity of the information regarding the connection to the foreign power and/or its activities related to that foreign power's interests.[44]

In investigations of international terrorism, the FBI generally has not sought to link domestic subjects of investigations to specific terrorist acts. It has not limited the predication (or basis) of its investigations to situations where there was suspicion of criminal activity. Instead, it has focused on links or associations, sometimes several stages removed from any suspected criminal conduct. The result, as in the LA 8 case, has been the investigation of organizations and individuals whose support for foreign groups or movements is wholly limited to these groups' lawful, nonviolent activities. Yet as this book goes to press, Attorney General John Ashcroft is reportedly considering relaxing the guidelines still further.

LOCAL LIMITS ON POLITICAL SPYING AND EFFORTS TO UNDO THEM

In the 1970s, activists in a number of cities undertook litigation and other efforts to constrain political spying by the FBI and its counterparts in local "Red Squads." Lawsuits were filed in New York, Chicago, Seattle, San Francisco and elsewhere, seeking to stop federal and local police spying and infiltration, to obtain restitution where possible, and to forestall future spying through local ordinances or court injunctions.[45] In Chicago, the litigation resulted in a court injunction against police and FBI spying. (The case is discussed further in Chapter 7, below.) In 1990,

San Francisco adopted a policy limiting political spying, after disclosures that the police had conducted a massive intelligence gathering operation before and during the 1984 Democratic national convention. At that time, police, FBI and other agencies had together collected intelligence on more than 100 political groups ranging from the KKK to the ACLU, "Gay Groups," and "Labor Coalitions." The 1990 policy required "reasonable suspicion" of a serious crime before permitting intelligence investigations of political or religious groups.

Almost as soon as these limits were put in place, however, the FBI began working to revoke them. In San Francisco, the FBI in 1996 proposed entering into a cooperative agreement with local police that would evade a San Francisco city policy that had limited police department collection of information on political groups, demonstrations and other First Amendment activities.[46] The FBI proposed that SFPD members would serve on a "Bay Area Counterterrorism Task Force," and would follow the more lenient Attorney General guidelines, which, as noted above, allow preliminary investigations, including the use of informants, in the absence of reasonable suspicion of a crime. In Chicago, the FBI and the police department began efforts to eliminate the controls of the settlement, filing a motion in September 1998 to effectively lift all restrictions against police spying.[47]

THE NCARL PETITION, H.R. 50, AND THE EDWARDS AMENDMENT

The evident limitations of other avenues for controlling the FBI led three of the nation's leading legal scholars in 1985 to draft a petition to Congress, calling for enactment of statutory controls to prevent the FBI and other federal law enforcement agencies from undertaking investigations that threatened or hindered the exercise of First Amendment rights. Professors Thomas I. Emerson of Yale and Vern Countryman of Harvard, veterans of the struggles against McCarthyism, were joined by Professor Carole Goldberg of UCLA. Working with NCARL, they circulated the petition to their colleagues at other law schools. Ultimately,

590 law professors at 147 law schools signed the petition. The petition (reprinted in the Appendix) called upon Congress to enact legislation —

> limiting FBI investigations to situations where there are specific
> and articulable facts giving reason to believe that the person has
> committed, is committing, or is about to commit a specific act
> that violates federal criminal law, and also limiting such investiga-
> tions to obtaining evidence of criminal activity; and provisions
> specifically prohibiting investigations of groups because of their
> members' exercise of First Amendment rights.

Representatives Don Edwards (D-CA) and John Conyers, Jr. (D-MI) embraced the petition by drafting and introducing H.R. 50, the FBI First Amendment Protection Act, first introduced in 1988.[48] It went nowhere.

H.R. 50 was reintroduced in several subsequent Congresses, but was never enacted. In 1994, however, Edwards succeeded in adding a small portion of H.R. 50 to the Violent Crime Control and Law Enforcement Act.[49] The opportunity arose when the Bush and later the Clinton Administrations supported a provision making it a federal crime to provide material support to anyone knowing that it would be used in the commission of one of a number of federal crim-inal offenses relating to terrorism. Edwards amended this "material support" provision by adding the following subsection, which closely tracked a provision in the law professors' petition:

> Activities Protected by the First Amendment. — An investigation
> may not be initiated or continued under this section based on
> activities protected by the First Amendment of the Constitution,
> including expressions of support or provision of financial support
> for the nonviolent political, religious, philosophical or ideological
> goals or beliefs of any person or group.[50]

President Clinton signed the provision into law as part of a massive crime bill in September 1994. Less than six months later, however, the President sent to Congress proposed anti-terrorism leg-islation. Among other things, the President's bill called for the repeal of the Edwards amendment and for the enactment of a much broader provision criminalizing support for lawful activities of "terrorist groups." The Clinton proposal drew none of the careful distinctions between support for criminal activity and support for political activity that Congress had insisted upon in 1994. Yet in 1996, Congress enacted both the repeal of the Edwards amendment and a provision criminalizing support of a terrorist group's lawful activities.

CONCLUSION

The history of the FBI has been one of an ongoing struggle between control and discretion, between efforts to limit monitoring of political dissent and efforts to preserve or extend FBI powers. Periods in which measures were adopted to control the FBI have been followed by efforts to repeal those limitations, to redefine them, or to expand powers in new areas.

In the 1940s, Presidential orders gave the FBI broad powers in the name of fighting subversion. From the 1950s through the 1970s, those powers were maintained and exercised in the name of fighting Communism. Following public disclosure of the COINTELPRO program and the abuses documented by the Church and Pike Congressional committees, the FBI came under new restrictions intended to limit its investigations of political activities. However, the reforms were limited and fragile. In the 1980s and 1990s, FBI powers were again extended. In the name of foreign counterintelligence and antiterrorism, the FBI continued to insist upon the authority to investigate legal activity that had a foreign nexus. The nationwide investigation in the early 1980s of peaceful activists opposing U.S. policy in Central America led to further criticism and reform. But, as Part III will show, the antiterrorism statutes of 1996 and 2001 have brought us full circle again, codifying guilt by association and making illegal the support of legal activities of certain foreign groups. As we enter 2002 engaged in a global struggle against terrorism, the FBI's powers to engage in political spying remain largely unrestricted by statute or executive regulation.

CHAPTER 7

CONSTITUTIONAL LIMITS —
THE ROLE OF THE JUDICIARY

The activities of the FBI are subject, of course, to constitutional constraints. The First Amendment's free speech and association guarantees, the Fourth Amendment's protection against unreasonable searches and seizures, and the Fifth Amendment's due process guarantee and its privilege against compelled self-incrimination impose limits on the FBI and other agencies. These restrictions, however, are often difficult to enforce for a variety of reasons, from doctrines extending immunity for official misconduct to the very secrecy that surrounds the FBI's activities. Moreover, while the Constitution has been interpreted to prevent prosecutions and other adverse action for First Amendment activities, the courts have been reluctant to block FBI investigations into First Amendment activities.

THE SUPREME COURT'S VIGOROUS PROTECTION OF SPEECH AND ASSOCIATION

In a series of landmark decisions over the past forty years, the Supreme Court has extended robust protection under the First Amendment to political speech and association. The Court has not always been sensitive to political freedoms, and it recently created a serious exception for aliens, but its current doctrine is otherwise staunchly protective. Taken together, its opinions frame a vision of a vigorous clash of ideas that is at odds with the FBI's counterintelligence model and its investigations aimed at monitoring and disrupting groups that support the political activities of disfavored causes.

Thus, the Court held in the 1969 case of *Brandenburg v. Ohio* that the government cannot punish statements advocating the use of force or other illegal conduct except where such advocacy is "directed to inciting or producing imminent lawless action and is likely to incite or produce such action."[1] Absent such a showing, which is difficult to make, speech advocating crime is constitutionally protected. In subsequent cases, the *Brandenburg* principle was reaffirmed and expanded, as the Court held that speech intended to stir anger and even speech that creates a climate of violence is protected under the First Amendment.[2] The Court has provided equally strong protection for political association, holding that the First Amendment protects association with a group engaged in legal and illegal activities so long as the individual's association is not specifically intended to further the group's unlawful aims.[3] As the Court explained in 1972:

> "guilt by association alone, without [establishing] that an individual's association poses the threat feared by the Government," is an impermissible basis upon which to deny First Amendment rights. The government has the burden of establishing a knowing affiliation with an organization pursuing unlawful aims and goals, and a specific intent to further those illegal aims.[4]

These constitutional standards sharply curtail the ability of the government to punish its political opponents. Individuals cannot be punished for advocating lawbreaking, as long as they avoid imminent incitement, and they are permitted to associate with groups engaged in illegal activity, as long as they do not specifically intend to further that illegal conduct. These principles require the government to focus on individual acts, not mere advocacy or affiliation.[5]

These precedents were significantly curtailed as to nonciti-zens in the Court's 1999 decision in *Reno v. American-Arab Anti-Discrimination Comm.*,[6] which denied aliens the right to object to deportations targeted against them in retaliation for activities that would be protected by the First Amendment if engaged in by U.S. citi-zens. (See Chapter 3, *supra*).

JUDICIAL BARRIERS TO RELIEF

Despite the Supreme Court's generally staunch protections for the rights of advocacy and association, the courts have erected procedural barriers that make it difficult for the victims of political spying to obtain judicial relief. For example, under a doctrine known as "standing," the Supreme Court in 1972 ruled that anti-Vietnam war protesters could not challenge an extensive government surveillance program.[7] The Court said that the protesters had alleged only a "subjective chill." It said that in order to obtain judicial relief ordering the government to stop its surveil-lance, an individual must show she "has sustained or is immediately in danger of sustaining a direct injury as the result of [a governmental] action." Although the case was decided only on threshold standing grounds, and did not purport to decide whether the surveillance was legal or not, it has been read (incorrectly) as allowing the government to investigate speech that could not constitutionally be prosecuted. On this basis, a federal appeals court refused to review a case in which Richmond police routinely surveilled demonstrations and meetings by maintaining a police presence and photographing participants, keeping the informa-tion on file, and sharing it with other law enforcement agencies such as the FBI.[8] Another appeals court rejected a challenge to undercover FBI surveillance of a convention of the Young Socialists of America.[9]

In practical terms, the standing doctrine means that much turns on the extent to which those challenging police or FBI surveillance can document the nature of the intrusion and show concrete evidence of injury. For example, while a Philadelphia court held that the mere photographing and compilation of records on political demonstrators gave rise to no First Amendment injury, it held that a tangible injury did occur when the police department publicly disclosed, in a network television broadcast, information concerning individuals and groups on whom police intelligence files were kept. [10] The court stated that disclosure of information concerning lawful First Amendment-protected activities to non-law enforcement groups chilled freedom of speech and association. Making such information generally available, the court found, could interfere with job opportunities, careers, or travel rights, and may dissuade others from joining unpopular groups under surveillance. [11]

The courts have also erected other procedural barriers to the enforcement of the First Amendment against the intelligence agencies. When 21 anti-Vietnam War activists sued the CIA in the 1970s for spying on them, a federal appeals court denied their requests for access to government files on the surveillance. This ruling made it impossible for the activists to demonstrate personal injury from the government's misconduct or the likelihood of future surveillance, and resulted in the dismissal of their claims for both damages and injunctive relief. [12]

On occasion, plaintiffs have succeeded in overcoming these barriers and establishing their "standing" to challenge FBI conduct. In one such case, Judge Thomas Griesa of the Southern District of New York ruled in 1986 that the FBI's COINTELPRO operations against the SWP, including the FBI's use of informants to obtain private information about political meetings and demonstrations and other lawful events of the SWP, were "patently unconstitutional and violated the SWP's First Amendment rights of free speech and assembly." [13] This victory, however, required extraordinary efforts by both plaintiffs and judge. The case lasted 13 years. In the course of the litigation, the FBI deliberately concealed from the plaintiffs and even from the U.S. Attorney's office that was representing the government information about FBI break-ins against the SWP and its members. The Bureau submitted to plaintiffs (and filed with the court) answers to interrogatories that were, in the words of the judge, "grossly deceptive." And the Attorney General refused to comply with the court's order to disclose information about informants.[14]

THE COURTS' RELUCTANCE TO LIMIT
FBI INVESTIGATIONS — THE CHICAGO LAWSUIT

A federal lawsuit in Chicago illustrates both the utility and the frustrations of constitutional litigation as a check upon FBI investigative activities. The case, *Alliance to End Repression v. City of Chicago*, began in 1974. Plaintiffs, including the ACLU, the Alliance to End Repression, and the Chicago Committee to Defend the Bill of Rights,[15] charged that the FBI had "conducted surveillance of, and compiled dossiers on, their lawful political and other lawful activities; gathered information about plaintiffs by unlawful means, including warrantless wiretaps and break-ins, unlawful use of infiltrators and informers, and by other unlawful means; [and] disrupted and harassed plaintiffs' lawful activities." After six years of sharply contested litigation, the parties proposed in late 1980 a settlement agreement, which the court approved.[16] The agreement set forth several principles the FBI was to follow while conducting domestic security investigations in Chicago. The agreement incorporated the rules set forth in the FBI guidelines issued by Attorney General Edward Levi, giving them the force of law in Chicago.

Eighteen months later, Attorney General William French Smith issued his revisions to the guidelines, described above in Chapter 6. The plaintiffs went back to federal court, and asked the judge to block implementation of the new guidelines in Chicago on the ground that they violated the settlement order. The trial judge agreed, finding that even though the introductory portion of the new guidelines included a prohibition against conducting an investigation solely on the basis of activities protected under the First Amendment, the practical effect of the revisions would be just the opposite. Specifically, the judge was concerned about the following provision in the new guidelines:

> When, however, statements advocate criminal activity . . . an investigation under these Guidelines may be warranted unless it is apparent, from the circumstances or the context in which the statements were made, that there is no prospect of harm.

The judge found the Smith guidelines deficient because they did not embody the *Brandenburg v. Ohio* test: they did not specify that the feared harm must be "imminent" and "likely" and they did not require that the speech be "directed" (i.e., intended) to cause imminent lawless action.

In 1984, the court of appeals overturned the decision of the trial judge, however, and the revised guidelines went into effect in Chicago.[17] The court of appeals stated that the FBI "has always investigated people who advocate or even threaten to commit serious violations of federal law, even if the violations are not imminent; and it always will. It 'has a right, indeed a duty, to keep itself informed with respect to the possible commission of crimes; it is not obliged to wear blinders until it may be too late for prevention.'" Accordingly, the appeals court held that the settlement order could be reasonably interpreted in a way that was consistent with the revised Smith guidelines:

> This interpretation is that the FBI may not base an investigation solely on the political views of a group or an individual; it must have a basis in a genuine concern for law enforcement. Thus it may not investigate a group solely because the group advocates Puerto Rican independence . . . but it may investigate any group that advocates the commission, even if not immediately, of terrorist acts in violation of federal law. It need not wait till the bombs begin to go off, or even till the bomb factory is found.

Up to a point, the appeals court was correct: the Constitution does not require the government to ignore the threats of those who advocate violence, even when the threat is not imminent. The standard for investigation need not be as stringent as the standard for prosecution. But like the guideline revisions adopted in the wake of the CISPES investigation, the appeals court's decision failed to distinguish carefully between the investigation of a *group* and the investigation of those *individual members* who threaten to engage in illegal activities. In saying that the FBI may investigate "any group that advocates the commission" of violent acts, the court endorsed the FBI's traditional intelligence model of monitoring the peaceful and political activities of groups whose members are also suspected of engaging in or planning violent activity.

Rarely, at least in the domestic context, does the FBI open a terrorism investigation without some indication that criminal conduct is being planned or advocated. First Amendment concerns develop when the FBI bootstraps that suspicion into a broad investigation of the group's political activities. In the international context, the FBI does not even need the predicate of a criminal or violent act, for the "agent of a foreign power" concept allows the FBI to investigate any and all activities "on behalf of" the foreign power, even if those activities are purely political and peaceful in nature.

The court of appeals in the Chicago case also reversed another lower court ruling that the FBI had violated the settlement agreement during its investigation of the Chicago chapter of CISPES from March 1983 to June 1985. The trial court had found that surveillance, photographing, attendance by government agents at public meetings, reviews of financial, utility, and telephone records, and checks of law enforcement records in the CISPES investigation had violated the settlement agreement. The court of appeals overturned the lower court ruling, holding that the settlement did not bar FBI investigations of First Amendment activities if the FBI conducted the investigation "for the purpose of routing out terrorist activity only to find that the basis for thinking that the organization was engaged in terrorism was flimsy or nonexistent." The court ruled that those who would bring suit under the settlement had to prove that the FBI *intended* to interfere with First Amendment rights or that the FBI engaged in a pattern of substantial noncompliance, whether or not it was intentional.[18]   Intent, almost always impossible to establish, is the wrong test. And if the CISPES investigation did not amount to substantial noncompliance, it is difficult to imagine what would. The correct test for evaluating FBI activities should be an objective one: Were the FBI's investigative activities reasonably calculated to obtain information about suspected violent activities? Surveilling and photographing public demonstrations is not reasonably calculated to produce evidence of criminal conduct committed before or after the demonstrations. The CISPES investigation was never really a search for terrorism. The stated purpose was routing out terrorism, but it was not conducted in a way likely to "rout out terrorist activity," even if such activity had existed.[19]

THE FOURTH AMENDMENT

Like the First Amendment, the Fourth Amendment's prohibition against unreasonable searches and seizures also imposes important limits on government conduct, but, as with the guarantees of the First Amendment, the courts have been reluctant to interpret the Fourth Amendment to rein in FBI investigations.

The courts have made it clear that wiretaps and physical searches by federal agents in criminal cases can generally be conducted only on the basis of judicial orders finding probable cause to believe that a crime has been, is being or is about to be committed and that the search will uncover evidence of the criminal activity. Thus, for example, Judge Griesa in the SWP case held that the FBI's surreptitious and warrantless entries ("black bag jobs," i.e., burglaries) under COINTELPRO were "obvious violations of the Fourth Amendment."[20]

This principle clearly applies to investigations of domestic terrorism, although the Justice Department once tried to claim that it did not. In 1972, in the landmark *Keith* case, the Supreme Court ruled that the warrantless wiretapping of domestic activists was unlawful under the Fourth Amendment. [21] Justice Powell, writing the Court's opinion, rejected the government's argument that there was a domestic security exception to the warrant requirement of the Fourth Amendment:

Security surveillances are especially sensitive because of the
inherent vagueness of the domestic security concept, the necessarily
broad and continuing nature of intelligence gathering, and the
temptation to utilize such surveillances to oversee political dissent.
We recognize, as we have before, the constitutional basis of the
President's domestic security role, but we think it must be exercised
in a manner compatible with the Fourth Amendment.

The courts, however, have divided on whether the Fourth Amendment permits warrantless searches where there is suspicion of involvement by a *foreign* government or group. (The issue has since been dealt with statutorily, as the FISA court has been granted authority over physical as well as electronic searches.) In one case arising out of the Watergate era, the courts flatly rejected the concept. The case involved two of President Nixon's assistants, who were prosecuted for conspiring to break into the office of a Los Angeles psychiatrist to steal medical records relating to one of his patients, Daniel Ellsberg, who was at the time under a Federal indictment for disclosing the Pentagon Papers to the press.[22] Nixon's aides sought to defend their actions by claiming that there was a "national security" exception to the Fourth Amendment warrant requirement.[23] The district court rejected the argument, and explained that recognizing such an exception would contravene "vital privacy interests" embodied in the Fourth Amendment:

The Court cannot find that [the recent, controversial ruling involving national security wiretaps] indicates an intention to obviate
the entire Fourth Amendment whenever the President determines
that an American citizen, personally innocent of wrongdoing, has
in his possession information that may touch upon foreign policy
concerns. Such a doctrine ... would give the Executive a blank
check to disregard the very heart and core of the Fourth
Amendment and the vital privacy interests that it protects.[24]

However, other lower court rulings approved warrantless searches in cases involving foreign counterintelligence. When Morton Halperin sued his former boss, National Security Advisor Henry Kissinger, for placing a wiretap on Halperin's home telephone without judicial approval while Halperin was a staffer at the National Security Council, the federal appeals court ruled that so long as objectively reasonable national security concerns prompted the wiretap, Kissinger was not liable.[25] And when the government sought to use information gleaned from a warrantless wiretap of an American citizen and a Soviet national to support their convictions for passing military secrets to the Soviets, the court deferred to the government's invocation of the concept of "national security."[26]

More significantly, the Supreme Court has allowed the FBI to do through informants or undercover agents what it could not do directly. Under the "invited informer" principle, the Court has reasoned that a person or political organization has no legitimate expectation of privacy in information voluntarily shared with a third party in the mistaken belief that the information will not be turned over to the government.[28] Thus, an informant can record his own phone conversations with activists who have invited him into their group or "wear a wire" to record conversations at meetings for the government, without any court order or probable cause showing. This principle was applied, for example, in a criminal case against members of a church who had provided a haven to Central American refugees fleeing civil wars in El Salvador and Guatemala. The church members were charged with violating U.S. immigration laws. The evidence against them included the testimony of an informant who had infiltrated their church. The federal appeals court in California held that infiltration into the church organization did not violate the Fourth Amendment since the defendants voluntarily and at their own risk revealed the information to the informant.[27]

DUE PROCESS

"There are literally millions of aliens within the jurisdiction of the United States. The Fifth Amendment, as well as the Fourteenth Amendment, protects every one of these persons from deprivations of life, liberty, or property without due process of law. Even one whose presence in this country is unlawful, involuntary, or transitory is entitled to that constitutional protection." *Mathews v. Diaz*, 426 U.S. 67, 77 (1976).

The due process clause of the Fifth Amendment is another critical constraint on government discretion in the name of fighting terrorism. A fundamental component of due process is the right to confront one's accusers. It is founded on the premise that the truth is most likely to emerge in an adversarial proceeding, where the accused, who is in the best position to defend herself, can confront the sources of evidence against her, and can challenge their veracity, reveal their bias, and catch them in contradiction.

Thus, it is well-established that in no criminal trial — even involving the most dangerous of crimes and the most secret of information — may the government rely on evidence not disclosed to the defendant. If the government wants to use an informant's testimony, the informant must take the witness stand. If the government wants to rely on classified information, it must reveal it in court. Even under the Classified Information Procedures Act, which permits the government to substitute as evidence an unclassified summary of classified evidence, the courts can accept the substitution only if it affords the defendant the same opportunity to defend herself as the full classified record would.[29]

The courts have ruled that the due process clause, which protects all persons living in the United States, citizens or noncitizens, whether here lawfully or unlawfully, bars the use of secret evidence to deport noncitizens living here.[30] Accordingly, deportation proceedings throughout our history have been conducted on the basis of evidence disclosed to the person, to afford her an opportunity to defend herself.[31]

In recent years, however, the INS, in the name of fighting terrorism, has repeatedly tried to assert the power to use secret evidence in deportation hearings. The federal courts have often rejected the efforts, but the INS persists. For example, when the INS sought to use secret evidence to expel Fouad Rafeedie, a permanent resident alien, the D.C. Circuit Court of Appeals rejected the government's effort, finding that "[i]t is difficult to imagine how even someone innocent of all wrongdoing could meet such a burden [of rebutting undisclosed evidence that he is a member of a terrorist group]."[32]

The INS sought to use secret evidence in the LA 8 case twice — first to justify detaining the eight and later to deny permanent resident status to two of them. The first time, the immigration judge refused to consider any evidence not disclosed to the eight. The second time, the aliens had to seek relief in the federal courts, which barred the INS from relying on secret evidence because to do so would violate due process.[33] The Ninth Circuit called the risk of error inherent in the use of undisclosed information "exceptionally high." It recalled the words of Justice Jackson in *United States ex rel. Knauff v. Shaughnessy:*

> The plea that evidence of guilt must be secret is abhorrent to free men, because it provides a cloak for the malevolent, the misinformed, the meddlesome, and the corrupt to play the role of informer undetected and uncorrected.[34]

Indeed, the court concluded, "one would be hard pressed to design a procedure more likely to result in erroneous deprivations." Balancing the risk of error against the government's asserted national security interests, the appeals court held that secret evidence could not be used: "[T]he fact that a given law or procedure is efficient, convenient, and useful in facilitating functions of government, standing alone, will not save it if it is contrary to the Constitution."

Notwithstanding these courtroom defeats, the INS continues to use secret evidence in immigration proceedings, as illustrated in Chapter 10.

CONCLUSION

The First Amendment serves as the single most important safeguard against infringements on political activity, and the Fourth and Fifth Amendments also offer important protections. But enforcing those guarantees is often difficult in the face of the secrecy that impedes the uncovering of improper behavior, judicially-erected barriers to recovery, and the willingness of the Justice Department to defend with tremendous resources the FBI, the INS, and other law enforcement agencies against citizen lawsuits seeking to impose limits on its investigative activity.

Frank Wilkinson's lawsuit lasted twelve years. The LA 8 case is in its fifteenth year.

Furthermore, the Chicago case shows the courts' reluctance to use the First Amendment to curb FBI surveillance. So long as courts refuse to acknowledge the chilling effect of FBI investigations, and so long as they are reluctant to limit FBI investigations of protected activities, the First Amendment will provide little meaningful protection against wasteful probes of political activity. This reluctance bodes ill for application of the Antiterrorism Act's provision making "support for terrorism" a crime, for even though political activity ultimately cannot be prosecuted, the FBI can spend considerable resources investigating it without judicial control.

There is an obvious tension between the Supreme Court decisions carefully protecting the rights of political speech and association and those allowing the government to engage in surreptitious surveillance and use of informants without probable cause. Government spying on lawful associational activities, such as public demonstrations or meetings, can have just as real a chilling effect on the exercise of the First Amendment right to associate as the compelled disclosure of membership lists that the Supreme Court blocked in cases involving the NAACP years ago.[35] Cases denigrating the chilling effect that FBI investigations have on First Amendment rights ignore the Supreme Court's warning: "[First Amendment] freedoms are delicate and vulnerable, as well as supremely precious in our society. The threat of sanctions may deter their exercise almost as potently as the actual application of sanctions."[36]

PART III

THE 1996 AND 2001
ANTITERRORISM ACTS:

CURTAILING CIVIL LIBERTIES IN THE
NAME OF FIGHTING TERRORISM

CHAPTER 8

PROLOGUE TO THE 1996 ANTITERRORISM ACT

On February 10, 1995, senior Democrats introduced the Clinton Administration's counterterrorism bill in the Senate and in the House of Representatives.[1] With the exception of habeas corpus "reform" provisions added subsequently, the Clinton proposal included all the critical elements of the antiterrorism law enacted one year later: it established a special court that would use secret evidence to deport noncitizens accused of association with terrorist groups; it gave the Executive Branch the power to criminalize fundraising for lawful activities conducted by organizations labeled "terrorist;" it repealed the Edwards amendment, which prohibited the FBI from opening investigations based on First Amendment activities; and it resurrected the discredited ideological visa denial provisions of the McCarran-Walter Act to bar aliens based on their associations rather than their acts. The bill also included provisions to create a new federal crime of terrorism, carve further exceptions in the time-honored posse comitatus law barring the U.S. military from civilian law enforcement, expand use of pre-trial detention, and loosen the rules governing federal wiretaps.[2]

The story of the Act's passage shows how easily civil liberties and constitutional principles can be cast aside under the influences of emotion and political posturing. The lessons of past FBI abuses from COINTELPRO through the CISPES investigation were ignored. The voices of likely victims of the statute's ideologically-based approach were never heard from, while those who opposed the legislation on the grounds that it was unnecessary or dangerously unconstitutional were marginalized. Instead, two incidents — the 1993 bombing of the World Trade Center and Timothy McVeigh's attack on the federal building in Oklahoma City — overwhelmed all rational discussion, and the law was enacted as an effort to do something in response to these two crimes. The fact that suspects were arrested soon after both incidents and later convicted, and the fact that the government could point to nothing in the Act that would have prevented or made it easier to prosecute either incident, proved irrelevant.

LONG SOUGHT AND LONG REJECTED

The most troubling provisions in the 1996 Anti-Terrorism Act — the resurrection of association as grounds for exclusion and deportation of noncitizens; the ban on supporting lawful activities of groups labeled "terrorist" by the Executive Branch; and the secret evidence provision — were developed long before the bombings that triggered their final enactment.

In the case of guilt by association, the Clinton proposal making mere membership in a terrorist group grounds for exclusion and deportation represented a return to the intolerant approaches of the 1950s. The McCarran-Walter Act, passed in 1952, made association with Communist or anarchist groups a ground for exclusion and deportation, and was used over the years against such luminaries as Gabriel Garcia Marquez, Graham Greene, Carlos Fuentes, Czeslaw Milosz, Yves Montand,

and Charlie Chaplin. In 1990, with much fanfare, Congress removed most of the ideological grounds for exclusion and deportation from the immigration law. But in the Clinton bill, they reappeared in the guise of a bar on anyone believed to be a member of a "terrorist organization."

The fundraising ban's history went back to 1984, when the Reagan Administration sent Congress a bill to make it a crime to "support" terrorism. Features of the Reagan proposal were remarkably similar to what was enacted in the 1996 Antiterrorism Act, including a provision granting effectively unreviewable discretion to the Secretary of State to designate foreign groups as "terrorist." The Reagan provision was opposed on constitutional grounds and was not enacted. The first Bush Administration proposed similar "support for terrorism" legislation, but again Congress rejected it. Finally, in the 1994 Clinton omnibus crime bill, a narrow support for terrorism provision was added, focused only on support for violent acts, and it was accompanied by the Edwards amendment, intended to prevent a repeat of the CISPES fiasco by precluding investigations based solely on activities protected under the First Amendment.[3]

Like the fundraising ban, the secret evidence provision also had a prior record, legislatively and judicially. The Clinton provision was a slightly modified version of a proposal offered during the prior Bush Administration, which Congress twice refused to enact. The INS had on several occasions sought to use secret evidence in immigration settings, but had been rebuffed by the courts. Undeterred by these losses in the courts on constitutional grounds, the Clinton Administration resurrected the Bush language in its 1995 proposal.

ONE-SIDED HEARINGS

From the outset, Congressional consideration of the legislation was largely one-sided. At the House Judiciary Committee's first hearing on the bill, in April 1995, the first six of the eight witnesses called to testify were strongly and uncritically supportive of the bill.[4] One of the other two witnesses raised questions about some aspects of the bill, but also called for repeal of the Executive Order banning the U.S. government from engaging in assassinations. Only one witness, Greg Nojeim of the American Civil Liberties Union, gave a consistently critical, constitutionally-based analysis of the legislation.

Absent from the hearings altogether were any of the people likely to be affected personally by the bill. Yet it was their stories that Congress should have heard. Any number of people could have been called to testify, from Fouad Rafeedie, a permanent resident alien the government sought to expel using secret evidence, to the LA 8 or Frank Wilkinson. The Committee also could have reached a little further back into American history to consider cases like that of Ellen Knauff, a World War II "war bride" held at Ellis Island for three years on secret evidence that she could not see and therefore could not rebut. Her case went all the way to the Supreme Court, where she lost on the ground that as an alien outside the U.S. she had no constitutional rights. When public pressure forced Congress to give Knauff a hearing, it came out that the "secret evidence" against Knauff was nothing more than a malevolent rumor sparked by a jilted former lover of Knauff's husband. Knauff was admitted to the United States, but not before spending three years in detention on Ellis Island. These were not the stories Congress chose to hear when it took up the Clinton terrorism bill.

The House Judiciary Committee's Subcommittee on Crime held a second hearing on May 3, two weeks after the Oklahoma City bombing.[5] Not surprisingly, given the emotional reaction to the bombing, this hearing was no more balanced than the first. Once again, those opposing the legislation were relegated, as one witness stated, to the "unenviable position of testifying on the [third and] last panel."[6]

In June 1995, the full House Judiciary Committee held two additional hearings and again the majority of the witnesses, and all of those on the first panels on each day, supported the legislation. Again, Greg Nojeim of the ACLU was the sole witness called to offer a comprehensive constitutional critique of the legislation.

The Senate hearings were even more one-sided. The first one was held barely one week after the Oklahoma City bombing. Not one of the ten witnesses allowed to testify criticized the legislation or warned of constitutional concerns. A second hearing was scheduled for May 24, 1995, at which two witnesses would have criticized the legislation, but that hearing was canceled.

Little attention was paid to whether the FBI was subject to standards that would prevent it from repeating past abuses of constitutional rights. Two exchanges between FBI Director Freeh and members of the House Judiciary Committee were particularly telling. Expressing concern that the legislation would invite a return to the days of COINTEL-PRO, Rep. Sheila Jackson Lee asked Director Freeh how successful he thought COINTELPRO was. Freeh's response: "I would really have to do some research to give you an intelligent answer."[7] The Director of the FBI should not have had to do "research" to discuss the worst period in his agency's history. Freeh should have jumped at the chance to distance himself and his organization from a program and philosophy universally condemned for violating civil liberties. He should have been able to outline concretely the principles and procedures by which agents avoid infringements on First Amendment rights. In the political climate at the time, however, Freeh felt no need to do so. When Rep. John Conyers asked Freeh to comment on the lessons of history and the difficulty of distinguishing violent rhetoric from terrorism, Freeh again declined to answer, stating "I don't think it's appropriate for me to comment on that." Freeh sensed that he would get the expanded powers he wanted, and he saw no need even to address these questions.

NO IDENTIFIABLE NEED
FOR ANTITERRORISM LEGISLATION

Despite the one-sidedness of the hearings, several members of the House Judiciary Committee, both Democrat and Republican, questioned the need for the legislation. They repeatedly asked Administration witnesses to identify the specific problems that the legislation would cure. The witnesses had remarkably little to offer and at times seemed confounded by the very question. When John Conyers of Michigan, the

House Judiciary Committee's senior Democrat and a veteran of many FBI scandals, specifically asked at the April 1995 hearing what lessons had been learned from the 1993 World Trade Center bombing that indicated that federal and state laws were deficient, Deputy Attorney General Jamie Gorelick at first refused to answer the question, saying only that there were a number of other cases, which she did not name, where there was inadequate federal jurisdiction. When Conyers pressed, Gorelick responded that if the facts of the World Trade Center bombing had been different, it could not have been investigated and prosecuted as a federal crime. At that, Conyers concluded:"I've never seen this much law created as a result of prosecutions that we agree worked very effectively, but you say that it may not have worked."[8]

Later, Republican George Gekas asked a similar question. Gorelick responded, "Well, speaking hypothetically . . . ." Gekas asked again,"My question is ... do we have any evidence that such things might — are brewing." Gorelick responded that she "was not at liberty" to share with the Congressman at the hearing information that would respond to that question. Howard Coble, a conservative Republican from North Carolina, questioned why law enforcement required new powers to combat terrorism and received equally unsatisfying answers. Congresswoman Sheila Jackson Lee asked what effect the legislation would have had on the Pan Am 103 case. Gorelick said she would have to submit an answer later. In that written answer, she admitted,"[W]e do not have examples of prosecutions that have been hampered by the lack of statutes of the type proposed in" the Administration's bill.[9]

At the House Subcommittee on Crime hearings on May 3, proponents of the legislation were once again unable to explain why new legislation was needed. Members asked how the new law would change current practices, and how this would improve the fight against terrorism. Again, Administration witnesses avoided answering these questions. When asked by Rep. Conyers how the proposed law would have affected the Oklahoma City bombing incident had it been in place at the time, FBI Director Freeh responded: "I really can't comment on that." [10]

IMPACT OF THE OKLAHOMA CITY BOMBING

The antiterrorism bill drew opposition from a broad-based coalition of groups who agreed that it would unnecessarily expand government power and infringe personal liberties. Irish American and Arab American groups felt particularly threatened, but all members of the coalition came to recognize the indivisibility of civil liberties. They knew the guilt by association concept could be redirected at any time for the foreign policy or internal political purposes of the government, and they feared that the practice of using secret evidence, once established, was likely to be expanded.

Editorial writers questioned the need for the legislation and opposed its liberty-threatening provisions. Most significantly, perhaps, public opinion polls showed widespread reluctance to give the government more powers. The legislation languished and seemed headed for defeat.

All that changed when, on April 19, 1995, a horrifying explosion destroyed the Oklahoma City federal building, killing 168 persons, including 19 children. Members of Congress immediately felt tremendous pressure to pass antiterrorism legislation. It did not matter that the proposals in the President's initial bill were directed largely against international terrorism, while the Oklahoma bombing was the work of homegrown discontents. Nor did it matter that, even after the bombing, polls still showed public reluctance to sacrifice liberties in an effort to purchase security. The President appeared on "60 Minutes" the Sunday after the bombing to offer his condolences to the victims' families and to set a tone of reassurance for the nation. He ended up promising further antiterrorism legislation and suggesting that it might be appropriate to use the occasion to "reform" habeas corpus.

POLITICS AND OTHER AGENDAS TAKE OVER

The antiterrorism bill soon became entangled in partisan politics. Democratic and Republican leaders introduced dueling versions of the legislation, and each party sought to blame the other for being unresponsive to terrorism.[11] Nonetheless, the House hesitated to act, in large part because of conservative opposition to expanded government wiretapping authorities and a proposal to regulate certain common explosives (seen by some as a step towards regulation of gunpowder and guns).

A different dynamic played out in the Senate, where Judiciary Committee chairman Orrin Hatch was eager to capitalize on the President's suggestion that habeas corpus reform be added to the antiterrorism package. For years, Hatch had sought to limit the right of habeas corpus, only to see his proposals dropped from every successive anticrime measure. The terrorism bill offered another chance to achieve this long-sought goal. Hatch's provisions gutting habeas corpus ended up in the Act, and are among its worst features, but they have nothing to do with terrorism. For the most part, the habeas reforms govern the standards that federal courts use in reviewing state court criminal convictions, and terrorism cases are almost never tried in state courts. What was really at issue in the habeas debate was whether state prisoners could obtain meaningful federal review of the constitutionality of the procedures by which they had been convicted and sentenced. Most of the debate centered around death penalty cases, but most of the changes sought by habeas opponents would apply to noncapital cases as well. Senator Hatch wanted to make it more difficult for federal courts to order retrials of prisoners where state courts had violated the U.S. Constitution.

The Senate acted quickly and passed the anti-terrorism bill, S. 735, by a vote of 91-8 in June 1995, after dropping the President's wiretap proposals and adding Hatch's provisions curtailing the right of habeas corpus. The Senate bill also included Clinton's proposals to exclude and deport aliens based on their association, to criminalize fundraising in the U.S. for designated groups, and to allow the military to assist in law enforcement efforts aimed at biological and chemical weapons.

In the House of Representatives, the legislation stalled for many months. But as 1996 — a Presidential election year — began, it became clear that President Clinton was going to use the terrorism issue politically. With the April 19 anniversary of the Oklahoma City bombing approaching, the House of Representatives ceded to the pressure and revived the bill. The version passed by the House omitted several troublesome provisions, reflecting the considerable opposition of a coalition of activists representing a broad spectrum of political, religious, and ethnic interests. From then on, however, the impending April 19 anniversary drove the issue. The conference committee that was appointed to reconcile the differences between the House and Senate versions was dominated by supporters of the legislation's more onerous provisions. A few objectionable provisions adopted by the Senate to expand wiretap authority were dropped, but these would have been incremental in their effect compared to the radical changes that were adopted: the prohibition on fundraising, a provision denying entry visas to members of terrorist groups, the secret evidence provisions, provisions to facilitate the denial of political asylum benefits and to expedite deportation of aliens arriving without proper documents, and limits on habeas corpus.

Eager to get the bill on the President's desk by the April 19 anniversary of the Oklahoma City bombing, the Senate adopted the conference report on April 17 in a 91-8 vote. The next day, the House also adopted the report by a vote of 293-133. On April 24, the President signed the Antiterrorism and Effective Death Penalty Act of 1996.

CHAPTER 9

THE 1996 ANTITERRORISM ACT'S CENTRAL PROVISIONS

The Antiterrorism and Effective Death Penalty Act of 1996[1] contained what were, prior to the 2001 antiterrorism measures, some of the worst assaults on civil liberties in decades. The Act was wide-ranging, dealing with everything from the making of plastic explosives to trading in nuclear materials. But it also attacked basic First Amendment and due process rights. This chapter focuses on the more troublesome provisions of the Act and describes what they purported to do. These provisions were unnecessary, unwise and unconstitutional. They were not justified by any deficiency in existing law nor, it has turned out, did they serve any legitimate purpose in deterring, investigating or punishing acts of violence. They have been directed against disfavored groups to the detriment of the civil liberties of all.

OVERVIEW

The Act made it a crime for citizens and noncitizens alike to provide any material support to the lawful political or humanitarian activities of any foreign group designated by the Secretary of State as "terrorist."[2] Thus, the Act reintroduced to federal law the principle of "guilt by association" that had defined the McCarthy era. People can be punished, the Act says, not for what they do or abet, but for supporting wholly lawful acts of disfavored groups. If this law had been on the books in the 1980s, it would have been a crime to give money to the African National Congress during Nelson Mandela's speaking tours here, because the State Department routinely listed the ANC as a "terrorist group."

This fundraising provision appeared to codify the focus on political ideology and association that had prompted the FBI's most intrusive investigations of political activists from COINTELPRO to CISPES. It gave the FBI reason to investigate any group or individual that supports even the wholly lawful activities of a designated foreign organization. The Act further encouraged politically-focused investigations by repealing the Edwards amendment, which had barred the FBI from opening or expanding investigations solely on the basis of First Amendment-protected activities.

Reversing another reform that had been years in the making, the Act revived the practice of denying visas to foreigners based on mere membership in undesirable groups, in this case, the same groups designated "terrorist" by the Secretary of State.[3] Congress repudiated such ideological exclusions (another form of guilt by association) in its 1990 reform of the immigration laws. The 1996 Act's provisions, however, allow exclusion based on membership alone, without any showing that the individual furthered any illegal acts of the group. Since an alien who was inadmissible at the time of entry is thereafter deportable, the change also gave the government grounds to deport a person who was a member of a designated organization at the time of his otherwise legal entry into the United States.[4]

The Act also created an unprecedented "alien terrorist removal procedure" designed to deny immigrants facing deportation the most basic of due process protections — the right to confront their accusers.[5] Under this provision, the government claims the authority to deport an alien alleged to be a terrorist without ever telling her the source of the evidence against her, a tactic that the courts have repeatedly ruled violates due process.[6]

Demonstrating the vulnerability of all rights in the face of the antiterrorism rhetoric, the Act included several destructive provisions having nothing to do with terrorism. One sharply curtailed the right of habeas corpus, the "Great Writ" by which federal courts have granted relief to people imprisoned as a result of constutional violations in state court criminal proceedings.[7] Others limited aliens' ability to claim political asylum and deprived them of due process rights if they entered the U.S. without going through immigration inspection, even if they are not suspected of any involvement in terrorist activity.[8]

TERRORISM IS WHATEVER THE SECRETARY OF STATE DECIDES IT IS

Perhaps the most troubling feature of the 1996 Act is its resurrection of guilt by association, criminalizing humanitarian support to any group blacklisted as "terrorist." Under the 1996 Act, the Secretary of State may designate a foreign group as a terrorist organization if she finds that the group "engages in terrorist activity" that threatens the "security of United States nationals or the national security of the United States." The Immigration and Nationality Act defines "terrorist activity" to include virtually any use of force, and the Antiterrorism Act defines "national security" as "the national defense, foreign relations, or economic interests of the United States." As a result, the Secretary of State can designate organizations that engage in both lawful and unlawful activity, based on a determination that the group's activities threaten our foreign policy or economic interests. Since courts are reluctant to second-guess the Secretary of State on what threatens our foreign policy, the law effectively gives the Secretary of State a blank check to blacklist disfavored foreign groups.

The Clinton Administration admitted in hearings leading up to enactment of the law that some of the groups it ultimately designated as "terrorist" were in fact broad-based organizations engaged in lawful social, political and humanitarian activities as well as violent activities. In 1994, the Clinton Administration testified against a bill that would have made membership in Hamas a ground for exclusion, arguing that because Hamas engages in "widespread social welfare programs" as well as terrorism, one could not presume that a Hamas member was a "terrorist" without indulging in guilt by association.[9] Yet by 1995, the Administration proposed to do just that for countless groups. The initial designations by the Secretary in October 1997 fulfilled that promise, including Hamas on the list.[10] Also on the list was the Popular Front for the Liberation of Palestine, which the trial court in the LA 8 case found was involved in a wide range of lawful activities, including the provision of education, day care, health care and social security. Notably, the list did not include any group headed by Osama bin Laden, illustrating the limitations of such a designation process as an antiterrorism measure.

Three consequences flow from the Secretary of State's decision to designate a foreign entity as a terrorist organization: (1) it is a crime for anybody to contribute money or other material support or resources to a designated group, even for its social, political or humanitarian activities;[11] (2) all members of the group are barred from entering the United States, and are deportable if they were members prior to entry, even if they have never been involved in illegal activities;[12] and (3) banks must freeze funds of any designated organization and its agents.

The designation authority invites selective enforcement. The Secretary of State can pick and choose which groups to designate, based on the politics of the moment. The Act's terms encompass groups whose activities threaten the security of U.S. nationals, meaning any U.S. tourist or corporate outpost anywhere in the world. There are literally hundreds if not thousands of groups worldwide that engage at least in part in violent activities. Practically speaking, the government must necessarily enforce such authority selectively. Introducing a further opportunity for politically motivated decisions, the Secretary of State can take an organization off the list whenever she decides that the national security of the United States warrants it, even if the organization is still involved in terrorist activity.

The decision of the Secretary of State to designate a group as terrorist can be based on classified evidence. An organization can challenge the Secretary's designation in federal court, but the scope and terms of judicial review are severely limited: a court can set aside the determination only if it finds it to be "arbitrary" or "capricious," unconstitutional, or "short of statutory right."[13] The review is to be "based solely upon the administrative record," and the statute provides no opportunity for a designated group to contribute to the administrative record. And the Secretary of State can defend her decision with secret evidence, making it impossible to mount an effective challenge. Most importantly, because courts will not second-guess the Secretary of State on what threatens our "foreign relations," the designation is effectively unreviewable. Yet the Act says that this one-sided review is the sole avenue for challenging determinations of what is and is not a terrorist organization. By the time the government brings criminal proceedings against someone for improper fundraising activity, it is too late to challenge the designation: the Act provides that "a defendant in a criminal action shall not be permitted to raise any question concerning the validity of the issuance of such designation as a defense or an objection at any trial or hearing."[14]

CRIMINALIZING SUPPORT FOR HUMANITARIAN AND POLITICAL ACTIVITIES

Once a group has been designated, it is a crime to provide any monetary or material support to it. [15] The law exempts medicine and religious materials, but all other humanitarian or political aid is prohibited. Congressional proponents of the measure referred to it as a ban on "terrorist fundraising." But rather than targeting fundraising for terrorist violence, the Act bans virtually *all* material support, even for humanitarian and political activities, of designated groups. This list-based approach to fighting terrorism produces some absurd results. For example, it is not a crime to raise and contribute money for violent conduct abroad that is not otherwise a crime under U.S. law, if carried out by a group that is not designated by the Secretary, but it is a crime to raise money for the peaceful activities of designated groups. Moreover, if a designated group renounces violence, it remains a crime to support its peaceful activities until the Secretary removes it from the list, but it is not a crime under the Act to give money to any splinter group that remains committed to terrorism, until that splinter group is designated. Increasingly, we are seeing terrorist activities for which credit is claimed by a "previously unknown group," yet it is impossible under the Act for the Secretary to bar support for a group that has no name.

This provision was entirely unnecessary. Prior to enactment of the 1996 Antiterrorism Act, it was already illegal to support the terrorist acts of any group or person if those acts were crimes under U.S. law. Aiding and abetting the commission of a crime is as illegal as the underlying crime itself. Additionally, in 1994 Congress passed a law specifically prohibiting material support of certain terrorist crimes at home or abroad (crimes against U.S. persons or interests wherever committed).[16]

The full scope of the 1996 Act prohibition is not entirely apparent. What if one knowingly gives money to an undesignated organization, but the government claims it was controlled by a designated organization? What if one gives money to an undesignated organization that has as a constituent member a designated organization? The significance of these questions lies not only in how they are answered, but also in the uncertainty that they create. Persons legitimately concerned about conditions in other countries, and seeking to support the political and humanitarian activities of ethnic or nationalist groups, will be more hesitant to exercise their First Amendment rights to support them if they fear criminal prosecution.

Furthermore, the uncertainty and ambiguity inherent in the fundraising prohibition invites the FBI to conduct wide-ranging investigations of lawful activities. The FBI can claim that it was merely trying to determine whether contributions to a non-designated organization were being diverted to a designated organization, or whether contributors "knew" where their contribution was ending up. On this thin reed, the FBI can try to justify wide-ranging investigations into certain communities, repeating — with legal sanction — the abuses of its past.

Indeed, the Clinton Administration was quite explicit in 1996 about its intention to investigate First Amendment activities. It sought and obtained repeal of the seemingly modest protections of the Edwards amendment, which prohibited investigations of "material support" to terrorism based solely on activities protected by the First Amendment. The Clinton Administration had agreed to the Edwards amendment in the 1994 crime bill.[17] Yet by early 1995, the Administration was claiming that this provision imposed "an unprecedented and impractical burden on law enforcement concerning the initiation and continuation of criminal investigations," and in the 1996 Act the Administration succeeded in obtaining its repeal, thus codifying the theory underlying the discredited CISPES and LA 8 investigations.

Simply put, the fundraising ban of the 1996 Antiterrorism Act ignores what has long been a fundamental precept of our constitutional law — that "a blanket prohibition of association with a group having both legal and illegal aims," without a showing of specific intent to further the unlawful aims of the group, is an unconstitutional infringement on "the cherished freedom of association protected by the First Amendment."[18]

THE 1996 ACT'S IMPACT ON IMMIGRATION LAW — IDEOLOGICAL EXCLUSION REVIVED

The First Amendment grants Americans the right to receive information and ideas, especially ideas the government finds objectionable. This right includes the receipt of information from abroad. One highly effective way of transmitting information remains the personal encounter, through speeches, conferences and meetings. Since the immigration law sets the standards both for excluding aliens from permanent admission and making them ineligible for visas for temporary visits, rendering a category of persons "excludable" on ideological grounds means that they cannot come here even temporarily to speak or engage in other activities implicating the First Amendment rights of U.S. citizens.

U.S. immigration policy for many years was dominated by the ideological exclusions of the McCarran-Walter Act. Colored by the Cold War, the Act barred from the U.S. not only suspected Communists but also critics of U.S. foreign and defense policy seeking to visit the U.S. to speak with U.S. citizens. The law was a constant source of embarrassment. Virtually every time the State Department denied a visa on ideological grounds, it was widely condemned, and ironically the speakers' views often gained greater attention than they might have received had they entered the United States. Through the 1980s, the ideological exclusions came under increasing challenge in the courts and in Congress.[19]

In the Immigration Act of 1990, Congress finally repealed the ideological exclusion provisions of the McCarran-Walter Act, repudiating the principle of guilt by association as a guiding principle in U.S. immigration law. Congress substituted a series of criteria focused largely on the criminal acts of individuals. Under the reforms, a foreigner could not be barred entry from the U.S. based on beliefs, advocacy or associations that would be protected under the First Amendment if engaged in by a person within the U.S. Rather, foreigners seeking to visit the U.S. to speak or lecture could be barred if there was reason to believe that they had engaged in criminal or terrorist conduct abroad or would do so here. From 1990 to 1996, aliens were excludable and deportable if they either engaged in a terrorist activity themselves, or if they provided material support to an individual, organization, or government "in conducting a terrorist act at any time." Terrorist activity was defined extremely broadly, to include virtually any use of a firearm or explosive with the intent to endanger person or property. However, the law required the government to prove that the individual it sought to deport or exclude had personally engaged in such activity, or had provided material support for the conducting of such activity.

The 1996 Antiterrorism Act reversed this reform. The Act eliminated the requirement that an excluded alien must individually have any connection to terrorist activity per se. It substituted guilt by association, barring entry to any alien who is a member or representative of a group designated by the Secretary of State as terrorist, even if the individual has participated only in the group's political or humanitarian activities.[20] It rendered aliens excludable (and deportable if their membership predated their entry to the United States) for associational activity otherwise protected by the First Amendment. Under this test, members of the African National Congress or the IRA would have been excludable, even if they were seeking to enter the United States specifically to pursue prospects for peace.

"ALIEN TERRORIST" REMOVAL PROCEDURES

In another section of the 1996 Antiterrorism Act, Congress gave the Department of Justice the authority to deport noncitizens on the basis of secret evidence. [21] The secret evidence provisions apply to a specially defined category of noncitizens called "alien terrorists."[22] But according to the INS, "alien terrorists" include not only those actually engaged in terrorism, but also those who have merely supported a terrorist organization's *lawful* activities.

Under the Act, the government can invoke the secret evidence provisions whenever the Attorney General determines that public disclosure of the evidence against an alleged "alien terrorist" would "pose a risk to the national security of the United States or to the security of any person."[23] It is likely that the government could make such claims whenever an informant is involved: all it needs to do is state that presenting the evidence in open court would disclose the informant's identity, and that the informant's security would be endangered. Similarly, any time any portion of the government's evidence is classified, it will be able to claim risk to the national security, since by definition classified information is information the disclosure of which would cause harm to national security. (In reality, of course, much of the information that is classified as secret would not in fact threaten national security if disclosed, but there are few checks on over-classification of information.)

The Act requires the government to provide the noncitizen with a summary of its classified information. The judge must determine that the evidence is "sufficient to enable the alien to prepare a defense."[24] It is difficult to see how a summary could ever be sufficient, however, because one cannot cross-examine a summary. If the judge determines that the summary is not sufficient, the Justice Department may immediately take an appeal to the Court of Appeals.

In a special removal proceeding, whether or not it involves the use of secret information, the alien is barred from seeking to suppress any evidence, even if it was unconstitutionally obtained, and has no right to discover information derived under the Foreign Intelligence Surveillance Act, which the government may use even if obtained in violation of FISA's provisions.[25] Aliens in such proceedings are also barred from applying for asylum or a form of relief known as "withholding of deportation," even if it is undisputed that they will be persecuted for their political ideas upon return to their country of origin.

The Act also provides for immediate detention without bail of all aliens subject to this procedure. Noncitizens here on student visas, tourist visas, or special labor visas are denied any hearing whatsoever regarding their detention. Lawful permanent resident aliens are entitled to a hearing, but the government is able to use classified information, and instead of the government having to prove that there are grounds for detention, the alien bears the burden of proving a negative: that there is no basis for detention.[26]

The secret evidence provisions are a recipe for error and a patently unconstitutional denial of fundamental due process. The courts have consistently declared unconstitutional INS attempts to use secret evidence to deport aliens, even where the government claimed that national security was at stake, [27] and our nation has survived quite well for over 200 years allowing citizens and noncitizens alike to confront their accusers. Perhaps not surprisingly given the law's many constitutional flaws, the Justice Department has never invoked it, finding other sources of authority for using secret evidence in immigration proceedings.

Chapter 10

The Impact of the 1996 Act

Surprisingly, the federal government was slow in implementing some of the 1996 Act's central elements, calling into question the urgency with which the Administration had urged its passage. Indeed, the "Alien Terrorist Removal Court" has never been used to deport a single alleged terrorist. It took the Secretary of State 18 months to issue her first list of designated foreign terrorist organizations. And as of December 2001, the government had prosecuted only three cases involving material support to terrorist organizations.

However, the government did aggressively pursue the use of secret evidence and guilt by association in related settings. From 1996 to 2000, it sought to use secret evidence to detain and deport about two dozen immigrants, almost all of them Muslims accused of vague associations with terrorist groups.[1] Over time, case by case, the government's evidence was revealed to be worthless, its legal theories were largely rejected, and virtually all of the accused aliens were released. As a result, prior to September 11, the practice of using secret evidence had nearly died out, a bill to end the practice had broad bipartisan support in Congress, and President Bush himself had publicly criticized the use of secret evidence.[2]

All of that progress ground to a halt, however, with the attacks of September 11. The Secret Evidence Repeal Act is widely considered dead in the water. The Justice Department has conducted a widespread campaign of secret immigration detentions. And the Administration has argued vigorously in court that it needs the authority to rely on secret evidence more than ever in the wake of September 11.[3]

In light of the government's renewed interest in using secret evidence, the history of its reliance on this tactic in the recent past is all the more important. That history demonstrates that the desire to use undisclosed evidence cannot be reconciled with the most basic demands of fairness.

SECRET EVIDENCE CASES

In the late 1990s, the INS selectively subjected a number of Arab immigrants to Star Chamber treatment, arresting them on the basis of minor immigration violations and then using secret evidence of their political associations to deprive them of their liberty, deny them immigrant status to which they are otherwise entitled, and deport them. In virtually every case, the government did not charge the aliens with any violent activity, but simply with associating with the wrong group. These proceedings were not brought under the terms of the 1996 Antiterrorism Act.[4] Instead, the Justice Department claimed that the tools of guilt by association and secret evidence were available to it under other provisions of the immigration law.[5] Most of the allegations in the secret evidence cases came from the FBI, reflecting heightened FBI scrutiny of U.S. Muslim communities.[6]

Nasser Ahmed

Most people assume that the Constitution prevents the government from arresting and jailing them without criminal charges, without bail, and without an opportunity to respond to the government's allegations. But according to the INS, an alien does not enjoy these rights. Nasser Ahmed, an Egyptian man and the father of three U.S. citizen children, spent three and a half years in a U.S. prison, on the basis of secret evidence that neither he nor his attorney ever saw. When Ahmed was arrested, in April 1996, he was charged with no crime. The government did not even allege that he facilitated or supported any criminal activity. Instead, the INS arrested him on routine charges of overstaying his visa. But claiming that Ahmed was a "threat to national security," the INS detained him on the basis of undisclosed classified evidence. It provided no summary of the evidence, maintaining that national security would be compromised even by describing it in general terms. One year later, the INS used secret evidence again, to oppose Ahmed's applications for asylum and withholding of deportation. This time the INS gave him a one-sentence summary: it stated only that the government had evidence "concerning respondent's association with a known terrorist organization." The government would not even identify the organization. The immigration judge called the summary "largely useless."

An electrical engineer, Ahmed has lived in New York City with his wife and children since 1986. He worshipped at the Abu Bakr Mosque in Brooklyn, where Sheik Omar Abdel Rahman occasionally preached, and which the FBI had under surveillance because of its members' political opposition to the government of Egypt. Ahmed came under FBI scrutiny while working as a court-appointed paralegal and translator for the legal team defending Sheik Abdel Rahman during the Sheik's trial for seditious conspiracy to bomb tunnels and buildings in New York City. The FBI and INS sought to convince Ahmed to join forces with them against the cleric, and threatened him with deportation if he refused to cooperate. Ahmed declined their offer. The INS carried out its threat on April 24, 1995 by arresting Ahmed for overstaying his visa. He was released on $15,000 bond three days later. Upon his release, Ahmed continued to work as a court-appointed member of the Sheik's defense team.

On April 23, 1996, as Ahmed entered the federal courthouse in New York for a routine hearing on his immigration case, the INS arrested him again. This time, the INS refused to release Ahmed on bail. He remained incarcerated until November 1999.

Ahmed feared returning to Egypt because of the persecution he would face as a result of his political and religious associations. The immigration judge hearing his case, Donn Livingston, ruled that he had "no doubt" Ahmed would be imprisoned and very likely tortured if returned to Egypt, and agreed that on the public record Ahmed deserved political asylum and withholding of deportation. Ordinarily this would have been the end of the inquiry, and Ahmed would have been entitled to remain in the country. However, despite his serious reservations about the constitutionality of considering secret evidence, Judge Livingston went on to conclude, on the basis of the secret evidence presented to him in a closed-door hearing outside the presence of Ahmed and his lawyers, that Ahmed was a threat to national security, and therefore he could not be released and was ineligible for asylum and withholding.

Ahmed then filed suit in federal court to challenge the constitutionality of the INS's actions. The INS responded by suddenly disclosing much of the information that it had previously claimed could not be disclosed without endangering national security. It named the group Ahmed was alleged to be associated with — al-Gama-al-Islamiya — and also charged that he was associated with Sheik Rahman. Significantly, the INS's summary contained no charge that Ahmed himself had ever engaged in any illegal activity or supported any illegal activity.

When both the federal district court judge and the Board of Immigration Appeals said that Ahmed should be given another chance to defend himself in light of the government's new disclosures, the government revealed still more of the previously classified evidence. With the newly released material in hand, Ahmed was able to rebut the charges. Judge Livingston, the same judge who earlier had found the secret evidence to be persuasive, concluded after the new hearing that Ahmed was not a danger to the national security. "Armed with a better understanding of the government's case," he wrote, Ahmed "was successful in rebutting most of the factual assertions." The remaining evidence was "double or triple hearsay," for which the FBI refused to provide any substantiation, so the judge concluded that it was not credible. The INS sought to bar Ahmed's release pending an appeal, but both the Board of Immigration Appeals and Attorney General Janet Reno rejected its requests, and Ahmed was released in November 1999.

Ahmed's case illustrates the dangers of relying on secret evidence. The chronology of the case suggests that the government often over-classifies evidence in the first instance. Each time the government was challenged about its use of secret evidence, it revealed a little bit more of the evidence. What the government ultimately disclosed could and should have been revealed the first time the evidence was used. Because it was not, Ahmed was denied the opportunity to confront any of the evidence used against him until almost three years after he was first detained. Judge Livingston specifically noted that some of the classified evidence used by the government also was available from non-confidential sources. Yet the government insisted on using the classified form, and Ahmed was not even told that the evidence existed in unclassified form. Secret evidence is almost by definition "unassailable," so short of a constitutional challenge, the government has little incentive to develop additional, public sources for its allegations.

In the end, the bulk of the evidence against Ahmed was nothing more than charges of association. In the secret hearing on Ahmed's asylum and withholding applications, the judge and the INS stated that the heart of the case was Ahmed's association with al-Gama-al-Islamiya. Yet once that was revealed, and Ahmed's lawyers were able to respond to it, both the judge and the INS admitted that association with al-Gama-al-Islamiya was not sufficient grounds to detain Ahmed or to deny him asylum and withholding.

Mazen Al Najjar

Mazen Al Najjar, a Palestinian professor from Tampa, Florida, also spent three and a half years in prison on the basis of secret evidence. Like Ahmed, Al Najjar was not charged with engaging in or supporting any illegal acts. The only basis for his detention was his political association. Like Ahmed, Al Najjar was given only a one-sentence summary of the classified evidence used against him. The summary stated that Al Najjar was associated with the Palestinian Islamic Jihad (PIJ). He was not accused of any illegal activity on the group's behalf.[7] He was not told how he was allegedly associated, what if anything he was alleged to have done with the group, where and when the association took place, or who made the allegation.

Al Najjar has resided in the United States since 1981. He came initially to pursue graduate studies, and later settled in Florida with his wife and three daughters. In 1995, the FBI began to investigate the World and Islam Studies Enterprise (WISE) in Tampa, Florida, a think tank affiliated with the University of South Florida, after its former administrator became head of the Islamic Jihad. The FBI claimed that WISE was a front for Palestinian terrorists. Al Najjar came under FBI scrutiny because he worked as the editor-in-chief of WISE's research journal.

The FBI and INS arrested Al Najjar on May 19, 1997, while he was in deportation hearings for overstaying his student visa, and detained him on the basis of secret evidence. Shortly thereafter, federal officials approached two people who knew Al Najjar and said that they would release him if he provided information about others in the community, suggesting that the government did not really believe that Al Najjar posed a threat to national security.

In 1999, Al Najjar filed a constitutional challenge to his detention in federal court. The court ruled that his detention violated due process because it was based on evidence that he had no meaningful opportunity to rebut, and that under immigration law, mere association with a terrorist organization, without more, was insufficient to justify detaining him. The district court ordered the INS to give Al Najjar a fair hearing on his custody status.

A two-week trial in immigration court ensued, in which the INS sought to show that Al Najjar had supported the Palestinian Islamic Jihad through his association with WISE and another Tampa-based organization, the Islamic Concern Project (ICP), which sponsored conferences on politics and Islam and raised money for indigent families in the Occupied Territories. At the close of the public portion of the trial, the same immigration judge who had initially ordered Al Najjar detained ruled that the INS had failed to offer any convincing evidence to support its assertions against Al Najjar.

Specifically, the judge found that there was "no evidence before the Court that demonstrates that either [ICP or WISE] was a front for the PIJ."[8] On the contrary, he found "that WISE was a reputable and scholarly research center and the ICP was highly regarded." And he concluded that "[b]ased on the evidence presented to this Court, it appears that Respondent's involvement with WISE and ICP amounted to cooperation with the organizations in lawful activities."

With respect to the assertion that Al Najjar raised money for terrorist organizations through WISE and ICP, the immigration judge again found no evidence to support the contention. Indeed, the INS's principal witness "admitted that there is no open source evidence that Respondent ever sent money to a terrorist organization or that he ever advocated terrorism." Despite the fact that the INS had seized the entire contents of the WISE and ICP offices, including financial records and over 500 videotapes of the two organizations' activities, the judge found that the INS had offered "no evidence that indicates that Respondent engaged in fundraising for the PIJ through WISE," through ICP, or indeed, "for any organization."

The INS then sought to present secret evidence against Al Najjar once again, but the immigration judge concluded that the INS's one-page summary was insufficient to provide Al Najjar a meaningful opportunity to defend himself, and therefore refused to consider the secret evidence. He ordered Al Najjar released on bond. The INS sought a stay of Al Najjar's release before the Board of Immigration Appeals and the Attorney General, but both rejected the INS's request, and in December 2000 Al Najjar was released.

In November 2001, however, after Al Najjar's deportation order became final, the INS re-arrested him and placed him in a maximum security prison under solitary confinement and 23-hour lockdown. To justify its actions, the INS issued a statement that did nothing more than repeat the very assertions that had been rejected as unfounded after a two-week hearing the previous fall. Al Najjar has once again challenged the constitutionality of his detention in federal court, and the challenge is pending.

Imad Salih Hamad

Imad Salih Hamad, a Palestinian born in Lebanon, has resided in the United States since 1980. He married a U.S. citizen in 1991, and sought permanent residence on that basis. The INS, however, alleged that he was affiliated with the Popular Front for the Liberation of Palestine, and sought his deportation. In 1997, the INS claimed to have classified evidence against him. An immigration judge evaluated the secret evidence behind closed doors, but concluded that it was insufficient to establish ties to any terrorist groups. In June 1998, while the INS's appeal of the immigration judge's ruling was pending, the INS declassified the secret evidence. It turned out to be material that the government had openly confronted Hamad with at an earlier stage in his proceedings.[9] Somehow, the material had become classified, and then declassified, in the meantime.

On February 19, 1999, the Board of Immigration Appeals affirmed the immigration judge's 1997 decision granting Hamad adjustment of status. The Board said that the evidence of Hamad's alleged connection with the PFLP was "vague, lacking in specificity and uncorroborated." The Board stated, "The classified information provided in camera may arouse suspicion, but would require much greater detail to convince the members of this Board that the respondent is in any way a supporter of a terrorist organization."

Anwar Haddam

Anwar Haddam has been for most of his adult life a member of the Algerian Islamic Movement. In 1991, he was elected to the Algerian parliament. After a military coup in January 1992 canceled the election, Haddam came to the United States and was politically active in Washington, D.C. on issues relating to Algeria. The INS arrested Haddam in December 1996 for violating his immigration status and sought to deport him to Algeria. Haddam produced evidence showing that he and his family would be tortured and executed for his political affiliations and beliefs if they were forced to return to Algeria. In fact, in March 1998 Algeria condemned Haddam to death in absentia. Nonetheless, the INS pushed for his expulsion on the basis of secret evidence. Haddam's lawyers were advised that the government was relying on telephone conversations recorded under the Foreign Intelligence Surveillance Act (FISA), but they were denied access to the tapes. The transcripts of the wiretaps were never actually produced for the immigration judge's examination either. Instead, the evidence was presented to the judge in summary form by an FBI agent who testified in the judge's chambers, off the record and without even being sworn in. Haddam's lawyers, who were excluded along with Haddam from the judge's chambers, protested this procedure on the grounds that it violated procedural due process and FISA. The judge heard the evidence over these objections.

After further hearings and appeals, Haddam was granted asylum. The Board of Immigration Appeals, after considering the secret evidence, concluded that it did not support the accusation that Haddam was a terrorist. Haddam was released in December 2000, having spent four years in detention.

Hany Kiareldeen

Hany Kiareldeen, an electronics store manager born in Gaza who has lived in the U.S. since 1990, was arrested in New Jersey in March 1998 and detained based on secret evidence. The summary of the evidence provided him said that he was a member of an unnamed terrorist organization, that he had relations with suspected terrorists, also unnamed, and that he had threatened Janet Reno. Kiareldeen denied all charges. From the outset, Kiareldeen suspected that one of the sources of the secret evidence (and perhaps the only source) against him was his estranged wife. Kiareldeen's lawyers made numerous unsuccessful attempts, over vigorous INS objections, to cross-examine her. She was engaged in a child custody dispute with him, and had on several occasions before leveled charges against him, all of which have been dismissed as unfounded.

In April 1999, an immigration judge ordered Kiareldeen released, on the ground that the secret evidence did not establish that he was a threat to national security. The INS appealed, however, and obtained a stay of Kiareldeen's release while the appeal was pending.

Kiareldeen was finally released from jail in October 1999, after a federal judge ruled the government's use of secret evidence unconstitutional and the Board of Immigration Appeals simultaneously found no basis for the government's allegations that Kiareldeen was a national security threat. It is rare for any judge — even an independent Article III judge — to reject a claim of national security by the federal government. Yet in Kiareldeen's case, seven immigration judges eventually reviewed the complete record, and all seven rejected the government's contention that he posed a threat to national security.

Although the judges were not allowed to reveal the substance of the confidential information, two judges directly discussed the quality of the government's secret evidence. Immigration Judge Daniel Meisner, who presided at the trial, stated that Kiareldeen had "raised formidable doubts about the veracity of the allegations contained in the [classified information]," and that in the face of repeated requests for more information, the INS had refused "to answer those doubts with any additional evidence, be it at the public portion of the hearing or even in camera."[10] He concluded that the classified evidence was "too meager to provide reasonable grounds to believe that [Kiareldeen] was actually involved in any terrorist activity."

BIA Judge Anthony Moscato, dissenting from a preliminary panel decision not to release Kiareldeen, wrote that the bare-bones character of the government's in camera evidence made it "impossible" for the BIA to exercise independent judgment in assessing "either the absolute truth or the relative probity of the evidence contained in the classified information."[11] Judge Moscato criticized the INS for having provided no original source material and "little in the way of specifics regarding the source or context of the classified information." He further noted that despite the immigration judge's continuing requests, the INS had provided "no witnesses, neither confidential informant nor federal agent, to explain or document the context of the actions and statements referenced in the classified information or to document the way in which the classified information became known to the source of that information."[12]

Iraqi Detainees

Perhaps the most unusual secret evidence case involved a group of Iraqi men who worked with the CIA in a plot to overthrow President Saddam Hussein, were then flown to the United States by the U.S. government in March 1997 after the CIA plan fell apart, and were only then ordered excluded from the United States on the basis of secret evidence.[13] Former CIA director R. James Woolsey volunteered to represent them pro bono upon hearing of their plight, and described their situation as follows:

> Six Iraqi men are sitting in a Los Angeles prison, bewildered by the U.S. government's decision to deport them. They are all enemies of Saddam Hussein, and after the Iraqi dictator's attack on northern Iraq in late 1996 the U.S. evacuated them and their families to Guam and then to Southern California. Now the Immigration and Naturalization Service argues that the six are a threat to U.S. national security, and an immigration judge has agreed that they should be sent back to Iraq, where they face nearly certain death. Though they struggled for freedom in Iraq, these men are being deprived of their basic rights to defend themselves.

> Would the INS charges that these men endanger national security
> stand up to scrutiny? It seems unlikely, given their personal histo-
> ries. But the charges against them are classified and neither the
> accused not their attorneys can see them. [14]

Upon their arrival in California, the men were separated from their families and placed in INS detention centers. The INS initiated exclusion proceedings against them for entering without a valid visa. Strangely, all of the family members who were transported with the men were granted political asylum. At a March 28, 1997 hearing, the INS stated that it denied the Iraqis' political asylum applications because they posed a security risk to the U.S., and the INS further indicated its intent to offer secret evidence showing the Iraqis ineligible for political asylum.

On March 9, 1998, a Los Angeles immigration judge, D.D. Sitgraves, found on the basis of the government's secret evidence that the men posed a threat to U.S. security. The judge's ruling was largely classified. As their cases proceeded though the courts, they remained in a Los Angeles detention facility. Woolsey wrote:

> Why does the INS insist on keeping them in prison facing deporta-
> tion and death? A case earlier this year, involving similar charges
> against another Iraqi evacuee, suggests that Justice Department
> incompetence may be a major factor. Hasim Qadir Hawlery was sin-
> gled out by the INS and imprisoned for a year after a botched inter-
> view by the FBI in Guam. Errors in translation and the interviewer's
> ignorance of Iraq led the INS to believe wrongly that Mr. Hawlery
> was lying about belonging to a particular opposition group. This
> mistake came to light only because the charges against Mr. Hawlery
> were unclassified, so the INS evidence had to be presented before
> both parties in an open hearing. He won his bid to stay in the U.S.
>
> Similar blunders may lie behind the charges against the six. Or dis-
> information may have been sown by informants among the larger
> group of Iraqi evacuees on Guam, some of whom may well have
> borne personal grudges or had other ulterior motives. Such errors
> will never come to light without a defense lawyer allowed to cross-
> examine government witnesses.[15]

As in Nasser Ahmed's case, much of the evidence initially classified and used in secret against the Iraqis has was later disclosed. As that evidence was declassified, it became clear that much of it was weak and based on unsubstantiated assertions by other Iraqis involved in the failed coup attempt.[16]

Ultimately, the government offered the men a settlement that would place them and their families in safe countries that agreed to accept them. Six of the men agreed and were released in the summer of 1999, subject to the condition that they remain in the Lincoln, Nebraska area until countries could be found that would accept them. However, two men, Dr. Ali Yasin Mohammed Karim and his brother, declined the offer and insisted on pressing their claim for political asylum in the United States. In May 2000, immigration judge D.D. Sitgraves ruled that Dr. Karim had presented "more than sufficient evidence" to rebut the government's claim that he should be excluded as a national security threat. Finally, in August 2000, after nearly four years in jail, Dr. Karim was released. Judge Sitgraves wrote in her opinion that Karim "has sufficiently demonstrated that the government's claims were ill-founded and has rebutted the presumption that he constitutes a risk to the security of the United States."[17]

Summary of Secret Evidence Cases

In a remarkable string of cases, then, the government repeatedly failed to justify its use of secret evidence. In some cases, it disclosed evidence that it initially said could not be disclosed, only to reveal that its charges were unfounded. In others, federal courts declared the government's reliance on secret evidence unconstitutional. And in others, it was harshly criticized by immigration judges for relying on insubstantial and unreliable evidence. As a result, the government even-tually grew more hesitant about using secret evidence. In the last years of the Clinton Administration, the Deputy Attorney General's office undertook a comprehensive review of all secret evidence cases, and in its last year the Clinton Administration filed no new secret evidence cases. As noted above, President Bush publicly criticized the practice during his presidential campaign. And a bipartisan bill to end the practice had substantial support in Congress. But the events of September 11 have brought unprecedented secrecy to immigration enforcement, and the Administration has argued in court that it needs the authority to use secret evidence to fight its new war on terrorism. Thus, while every federal court to address the use of secret evidence in the last decade has declared the practice unconstitutional, it is likely to continue.

STATE DEPARTMENT DESIGNATION OF FOREIGN TERRORIST GROUPS

A year and a half after President Clinton signed the 1996 Antiterrorism Act, the State Department designated 30 groups as foreign terrorist organizations.[18] The long delay in issuing the list belied the government's claim in 1995 that enactment of the fundraising ban was urgently needed to fight terrorism. Without a designation, the ban on domestic fundraising for terrorist organizations had no effect. The list was issued in October 1997 only after political pressure was applied by private groups.[19]

Now that groups have been designated, anyone who provides funds or other support to the listed groups can be prosecuted. American financial institutions that have assets of these groups under their control must freeze them. Known members of such organizations are not eligible for visas. When the State Department designated the groups, its spokesperson James P. Rubin noted that "the goal of this law was more deterrence than confiscation." But in seeking deterrence, the government cast a wide net chilling speech and punishing individuals for constitutionally protected associational activities.

The perverse quality of the material support provision is best captured by its application to the Humanitarian Law Project (HLP), a 30-year old human rights organization based in Los Angeles. Since 1991, the HLP has, among other things, focused on the plight of Turkey's Kurdish minority, encouraging recognition of their basic human rights, and promoting a peaceful resolution of their conflict with Turkey's government. To that end, the HLP has worked with the Kurdistan Workers Party (PKK), the principal political organization representing the Kurds in Turkey, specifically by training and assisting them in human rights advocacy. But because it constitutes "material support," that work became a crime when the Secretary of State designated the PKK a terrorist organization.

In March 1998, HLP joined with a number of U.S. groups of Sri Lankan Tamils to challenge the Act. The Tamils are an abused ethnic minority in Sri Lanka. U.S.-based Tamil groups seek to provide humanitarian and political support to the Liberation Tigers of Tamil Eelam (LTTE), which represents Tamils and is engaged in a civil war against the Sri Lankan government. As one of the leading organizations advocating for human rights and the right to self-determination for the Tamils, the LTTE provides humanitarian aid to Tamil refugees fleeing from Sri Lankan armed forces, engages in political organizing and advocacy, provides social services and economic development through a quasi-governmental structure in Tamil Eelam, administers a chain of orphanages, and seeks to defend the Tamil people from Sri Lankan human rights abuses. But when the Secretary of State designated the LTTE a terrorist group under the Antiterrorism Act, it became a crime to support any of this work.

The groups' lawsuit argued that the ban on material support violated their First Amendment right to political association, because providing material support to a group is a constitutionally-protected form of association, and the law criminalizes such association even where it is undertaken for wholly peaceful and nonviolent purposes.[20]

In June 1998, the district court granted HLP a preliminary injunction, declaring that the law's bans on providing training and personnel were unconstitutionally vague. However, the court declined to enjoin the remainder of the statute, including the ban on providing any other kind of monetary support. The U.S. Court of Appeals for the Ninth Circuit upheld the district court's order.[21] Both courts acknowledged that the First Amendment protects the right to associate with "terrorist organizations," but reasoned that a ban on monetary support was justified because money is fungible. But if the right to associate does not include the right to pay dues, raise money, or provide any material support to one's group of choice, the right is an empty formalism. Associations cannot exist without the material support of their members.

In September 2001, the district court made its preliminary injunction against the "training" and "personnel" provisions final, and again refused to enjoin the rest of the statute. Both sides have appealed.

Meanwhile, in the now five years that the 1996 Antiterrorism Act has been on the books, the United States has brought only three prosecutions for providing material support to a designated terrorist organization. The first was abandoned when the defendant absconded. Two are currently pending, one in North Carolina against a man accused of raising money for Hizbollah in Lebanon, and the other in Los Angeles against a group of persons accused of soliciting contributions at Los Angeles Airport for the People's Mujahedin Organization of Iran. As of December 2001, neither case had yet come to trial.

FREEZING ASSETS OF DESIGNATED "FORIGN TERRORIST ORGANIZATIONS"

The 1996 Antiterrorism Act requires any financial institution that "becomes aware that it has possession of, or control over, any funds in which a foreign terrorist organization, or its agent, has an interest," to freeze the assets and report them to the Treasury Department. The first case to arise under this provision resulted in a court order requiring the bank to unfreeze the account of a U.S.-based distributor of Mojahed, a newsletter published in Europe by the People's Mojahedin Organization of Iran.

Crestar Bank of Virginia received an anonymous electronic mail message informing it that one of its accounts, held by Nasher Ltd., belonged to a designated terrorist group. Crestar promptly contacted the Office of Foreign Assets Control (OFAC) of the Department of Treasury, which, according to Crestar, informed the bank by telephone that Nasher Ltd. was a "front or conduit" for a listed terrorist group, and told Crestar to freeze the account, which had between $5,000 - $6,000, and to turn over the account holder's records.[22]

Nasher Ltd. challenged the freezing of assets on First Amendment grounds, arguing that distributors and publishers are protected by the First Amendment. Nasher also sought to prevent disclosure of any account records that would reveal the identities of subscribers to the newsletter, many of whom had already endured persecution in Iran on account of their political beliefs, and feared retribution against family members in Iran or themselves were such information shared with Iran.

Federal district court judge Leonie Brinkema granted the injunction to unblock the account, and ordered Crestar not to reveal to OFAC the names and/or addresses of any subscribers to the newsletter.[23] In doing so, Judge Brinkema held that Nasher Ltd. and its subscribers had significant First Amendment and personal security interests, and that they would suffer "irreparable injury" if the injunction was not granted. In a strange turn of events, OFAC actually denied asking the bank to freeze the account or turn over records.[24] Since both the bank and the government said that they did not oppose unfreezing the account, the judge disposed of the case without deciding the First Amendment claims. But she indicated that the evidence presented by Nasher, Ltd. demonstrated a "definite indication of likelihood of success on the merits."[25]

In a still more bizarre case, the United States has effectively subjected a U.S. citizen, Mohammed Salah, to a form of internal banishment. In 1998, President Clinton added Salah's name to an Executive Order that, like the 1996 Antiterrorism Act, bars financial transactions with terrorist organizations. The Executive Order, however, also designates individuals, and Salah was so designated. As such, it became a crime for anyone in the United States to have any financial dealings with Salah. He cannot buy a sandwich, pay his mortgage, get a job, or go to the doctor without a special exemption issued by the Treasury Department.[26] The order even bars donations to Salah. Thus, if literally enforced, the order would require Salah to starve to death in his own country. Yet this punishment was imposed without a trial, without a hearing, and without any provision of reasons for its imposition.

FURTHER LEGISLATIVE DEVELOPMENTS

Several controversial provisions dropped from the 1996 terrorism bill were subsequently enacted in other legislation. Among them were changes to the posse comitatus law, which prohibits use of the U.S. military in domestic law enforcement. The posse comitatus changes were enacted later in 1996, on the Department of Defense Authorization Act for fiscal 1997.[27] The provision authorized use of the military to assist the Department of Justice in domestic law enforcement investigations "during an emergency situation involving a biological or chemical weapon of mass destruction." (Similar authority had previously been granted for situations involving nuclear materials, and major changes to the posse comitatus law had been enacted in the 1980s, allowing use of the military in drug interdiction and other anti-narcotics activities.) The 1996 changes allow the military to carry out arrests, conduct searches and seizures, and collect intelligence for law enforcement purposes, if the action "is considered necessary for the immediate protection of human life, and civilian law enforcement officials are not capable of taking the actions."

The Clinton Administration had also offered with its terrorism package a proposal to weaken the standards for government use of so-called roving wiretaps, potentially very wide-ranging wiretaps that follow a target as he moves from phone to phone. Congress eventually enacted a broadened roving tap authority in October 1998, in the Intelligence Authorization Act for Fiscal Year 1999.[28] In what was basically a legislative sneak attack, the provision was added behind closed doors by the conference committee after it had been left out of the bills passed by both the House and the Senate. The change adopted in 1998 was even broader than the one Congress had rejected two years earlier. Under prior law, investigators had been able to obtain a roving tap only when they could show to a judge that the target of surveillance was changing telephones (e.g., by using different pay phones) with the purpose of avoiding interception. Under the 1998 law, it is now sufficient to show merely that any of the person's actions could have the effect of thwarting interception. Moreover, the roving tap may remain "for such time as it is reasonable to presume that the person [identified in the order] is or was reasonably proximate to the instrument through which such communications will be or was transmitted." This means the government can tap the phones in the homes and offices of friends, relatives and business associates visited by a suspect, despite the Fourth Amendment's requirement that the government specify with particularity the person or place to be searched.

The fiscal 1999 intelligence authorization act also included other enhancements of FBI authority, creating explicit authority to use pen register and trap and trace devices in counterintelligence and international terrorism investigations and granting the government access to hotel, car rental, bus, airline and other business records.[29] Interestingly, the changes were not as discretionary as the FBI had wanted. The pen register and trap and trace authority adopted in 1998 required the approval of the FISA court and the standard was in some ways more stringent than the standard for pen registers and trap and trace devices in a criminal case, requiring investigators to provide information that "demonstrates" that the surveilled line has been or is about to be used in communication about activities that "involve or may involve a violation of the criminal laws." As to accessing business records concerning hotels, transportation, car rental and similar services, the FBI had originally sought authority to issue so-called administrative subpoenas, basically a piece of paper signed by an FBI official compelling a business to turn over records on its customers. Instead, the provision included in the intelligence authorization act required the issuance of an order by the FISA court. Again, in some respects, this standard was tougher than the standard for access in criminal cases, where a grand jury subpoena can be issued without any effective judicial control. (Those limitations, as we explain in Chapter 11, were abandoned in the 2001 antiterrorism legislation.)

NO POSITIVE RESULTS

In February 1998, a Senate subcommittee looked at the status of counterterrorism efforts in the U.S.[30]   Dale L. Watson, Section Chief for International Terrorism Operations at the FBI, admitted that the fundraising ban had produced no tangible results. Watson speculated that even though the ban had no discernible impact to date in disrupting the activities of terrorist groups, the deterrent effects of the ban alone may indicate its effectiveness.

The fact is that the government has not made much use of the authorities in the Antiterrorism and Effective Death Penalty Act of 1996, despite the urgency with which the Administration said they were needed. The much-touted gains in law enforcement powers from the Antiterrorism Act of 1996 have produced no visible concrete results in the fight against terrorism. And the principles espoused in the Act — especially reliance on secret evidence and guilt by association — were shown in case after case to be both unconstitutional and ineffective in the fight against terrorism.

CHAPTER 11

FIGHTING A WAR AGAINST TERRORISM, AT HOME AND ABROAD

When terrorists hijacked four airplanes on a crisp Tuesday morning in September 2001, turning them into devastating explosives directed at the World Trade Center, the Pentagon, and a third location still unknown, they not only killed thousands of innocent civilians in the most brutal act of terrorism mankind has yet perpetrated, but they also threatened to change the fabric of American life. Before September 11, we had been relatively free of foreign attacks on our soil, at least since Pearl Harbor. After September 11, we all confront a new vulnerability. Before September 11, terrorists had done many unspeakable things, but never had they committed an act so heinous and so devastating. The attacks of September 11 made the unthinkable gruesomely real. The anthrax scare that followed in the ensuing weeks only exacerbated the threat.

In the wake of these attacks, calls for new security measures are undoubtedly warranted, particularly in light of the ongoing threats that the country faces as it fights a war against terrorism, and specifically against Osama bin Laden and his al Qaeda network. Airport security has been a particular focus, but to stop there would fail to address the threat that the next attack will likely take a very different form. We must improve all of our defenses against terrorism, by improving intelligence and law enforcement capabilities. The fact that the U.S. intelligence agencies apparently had no foreknowledge of the September 11 attacks points to a failure of intelligence with massive consequences.

But in responding to the threat of terrorism, we must not trample upon the very freedoms that we are fighting for. Nothing tests our commitments to principle like fear and terror. Precisely because the terrorists violated every principle of civilized society and human dignity, we must maintain our commitment to principle as we fashion a response.

Three principles in particular should guide our response. First, we should not overreact in a time of fear, a mistake we have made all too often in the past. Second, we should not sacrifice the bedrock foundations of our constitutional democracy — political freedom, due process, and equal treatment — absent compelling showings of necessity. And third, in balancing liberty and security, we should not trade a vulnerable minority's liberties, namely the liberties of immigrants in general or Arab and Muslim immigrants in particular, in a misguided effort to obtain security for the rest of us.

Unfortunately, the immediate response to the events of September 11 has violated all three principles. Some measures in the anti-terrorism legislation enacted hastily in October 2001 were undoubtedly justified — in particular those that seek to reduce barriers to coordination between law enforcement and intelligence in terrorism investigations, to shore up airport security, border control and visa review procedures, and to improve controls over biochemical toxins. But in several critical areas, Congress has given the Executive Branch (and the Executive Branch has claimed for itself) broad new powers that go far beyond the fight against terrorism, and that infringe on fundamental liberties.

The government has detained over 1200 persons in connection with its investigation of the attacks of September 11, yet as of late December only one had been charged with any involvement in the crimes under investigation, and the government claims that only ten or twelve of the detained are members of al Qaeda, the organization said to be responsible for the attacks. The vast majority are being held on routine immigration charges under unprecedented secrecy. The government will not disclose most of their names, their trials are held in secret, and their cases are not listed on any public docket.

At the same time, ethnic profiling is being broadly engaged in, and widely defended as reasonable. The Justice Department has assumed the authority to listen in on attorney-client communications without a judge's approval and is considering relaxing the limits on FBI spying that were created in the wake of COINTELPRO. And President Bush has authorized the use of military tribunals, not only against al Qaeda members captured abroad, but against any of the 20 million noncitizens residing among us whom the President accuses of engaging in "international terrorism" or of harboring someone who has so engaged. In such tribunals, the military would be prosecutor, judge, jury and executioner, the trials could be held in secret, classified evidence could be used against the defendant without affording him an opportunity to confront it, and there would be no judicial review. And these responses mark only the first three months of the new "war on terrorism." Already, we fear, the government has overreacted in a time of fear, assuming powers in the name of fighting terrorism that are in no way limited to counterterrorist investigations. It has not shown that the new powers it has asserted are necessary to fight terrorism. And it has targeted the lion's share of its infringements on liberty at immigrants, and particularly Arab and Muslim immigrants.

REPEATING HISTORY

Before turning to the specifics of the post-September 11 response, it is worth reviewing a little history, and assessing what powers government already has in the fight against terrorism. Both assessments are critical to asking whether the government's response to September 11 is measured and likely to be effective.

This is not the first time our nation has responded to fear by targeting immigrants and treating them as suspect because of their group identities rather than their individual conduct. In World War I, we imprisoned dissidents for merely speaking out against the war, most of them immigrants. In 1919, the federal government responded to a politically motivated bombing of Attorney General A. Mitchell Palmer's home in Washington, DC by rounding up more than 6,000 suspected immigrants in 33 cities across the country — not for their part in the bombings, but for their political affiliations. They were detained in overcrowded "bull pens" and beaten into signing confessions. Many of those arrested turned out to be citizens. In the end, 556 immigrants were deported, but for their political affiliations, not for their part in the bombings.

In World War II, we interned 110,000 persons, over two-thirds of whom were citizens of the United States, not because of individualized determinations that they posed a threat to national security or the war effort, but solely for their Japanese ancestry. And in the fight against Communism, which reached its height in the McCarthy era, we made it a crime even to be a member of the Communist Party, and passed the McCarran-Walter Act, which authorized the government to keep out and expel noncitizens who advocated Communism or other proscribed ideas, or who belonged to the Communist Party or other groups that advocated proscribed ideas. As noted above, under the McCarran-Walter Act, the United States denied visas to famous writers and artists, as well as to Nino Pasti, former Deputy Commander of NATO, simply because he was coming to speak against the deployment of nuclear cruise missiles. And as the preceding chapters of this book have illustrated, misguided enforcement directed at political dissidents rather than criminals has continued into the present day.

All of these past responses are now seen as mistakes. Yet while the post-September 11 response does not yet match these historical overreactions, it nonetheless features some of the same mistakes of principle — in particular, targeting vulnerable groups not for illegal conduct, but for political speech, political activity, or group identity, and relying on broad investigatory sweeps rather than focusing on objective individualized suspicion. The present story begins with the awkwardly titled "United and Strengthening America by Providing Appropriate Tools Required to Intercept and Obstruct Terrorism Act of 2001"[1] — the PATRIOT Act for short — enacted within six weeks of the fateful attacks.

THE PATRIOT ACT

In legislative time, Congress enacted the PATRIOT Act virtually overnight. Attorney General John Ashcroft, its principal proponent, exerted extraordinary pressure, essentially threatening Congress that the blood of the victims of future terrorist attacks would be on its hands if it did not swiftly enact the Administration's proposals. The bill was never the subject of a Committee debate or mark-up in the Senate. There was a truncated process in the House, which heard no official testimony from opponents of the bill but at least held a full Committee mark-up. But the result of that process was put aside by the Administration and the House leadership and never brought to a vote in the full House. Instead, after three weeks of behind-the-scenes discussions between a few Senators and the Administration, a bill was introduced in the Senate on October 5 that included essentially all of the Administration's proposals. That bill passed the Senate on October 11, following a brief debate that made it clear that even supporters of the legislation had not read it and did not understand its provisions. The next day, a slightly different bill was introduced in the House, and was taken up and passed the same day under a procedure barring the offering of any amendments. It is virtually certain that not a single member of the House read the bill for which he or she voted. Differences between the two bills were reconciled without the normal convening of a conference committee. The President signed the bill into law on October 26.

Some measures in the omnibus act make sense. These include provisions ensuring adequate personnel on the northern border, some provisions strengthening the laws on money laundering, some provisions intended to break down institutional barriers that had limited the sharing of information between law enforcement agencies and intelligence agencies, and provisions intended to improve the processing of visas. (Making these things actually work, however, is largely beyond Congress's control.) Some of the expanded electronic surveillance provisions would also have made sense had they included appropriate limitations and judicial controls.

But in many respects, the PATRIOT Act reflects an overreaction all too typical in American history. It casts a cloak of secrecy over the exercise of government power by removing limitations and judicial controls on investigative authorities, and short-circuits procedures designed to protect the innocent and punish the guilty. It violates core constitutional principles, rendering immigrants deportable for their political association and excludable for pure speech. It fundamentally alters the power of the FBI and the role of the CIA within the United States, without adequate checks to protect against abuses. And by reserving its harshest measures for immigrants, measures that in the immediately foreseeable future will be directed predominantly at Arab and Muslim immigrants, it sacrifices commitments to equality by trading a minority group's liberty for the majority's purported security — a trade that will in all likelihood be ineffective. Painting with a broad brush is simply not a good law enforcement tool; it wastes resources on innocents and alienates communities, making it all the more difficult for law enforcement to distinguish the true threats from the innocent bystanders.

The PATRIOT Act: (1) imposes guilt by association on immigrants, extending the reach of that philosophy beyond the 1996 Act; (2) authorizes executive detention on mere suspicion that an immigrant has at some point engaged in a violent crime or provided humanitarian aid to a proscribed organization; (3) authorized the government to deny entry to aliens for pure speech, resurrecting yet another long-interred relic of the McCarthy era; (4) expands the government's authority to conduct criminal searches and wiretaps without first showing probable cause that the subject is engaged in criminal activity; (5) authorizes secret searches in cases having nothing to do with terrorism; (6) gives the Central Intelligence Agency access to the awesome power of criminal grand juries; and (7) reduces judicial oversight of intrusive information-gathering powers and expands the scope of FBI access to a wide range of records, essentially sanctioning fishing expeditions.

GUILT BY ASSOCIATION

Building on the 1996 Antiterrorism Act, the PATRIOT Act expands guilt by association, a McCarthy-era philosophy which the Supreme Court has condemned as "alien to the traditions of a free society and the First Amendment itself,"[2] but which has been making a strong comeback in recent years under the guise of cutting off funding for terrorism. Under the immigration law that existed before September 11, aliens were deportable for engaging in or supporting terrorist *activity*. The PATRIOT Act makes aliens deportable for wholly innocent associational activity with a "terrorist organization," irrespective of any nexus between the alien's associational conduct and any act of violence, much less terrorism.[3] The new law defines "terrorist activity" to include virtually any use or threat to use violence, and defines "terrorist organization" as any group of two or more persons that has used or threatened to use violence. Thus, the Act's proscription on associational activity potentially encompasses every organization that has ever been involved in a civil war or a crime of violence, from a pro-life group that once threatened workers at an abortion clinic, to the African National Congress, the Irish Republican Army, or the Northern Alliance in Afghanistan.

Like the criminal "material support" provisions of the 1996 Antiterrorism Act, the new law contains no requirement that the alien's support have any connection whatsoever to a designated organization's violent activity. Thus, an alien who sent coloring books to a day-care center run by a designated organization would apparently be deportable as a terrorist, even if she could show that the coloring books were used only by 3-year olds. Indeed, the law apparently extends even to those who seek to support a group in the interest of *countering* terrorism. Thus, an immigrant who offered his services in peace negotiating to the IRA in the hope of furthering the peace process in Great Britain and forestalling further violence could be deported as a terrorist if the Secretary of State chose to designate the Irish Republican Army (IRA) as terrorist.

The PATRIOT Act expands the "guilt by association" provisions of the 1996 Antiterrorism Act in several ways. It makes associational support a deportable offense, whereas the 1996 Act imposed criminal penalties. Unlike the 1996 Act, the new law makes no exception even for medicine or religious materials. And it expands the government's authority to blacklist groups, by permitting the designation of domestic groups, requiring no notice to Congress, and providing no opportunity for groups to challenge their designation.

Some argue that the threat from terrorist organizations abroad, and the fungibility of money and support, require us to compromise the constitutional principle that prohibits guilt by association. But the principle prohibiting guilt by association was developed in the crucible of a battle against what appeared to be an even more formidable foe — the Communist Party, an organization that Congress found to be, and the Supreme Court accepted as, a foreign-dominated organization that used sabotage and terrorism for the purpose of overthrowing the United States by force and violence.[4] If association with such an organization deserves protection, surely association with much less powerful groups that have threatened or used some violence at some point deserves similar protection.

The fungibility argument rests on a faulty factual assumption. It maintains that because money is fungible, even a donation of blankets to a hospital will free up resources that will then be devoted to terrorism. But this argument assumes that a group engaged in a political struggle that uses both legal and illegal ends will necessarily devote every marginal dollar to its illegal ends. On this assumption, every dollar donated to the African National Congress (ANC) for its nonviolent opposition to apartheid freed up a dollar that the ANC would then spend on violent, terrorist ends. While some groups may be so committed to violence that all else is only a front for terrorism, that is not likely to be true for most organizations that use violence. For most groups, violence is but one means to a political end. This is not to excuse the violence in any way, but to insist that one must distinguish between a group's lawful and unlawful activities.

Consider Hamas, for example, which has been designated as a terrorist group. The Israeli government itself estimates that Hamas devotes 95 percent of its resources to legal social service activity and only 5 percent to violent or military activity. For that reason the State Department in 1994 opposed making membership in Hamas a ground for denying visas. If Hamas sought to devote every marginal dollar to terror, one would expect to see the distribution between illegal and legal activities reversed. Should a person who sends blankets or medicine to a Hamas-run hospital be condemned as a terrorist? Is it really plausible that every blanket provided will lead to more money being spent on terrorist attacks? If it could be shown that a group's "legitimate" activities were a cover for its illegal activities, action against its legitimate enterprises would be justified, just as federal law allows the government to seize legitimate businesses if it can show that they are fronts for organized crime. But short of such a showing, we can and should distinguish between lawful and unlawful activities.

The fungibility argument also proves too much as a legal matter. The Supreme Court has repeatedly struck down laws that penalized association with the Communist Party absent proof that the individual specifically intended to further the group's illegal ends. If the provision of material support to a group were somehow different, then all of the anti-Communist measures declared invalid by the Supreme Court could have simply been rewritten to hinge punishment on the payment of dues, the volunteering of time, or any of the other material manifestations of political association. The right of association, in other words, would be left a meaningless formality.

DETENTION VS. DUE PROCESS

The PATRIOT Act gives the Attorney General unprecedented power to lock up any immigrant that he certifies as a "suspected terrorist."[5] Such persons are subject to potentially indefinite detention. While "suspected terrorists" may sound like a class that should be locked up, there are several problems with this measure. It applies to "suspected" terrorists, not "proved" terrorists. It allows the Attorney General to lock up individuals where he has "reasonable grounds to believe" that they have committed any of a wide range of immigration violations, without a hearing to determine whether they actually pose any real threat. And the legislation defines "terrorist activity" so expansively that it includes virtually every immigrant who is suspected of being involved in a barroom brawl or domestic dispute, as well as aliens who have never committed an act of violence in their lives, and whose only "crime" is to have provided humanitarian aid to an organization disfavored by the government. The law further provides that such persons may be detained indefinitely, even if they are "granted relief from removal," and therefore have a legal right to remain here permanently. The INS has never before had power to detain persons that it has no authority to expel, yet this law gives it exactly that.

To appreciate the extraordinary breadth of this unprecedented power, one must consider that under pre-existing law, the INS already had authority to detain any alien in deportation or exclusion proceedings who presented either a threat to national security or a risk of flight. Thus, what the new legislation adds is the authority to detain aliens who do *not* pose a current danger or flight risk, and who are *not* removable because they are entitled to asylum or some other form of relief.

This provision raises several constitutional concerns. First, it permits preventive detention of persons who pose no threat to national security or risk of flight. The Supreme Court has upheld preventive detention of accused criminals, but only where there is a specific reason for the detention — namely, that they pose a danger to others or a risk of flight.[6] Under the PATRIOT Act, however, if the Attorney General says that he has reasonable grounds to believe that an alien has threatened to use a weapon, the alien is presumptively detained, whether or not he poses any continuing threat to anyone. Preventive detention without a showing that the alien needs to be detained violates due process.

Second, the legislation allows the government to detain aliens indefinitely, *even where the alien has prevailed in his removal proceedings.* But once an alien has prevailed in his removal proceeding, and has been granted relief from removal, he has a legal right to remain here. At that point, the INS has no legitimate reason to keep him in jail. Detaining such a person would be akin to keeping a prisoner locked up even after he has been pardoned for all of the charges against him. The INS's authority to detain has always been incidental to its authority to deport, yet under this provision, the INS would have freestanding authority to detain indefinitely persons never convicted of a crime and legally residing here.[7]

Third, the evidentiary standard for detention raises serious constitutional concerns. It is important to keep in mind that the law authorizes potentially *indefinite* detention. That is a far more severe deprivation of liberty than holding a person for interrogation or trial. Yet the INS has in litigation argued that the "reasonable grounds to believe" standard now required for detention is essentially equivalent to the "reasonable suspicion" required for a brief stop and frisk under the Fourth Amendment. But if "reasonable suspicion" does not even authorize a full arrest in criminal law enforcement, it surely cannot authorize indefinite detention in immigration law enforcement.

Fourth, and most importantly, it is critical to the constitutionality of any detention provision that the government bear the burden of justifying any preventive detention promptly in a scrupulously fair proceeding. Few intrusions on liberty are more severe than being locket up. Yet the PATRIOT Act imposes no affirmative burden of proof on the government, provides for no hearing, and authorizes detention on the Attorney General's say-so. The only "process" the alien is afforded is the right to go to federal court and sue the government for its actions. But due process requires that the agency seeking to deprive a person of his liberty afford him a fair procedure in which to be heard; the availability of a lawsuit after the fact is not sufficient.

Finally, the PATRIOT Act permits detention of certified aliens for up to seven days without the filing of any charges. Yet the Supreme Court has ruled in the criminal setting that charges must be filed within 48 hours except in the most extraordinary circumstances.[8] The new law extends blanket authority to detain for seven days on mere certification that an alien was at one time involved in a barroom brawl. Such overbroad authority does not meet the Supreme Court's requirement that any preventive detention authority be accompanied by heightened procedural protections and narrowly drawn laws.[9]

IDEOLOGICAL EXCLUSION

The PATRIOT Act also expands ideological exclusion, authorizing the government to deny entry to aliens for pure speech.[10] It excludes aliens who "endorse or espouse terrorist activity," or who "persuade others to support terrorist activity or a terrorist organization," if the Secretary of State determines that such speech undermines U.S. efforts to combat terrorism. It also excludes aliens who are representatives of groups that "endorse acts of terrorist activity" in ways that similarly undermine U.S. efforts to combat terrorism.

While the Supreme Court has long ruled that aliens outside our borders — in contrast to aliens living among us — have no constitutional rights, such ideological exclusions nonetheless raise constitutional concerns. The First Amendment is designed to protect a wide-open and robust public debate, and if our government can keep out persons who espouse disfavored ideas, our ability as Americans to hear and consider those ideas will be diminished. More broadly, excluding people for their ideas is contrary to the spirit of freedom for which the United States stands. It was for that reason that Congress repealed all such grounds in the Immigration and Nationality Act in 1990, after years of embarrassing politically-motivated visa denials. We are a strong enough country, and our resolve against terrorism is strong enough, to make such censorship wholly unnecessary. Yet we have now returned to the much-criticized ways of the McCarran-Walter Act, targeting people not for their acts but for their words.

SECRET SEARCHES WITHOUT CRIMINAL PROBABLE CAUSE

The PATRIOT Act also makes many changes in the rules that govern the collection and sharing of information by law enforcement and intelligence agencies. The Administration argued that it needed broader search and seizure authority, and needed to be able to share the information it gained through criminal investigations more broadly with intelligence agencies. While some of the Administration's criticisms about existing law made sense, the changes adopted in most instances go far beyond what was needed to respond to terrorism. In many instances, the changes are not limited to terrorist investigations at all, but apply across the board to all criminal investigations. And while Congress imposed a four-year sunset on some of the changes, permitting reevaluation in light of their implementation, many of the surveillance and information-gathering provisions are permanent. The changes to the rules governing surveillance, information-gathering, and intelligence-sharing potentially affect all citizens, although their principal targets, at least initially, are likely to be Arab and Muslim immigrants.

One of the most significant changes has the effect of authorizing warrants for secret searches (so-called black bag jobs) and wiretaps in criminal investigations without probable cause of criminal conduct.[11] The Fourth Amendment generally permits the government to conduct searches or wiretaps only where it has probable cause to believe that an individual is engaged in criminal activity or that evidence of a crime will be found. But the PATRIOT Act allows the government to evade that requirement wherever it says that its investigation also has a significant foreign intelligence purpose.

The PATRIOT Act does this by amending the Foreign Intelligence Surveillance Act (FISA).[12] FISA creates a limited exception to the probable cause rule for foreign intelligence gathering. It authorizes the FBI to conduct electronic surveillance and secret physical searches without a criminal predicate, on the theory that foreign intelligence gathering is not designed to detect crimes but to gather information about foreign agents. Accordingly, it authorizes warrants not on a showing of probable

criminal conduct, but on a showing that the target of the intrusion is an "agent of a foreign power." "Agent" is defined broadly to include any member of a foreign organization, so that a member of Amnesty International could be an "agent." If the suspected agent of a foreign power is a U.S. citizen or permanent resident alien, the government is not allowed to base its warrant on First Amendment-protected activities, but even as to citizens the standard is looser than that applicable to ordinary wiretaps in criminal cases. The First Amendment limit does not apply to noncitizens here on temporary visas.

Searches and wiretaps under FISA may be kept secret from the target, in most cases forever. (Targets of criminal searches and wiretaps, by contrast, must be notified eventually of the search.) Under FISA, a person is notified of surveillance only if he or she is later prosecuted using the evidence seized. Even then, defendants have little opportunity to challenge the validity of the search, for they are not provided the affidavit that served as the basis for the surveillance. Where individuals are not prosecuted — those cases where the likelihood of government overreaching is greatest — notice is never provided, and therefore the search cannot be challenged.

The extraordinary authority provided by FISA was justified on the ground that intelligence gathering is different from criminal law enforcement, and that the FISA authority would not be used for the purpose of investigating crime. Congress recognized, however, that evidence of crimes might be obtained during foreign intelligence gathering — espionage, for example, is a crime — and therefore allowed the use of FISA evidence in criminal cases. But in order to obtain a FISA warrant, the "primary purpose" of the investigation had to be the collection of foreign intelligence, *not* criminal law enforcement. Otherwise, the statute would serve as an end-run around the probable cause requirements of the criminal wiretap statute.

In the PATRIOT Act, Congress eliminated the primary purpose test, amending FISA to allow wiretaps and physical searches without probable cause in criminal investigations so long as "a significant purpose" of the intrusion is to collect foreign intelligence. The express justification for this amendment was to permit the government to initiate wiretaps under FISA's lower standard where the investigation's primary purpose was to collect criminal evidence. The potential scope of this loophole is enormous. For example, in an investigation of foreign contributions to a US political campaign, the Justice Department could conduct a criminal investigation involving FBI wiretapping and secret searches without probable cause of criminal conduct. If it did not initiate a prosecution, the government would never need to notify the politician whose phones were tapped or offices were searched. Yet, as will be detailed later, the FBI could share that information with the CIA, the National Security Council staff, and the Pentagon. And as this example shows, this extraordinary expansion of surveillance authority is in no way limited to the investigation of terrorism, but applies to any federal criminal investigation in which the government can also assert a "significant" foreign intelligence interest.

"SNEAK AND PEEK" SEARCHES

Another provision of the PATRIOT Act expansively alters the rules that govern searches in ordinary criminal investigations. Criminal searches have long been subject to the "knock and announce" rule, under which law enforcement officers executing a search warrant must generally knock on the door of the place to be searched and give notice to the owner that the search is to be conducted. The purpose of this longstanding requirement has been to allow owners to ensure that the warrant is being executed at the proper address, to monitor the scope of the search to ensure that it does not extend beyond the terms of the warrant, and in the case of a prolonged search, to seek judicial intervention to narrow the scope of the search.

The PATRIOT Act effectively threw out this concept.[13] It allows the FBI to delay notification of searches whenever notification would "seriously jeopardize" an investigation. Government officials could almost always claim that notice would jeopardize the investigation, and thus this exception to the "knock and announce" rule threatens to swallow the rule. Under a "sneak and peek" warrant, FBI agents can secretly enter an apartment or home while the owner is asleep or away, take, alter or copy things, and not tell the owner that they were there for a "reasonable period thereafter." The Justice Department has stated in its *Field Guidance on New Authorities (Redacted) Enacted in the 2001 Anti-Terrorism Legislation* that 90 days could be a "reasonable period."[14]

Instead of crafting specific standards for such searches, Congress merely incorporated by reference a delayed notice provision governing the reading of stored e-mail, a less intrusive search. And the provision is not limited to terrorism cases, but applies to any federal crime, from drug cases to giving false information on a student loan application. Moreover, it is not subject to the 4-year "sunset" provision, but marks a permanent change. Thus, in this instance, the Administration used the emergency atmosphere generated by the September 11 attacks to make a permanent, fundamental change in law enforcement procedures having nothing to do with terrorism.

ELIMINATING BARRIERS BETWEEN LAW ENFORCEMENT AND INTELLIGENCE

One of the purposes of the PATRIOT Act was to promote the sharing of information between law enforcement agencies and intelligence agencies. That goal is not illegitimate. Many experts suggested that one of the reasons for our failure to learn about the September 11 plot before the damage was done was that the many federal agencies that engage in intelligence and law enforcement did not communicate among themselves very effectively. One reason for this, and probably the most difficult to address, is the turf wars that large bureaucracies inevitably engender. But another reason consisted of legal barriers to the sharing of certain information. The PATRIOT Act did nothing to address the first problem, but did seek to address the second. However, in doing so Congress may well have overcompensated, creating the risk that intelligence agencies such as the CIA will now have substantial access to domestic criminal law investigatory tools. And history suggests that when the CIA gets involved in domestic activity, abuses are likely to follow. The agency is simply not trained in adhering to domestic legal limits on its conduct, because its principal field of operation is espionage overseas, where domestic rules do not apply. The PATRIOT Act allows law enforcement officials to share with the CIA the fruits of its grand jury investigations, its wiretaps, and any other information it collects if it constitutes "foreign intelligence." These changes give the CIA and other intelligence agencies a much greater domestic role, while leaving them shrouded in secrecy and largely immune to judicial or public oversight.

When the Central Intelligence Agency was created in 1947, Congress explicitly said that the Agency was to have no subpoena or domestic police powers.[15] Congress did not want this secret intelligence agency engaged in domestic security activities. Instead, the CIA's operations were intended to be directed overseas, focused on foreign nationals, in the world of spy-versus- spy and relations between states, where the criminal law was largely inapplicable. The information the CIA secretly collected was intended to inform the President in carrying out foreign affairs and national defense, not to be used to arrest people or prosecute crimes. The secrecy with which the CIA operated — collection activities could go on for years, even decades, without being publicly revealed — was fundamentally incompatible with the criminal justice system, where investigations must have a clear criminal objective, and the information collected and the means by which it is acquired must in most cases ultimately be shared with the accused and tested in open court.

Since the CIA was not supposed to engage in law enforcement, and since its agents were not supposed to appear in court, the CIA was not granted law enforcement powers. Those law enforcement powers are awesome — in some ways more awesome than the powers of the intelligence agencies — but they are subject to checks and balances unknown to the world of foreign espionage.

One of the most powerful tools of the criminal justice system is the grand jury — an institution originally designed to protect against prosecutorial abuse but since turned into an investigative tool. The grand jury can compel anyone to testify before it under oath. Anyone who refuses to testify can be sent to jail. A witness who lies can be prosecuted for perjury. The grand jury can compel anyone with any record or tangible thing to produce it, irrespective of probable cause, again with the threat of jail time for those who refuse. Neither the Fourth nor the Fifth Amendment protects against the compelled disclosure of records. Witnesses before the grand jury are not entitled to have a lawyer with them in the room while they testify. In practice, the grand jury operates as the arm of the prosecutor who convenes it. While technically subject to the oversight of a judge, the prosecutor issues subpoenas without the prior approval of the judge. In fact, the subpoenas are often issued in blank to FBI agents, who fill them in, serve them, and collect the records. The judge usually never sees what is turned over. Much of it is never shown to the grand jurors.

These powers are subject, however, to two important controls: anything from the grand jury that the government uses in a criminal case must satisfy the full panoply of due process protections, while anything not used in open court can be disclosed only for law enforcement purposes and otherwise must be kept secret.[16] The rules of due process ensure that evidence collected by the grand jury cannot be used against a person without the full vetting guaranteed by the confrontation clause, and must ultimately satisfy the government's burden of proof beyond a reasonable doubt. The rule of grand jury secrecy has two purposes. First, it protects the innocent: much of what the grand jury collects turns out to be about innocent conduct. Some of the testimony is wrong, honestly or intentionally so, some is misleading, some irrelevant. If disclosed, especially if taken out of context, it could lead to wrong conclusions and harm reputations. A second reason for grand jury secrecy is security: witnesses could be endangered if the substance of their testimony were disclosed and investigations could be derailed if news of their direction were prematurely released.

The PATRIOT Act cast aside this set of limitations and controls, giving the CIA the benefit of the grand jury's powers with none of the protections of the criminal justice system.[17] Section 203 amends Rule 6(e) of the Federal Rules of Criminal Procedure to allow information collected by grand juries to be shared with the CIA and other intelligence agencies, as well as any national defense or national security official, without the prior approval of a judge. In effect, CIA agents working with law enforcement officers can now jointly draw up subpoenas, obtain the fruits of the grand jury's power, and never have to appear in open court or explain how they used the information.

At its core, this provision addresses a real problem. The grand jury that investigated the role of Osama bin Laden and al Qaeda in the bombing of the U.S. embassies in Africa, for example, collected some of the most comprehensive information available anywhere in the U.S. government on the operations of al Qaeda. The CIA could have used such information to pursue leads overseas beyond the scope of the criminal case. Thus, information sharing is justified in certain settings.

But Section 203 creates no limits on the sharing of information. A better solution would have required judicial approval for the sharing of grand jury information, but Congress acceded to the Bush Administration's insistence that law enforcement agencies should be free to act without judicial approval. In addition, the sharing of information should have been limited to cases of terrorism. But the PATRIOT Act allows the government to share any grand jury information that "involves" foreign intelligence or counterintelligence. And foreign intelligence is expansively defined to include any "information relating to the capabilities, intentions, or activities of foreign governments or elements thereof, foreign organizations, or foreign persons."[18] Thus, while the sharing of information makes sense, Congress essentially removed any checks on the mixing of intelligence and law enforcement functions, failing to address the very real concerns that the foreign intelligence approach may lead to serious invasions of liberty of people residing here.

INTELLIGENCE ACCESS TO RECORDS — THE DRAGNET APPROACH

Finally, the PATRIOT Act greatly expands the government's ability to collect information under the rubric of investigating terrorism or clandestine intelligence activities. Section 215 of the Act authorizes the government to seize "any tangible things (including books, records, papers, documents, and other items)" where those items are sought for an investigation "to protect against international terrorism or clandestine intelligence activities."[19] The subject of the order need not be suspected of any criminal wrongdoing whatsoever; indeed, the order need not be limited to the records of a particular person but may encompass entire collections of data related to many individuals.

In general, the government can obtain a person's records from a bank, credit bureau, telephone company, hospital, or library only if there is reason to believe that the individual is engaged in some wrongdoing or that the records are evidence of a crime. Over time, Congress has given the FBI power to compel disclosure of various records for intelligence and counterintelligence investigations. Each of these authorities was carefully considered by Congress and was enacted based on a showing by the FBI that the particular category of records was especially relevant to the conduct of counterintelligence investigations. For example, telephone toll records may be useful in identifying members of the circle around a known or suspected hostile foreign agent. Bank and credit records have obvious utility in tracing the money flow, and, in the case of suspected spies, identifying any unexplained income or spending. But in each instance, Congress applied a simple rule: the government had to have reason to believe that the records being sought pertained to an agent of a foreign power — an intelligence officer, for example, or a member of an international terrorist organization.

The PATRIOT Act eliminated the "agent of a foreign power" standard from all of the authorities giving the FBI access to specific categories of records in intelligence investigations, and created a massive catch-all provision, giving the FBI the ability to compel anyone to disclose any record or tangible thing that the FBI claims is relevant to an investigation of international terrorism or "clandestine intelligence activities," even if the record does not pertain to a suspected spy or international terrorist.

The implications of this change are enormous. Previously, the FBI could get the credit card records of anyone suspected of being a foreign agent. Under the PATRIOT Act, the FBI can get the entire database of the credit card company. Under prior law, the FBI could get library borrowing records only by complying with state law, and always had to ask for the records of a specific patron. Under the PATRIOT Act, the FBI can go into a public library and ask for the records on everybody who ever used the library, or who used it on a certain day, or who checked out certain kinds of books. It can do the same at any bank, telephone company, hotel or motel, hospital, or university — merely upon the claim that the information is "sought for" an investigation to protect against international terrorism or clandestine intelligence activities.

These changes permit the FBI in international terrorism cases to cast its net far wider than ever before. As we have shown above, the FBI has historically focused far too much of its counterterrorism effort on the monitoring of overt political activity. The issue is not whether the FBI can investigate people who say that they want to kill Americans — they can clearly be investigated. The issue is whether the FBI can investigate people who merely say that they support a Palestinian state. What was striking about the September 11 attackers is that they had no overt political inclinations — they never engaged in the type of political or associational activity that the FBI has traditionally made the focus of its counterterrorism efforts. Yet the new authorities in the PATRIOT Act will almost certainly result in broader collection of data on persons suspected of no wrongdoing and engaged only in political activity. The FBI and the other intelligence agencies are already awash in information that they cannot digest. Drawing in even more information on more innocent people is unlikely to make the picture any clearer.

In sum, the PATRIOT Act radically transformed the landscape of government power, and did so in ways that virtually guarantee repetition of some of law enforcement's worst abuses of the past. The PATRIOT Act itself, however, was only part of the government's response to September 11. Other actions, detailed below, raise still further questions about the appropriate balance between liberty and security.

ETHNIC PROFILING

One of the most dramatic responses to the attack of September 11 was a swift reversal in public attitudes about racial and ethnic profiling as a law enforcement tool. Before September 11, about 80 percent of the American public considered racial profiling wrong. State legislatures, local police departments, and the President had all ordered data collection on the racial patterns of stops and searches. The U.S. Customs Service, sued for racial profiling, had instituted measures to counter racial and ethnic profiling at the borders. And a federal law on racial profiling seemed likely.

After September 11, however, polls reported that 60 percent of the American public favored ethnic profiling, at least as long as it was directed at Arabs and Muslims. The fact that the perpetrators of the September 11 attack were all Arab men, and that the attack appears to have been orchestrated by al Qaeda, led many to believe that it is only common sense to pay closer attention to Arab-looking men boarding airplanes and elsewhere. And the high stakes — there is reason to believe that we will be subjected to further terrorist attacks — make the case for engaging in profiling stronger here than in routine drug interdiction stops on highways. Thus, Stuart Taylor, a columnist for Newsweek, the National Journal, and Legal Times, wrote shortly after the attacks in favor of ethnic profiling of Arab men on airplanes.[20]

Press accounts made clear that whether as a matter of official policy or not, law enforcement officials were paying closer attention to those who appear to be Arabs and Muslims. And in November, the Justice Department announced its intention to interview 5,000 young immigrant men, based solely on their age, immigrant status, and the country from which they came. Virtually all of those interviewed were Arabs and Muslims, and the list looked uncomfortably like one generated to identify Arab and Muslims without explicitly relying on ethnicity. Several police departments around the country refused to participate in the interviews on the grounds that they appeared to constitute ethnic profiling.

There is no question that the immediate aftermath of September 11 called for greater urgency than the ongoing war on drugs, and that the immediate threat posed to our national security was greater. But that does not answer whether ethnic profiling is a legal, much less an effective, response. The argument that we cannot afford to rely on something other than racial or ethnic proxies for suspicion, after all, is precisely the rationale used to intern 110,000 persons of Japanese ancestry during World War II. While subjecting an individual to closer inspection and a possible search is less extreme than detention, the rationale — that we should rely on ethnic background as a proxy for suspicion — is the same.

Precisely because of the history of racial discrimination in this country, the Equal Protection Clause of the Constitution presumptively forbids government authorities from relying on explicit racial or ethnic distinctions. Such actions trigger "strict scrutiny," a stringent form of court review that requires the government to justify its racial distinctions by showing that they are "narrowly tailored," or "necessary," to further a "compelling government interest." There is no question that protecting citizens from terrorism is a compelling government interest, but so too is drug interdiction — in fact, all criminal law enforcement would likely be viewed as a compelling state interest.

The real question from a constitutional perspective is whether the means adopted — reliance on ethnic appearance as a proxy for suspicion — is narrowly tailored to further that interest. It is highly unlikely that profiling could satisfy that scrutiny. First, the vast majority of persons who appear Arab and Muslim — probably well over 99.9 percent — have no involvement with terrorism. Arab and Muslim appearance, in other words, is a terribly inaccurate proxy for terrorism. In the sex discrimination context, where the Supreme Court applies less stringent scrutiny than it does to ethnic or racial discrimination, the court held that statistics showing that 2 percent of young men between the ages of

18 and 21 had been arrested for drunk driving did not justify denying men of that age the right to purchase an alcoholic beverage.[21]

Second, the use of ethnic stereotypes is certainly not "necessary" to effective law enforcement. In fact, it is likely to be bad law enforcement. When one treats a whole group of people as presumptively suspicious, it means that agents are more likely to miss dangerous persons who take care not to fit the profile. In addition, the fact that the vast majority of those suspected on the basis of their Arab or Muslim appearance are innocent will inevitably cause agents to let their guard down.[22] Overbroad generalizations, in other words, are problematic not only because they constitute an unjustified imposition on innocents, but because they undermine effective law enforcement.

Profiling undermines effective law enforcement in still another way. It is virtually certain to alienate members of the targeted communities. Studies of policing have shown that it is far more effective to work with communities than against them. Where a community trusts law enforcement, people are more likely to obey the law, and more likely to cooperate with the police in identifying and bringing to justice wrongdoers in their midst. If we have reason to believe that there are potential terrorist threats within the Arab and Muslim community in the United States, we should be seeking ways to work with the millions of law-abiding members of those communities to help identify the true threats, not treating the entire community as suspect.

The ethnic profiling issue is complicated in the wake of the September 11 attacks by the fact that some use of ethnicity is probably permissible. When a bank reports a robbery, and describes the robbers as three white men in their thirties wearing blue shirts, the police can rely on race in seeking to identify and catch the suspects. In that setting, the use of race does not carry negative stereotyped connotations, but is simply an identifying marker, like the fact that they were wearing blue shirts. Moreover, as one of the few identifying characteristics, reliance on race in that setting is narrowly tailored to the compelling interest of catching the robbers. Ethnic or racial profiling, by contrast, consists of the reliance on race as a generalization about future behavior — the assumption that because an individual is black, he is more likely to rob a bank. Such reliance on generalizations is probably always impermissible, whereas reliance on race as an identifying criterion is usually permissible.

In the aftermath of September 11, it was often difficult to separate out these two uses of ethnicity. If law enforcement agents had reason to believe that there were others involved in the planning and carrying out of the attacks or that their associates might have been planning further attacks, and that these others were Arab or Muslim men, then relying on ethnic criteria to identify the guilty parties may have been permissible.

However, to the extent that law enforcement agents rely on ethnicity as a predictor of future behavior, they are using impermissible generalizations. Where the perpetrators are thought to be planning future attacks, the distinction between an identifying criterion and a prospective generalization is particularly difficult to draw. Therefore, where ethnicity is being accorded a dominant role in investigative activities, two other factors become very important. First, the use of an ethnic identifying factor becomes more objectionable when it is applied on a nationwide basis over an extended period of time. It is one thing to say that the police, having only the information that three white men robbed a bank, can stop and question all white men in the vicinity of the bank immediately after the robbery. It would be another matter for the police nationwide to keep interviewing white males until they find the bank robbers.

Second, when the government relies on ethnic identifying characteristics, it is critical that it act quickly to resolve its suspicions and to determine whether other, non-ethnic factors justify or disprove its selection of certain people for scrutiny. What is particularly troubling about the government's response to September 11 is that government officials seemed determined to apply ethnic profiling on a nationwide, seemingly arbitrary basis and failed to resolve promptly their selection of certain individuals for the worst form of ethnic-based action: detention without serious criminal charges.

THE INVESTIGATION OF THE SEPTEMBER 11 ATTACK

As this book goes to press, the government's investigation of the September 11 attacks remains shrouded in secrecy. The government has detained well over 1,200 persons in connection with the investigation — it stopped issuing a running tally in early November, when the number was over 1100, as criticism of the breadth of its detentions was growing. The detentions have been conducted under an unprecedented veil of secrecy. Initially, the Justice Department refused to issue any details about the detainees. In November, it said that over 600 persons were in federal custody, the vast majority of them held on immigration charges. About fifty were being held on federal criminal charges, and an undisclosed number were held as material witnesses. The government has refused to disclose how many detainees are held on state or local criminal charges. And the government has refused to reveal the identities of any of the immigration or material witness detainees. This secrecy makes it virtually impossible to know to what extent the government is adhering to or violating the law in the detentions.

Some stories have been told, however, and they are not very encouraging. They include accounts of persons interrogated while blindfolded and handcuffed, of families being unable to verify whether their family members have in fact been detained, of lawyers having great difficulty even locating their clients as the clients are transported from prison to prison, and of inmates being beaten. Moreover, the very fact that over 1200 people have been detained and that as of December 2001 over 500 were still being incarcerated raises questions about the government's motives. Only one of the detainees, Zaccarias Moussaoui, has been charged with involvement in the crimes being investigated. And the government says that it thinks ten or twelve of the detainees, including Moussaoui, are members of al Qaeda. But if that is the case, what justifies holding the other 490 in jail?

The immigration detainees are being tried in secret trials, in proceedings that are closed to the public, the press, observers, and even family members. Their cases are not listed on the public docket, and immigration judges have been instructed to refuse to confirm or deny that such a case exists if asked. This unprecedented use of secret proceedings raises fundamental questions of fairness, because the rule of law requires public scrutiny to be effective. Yet hundreds of aliens are being tried in secret.

At the same time, the INS has given itself expanded powers to detain aliens in immigration proceedings. Before September 11, the INS had to satisfy an immigration judge that the alien posed a threat to national security or a flight risk to hold him while his deportation proceedings were pending. But in October, the Justice Department issued a new regulation authorizing INS prosecutors, or District Directors, to keep aliens locked up even after an immigration judge had ruled that there was no basis for his detention. Simply by filing an appeal to the Board of Immigration Appeals, the INS obtains an "automatic stay" of the alien's release for as long as it takes to resolve the appeal. Appeals typically take many months, and often well over a year, to decide. Thus, this regulation gives the INS prosecutor the authority to ignore an immigration judge's ruling that an alien should be released and keep the alien locked up for many months, without any showing that the INS is likely to succeed on appeal.

The secrecy surrounding the "material witnesses" also makes assessment of the legality of the government's conduct difficult. The "material witness" law permits the government to lock up a person if it shows that he or she has information material to a trial or grand jury proceeding, and that the person would flee if served with a subpoena to testify. The "material witness" authority, which incarcerates persons without even a charge of wrongdoing, is used only rarely. Its purpose is solely to ensure that a witness be available for testimony. It is not designed to allow the government to detain someone without probable cause while it searches for more evidence, or to detain someone it thinks might be dangerous but as to whom it has no evidence of illegal conduct.

Finally, the government has asserted the authority to listen in on attorney-client conversations of persons in federal incarceration where it has reasonable suspicion that the communications might further terrorism. Attorney-client conversations have long been subject to a strong presumption of confidentiality, yet under this regulation the government need obtain no warrant, and need not have probable cause of criminal wrongdoing, in order to listen in on one of the most traditional of private communications. The government has always had the authority to listen in on attorney-client communications where it obtains a warrant based on probable cause that the relationship is being used to further a crime. But here the Justice Department has departed from that exception, asserting the right to listen in without probable cause or a warrant.

In its current investigation, then, the Justice Department has detained hundreds of people not charged with the crime being investigated and not thought to be members of al Qaeda, has refused to reveal even the names of the vast majority of those detained, has conducted immigration trials in secret, has listened in on attorney-client communications, and has assumed the authority to keep immigrants locked up even after a judge has ordered their release. It has not justified these measures as necessary to deter terrorism or to find the perpetrators of the September 11 attacks. And it has reserved its most harsh treatment for those who have the least voice in our political process, noncitizens. In short, we have already begun to repeat the mistakes of the past.

CONCLUSION

We must respond to the new terrorist threat, but in doing so we must ensure that our responses are measured, balanced, and effective. Judged by these standards, is our anti-terrorism effort improved by making deportable anyone who provides humanitarian aid to any organization engaged in a civil war? Is it effective or balanced to label every domestic dispute or barroom fight with a weapon by an immigrant an act of terrorism? Are we made more secure by subjecting anyone suspected of such activity to mandatory detention, without any procedural protections, and without any showing that he poses any current danger? Is it necessary to try immigrants in secret, and to hold them in detention even after judges have ordered their release? Is it measured to restore the authority to deny visas for the mere expression of ideas we dislike? Is it balanced to authorize wiretaps and searches in criminal investigations without probable cause of a crime? Have we adequately considered constitutional rights when we allow secret searches in cases having nothing to do with terrorism? Is it effective to authorize the government to engage in fishing expeditions, with no particularized suspicion that the vast quantities of data being swept in have any connection to persons suspected of engaging in terrorism? Is it measured to engage in profiling based on the color of one's skin? And is it fair to detain over hundreds of people in connection with a criminal investigation when only one has been changed with the crime?

It is too early to judge how the United States as a country will in the long run react to the new threat of terrorism manifested by the attacks of September 11. But our early responses unfortunately reflect the pattern of overreaction that we have so often seen in the past. Many of the expansive authorities that the new law grants, however, are not likely to make us more safe. To the contrary, by penalizing even wholly lawful, nonviolent, and counterterrorist associational activity, we are likely to waste valuable resources tracking innocent political activity, drive other activity underground, encourage extremists, and make the communities that will inevitably be targeted by such broad-brush measures far less likely to cooperate with law enforcement. As Justice Louis Brandies wrote nearly 75 years ago, the Framers of our Constitution knew "that fear breeds repression; that repression breeds hate; and that hate menaces stable government."[23]

CHAPTER 12

CONCLUSION

> In times of crisis, the Government will exercise its power to conduct domestic intelligence activities to the fullest extent. The distinction between legal dissent and criminal conduct is easily forgotten. Our job is to recommend means to help ensure that the distinction will always be observed.[1]

As September 11 dramatically demonstrated, the United States faces a real terrorist threat from abroad. At the same time, however, the United States itself has not been a fertile breeding ground for home-grown terrorism. This may well be because values central to our system of democratic governance make it difficult to nurture within this country the ideological, ethnic or religious hatred that fuels much terrorism. These values include appreciation of diversity and religious and ethnic tolerance, reflected in our repeated absorption of large influxes of immigrants. They also include constitutional limits on government powers, checks and balances, access to government information, accountability of public officials, and due process accorded in judicial proceedings open to public scrutiny, all of which increase public confidence in government. Perhaps most important is our strong protection for political freedoms of speech and association, with a nearly unlimited right to criticize government and government officials, and a nearly insurmountable presumption against prior censorship, assuring the disaffected that their concerns can be heard without violence.

Unfortunately, much of our official response to the threat of terrorism is incompatible with these core civil liberties values. The 1996 Antiterrorism Act, for example, deems people guilty not on the basis of what they have done, but on the basis of the groups with which they are associated. It denies one of the most fundamental elements of due process — the right to confront one's accusers in open court. And measures taken after September 11 have similarly threatened basic values — imposing guilt by association, conducting trials in secret, engaging in ethnic profiling, and intruding on the privacy of innocent persons. The question is whether we can respond effectively to the new threat of terrorism without jeopardizing the very freedoms that have contributed to our security at home.

THE FALSE TRADE-OFF — CURTAILING LIBERTY WILL NOT ENHANCE SECURITY

In the ongoing debate over responding to terrorism, many argue that civil liberties must be sacrificed in order to ensure the safety of our democratic way of life. Something unique about the threat of terrorism, it is argued, requires us to alter the constitutional balance we have long struck between government power and personal freedoms. The premise of this argument — so unquestioningly accepted that it often goes unstated — is that antiterrorism measures infringing civil liberties will work.

Efficacy, of course, does not determine the outcome of the constitutional debate. Even if a police state were efficient, it would not reflect our fundamental values. But many of the rights we have discussed in this book actually promote governmental efficacy in defending the common good. We guarantee the right to confront one's accusers, for example, not only as an element of human dignity but also because we know that cross-examination is an effective engine of truth. Relying on untested evidence not only risks convicting the innocent, but it also means that the search for the truly guilty party may be called off prematurely. We subject executive decisions to judicial review not only because the judicial system gives a voice to individuals but also because we know that the adversarial process can produce a fuller factual record, exposing faulty assumptions, and because deliberative review by life-tenured judges can protect against the rash decisions resulting from the pressures felt by elected officials. We reject guilt by association not only to protect political freedom, but also because a system that holds individuals responsible for their own actions is more closely tailored to deterring crime. We protect freedom of speech not only because it allows room for personal self-expression, but also because the availability of channels for peaceful change promotes stability. We have more to fear from the pressure-cooker of repressed dissatisfaction than from the cacophony of dissent. For these reasons, many of the counterterrorism measures that we have criticized are not only unconstitutional, but are also likely to be counterproductive.

Curtailing civil liberties does not necessarily promote national security. In COINTELPRO, the FBI experimented with the massive monitoring of political dissent. It failed to produce any substantial evidence of violent conduct, proving that politics is a poor guide and extensive monitoring an ineffective strategy for counterterrorism investigations. Other more recent examples here and abroad have shown that racial and ethnic stereotyping is a poor basis for security policy. The assassin of Yitzak Rabin escaped detection because the Prime Minister's bodyguards were on the lookout for Arab assailants. If police had listened only to those who claimed that the Oklahoma City bombing bore the trademarks of Muslim fundamentalists, they might not have captured Timothy McVeigh as he fled from the crime.

Violations of civil liberties "work" only in a narrow sense: random or door-to-door searches will uncover contraband in some houses, and torture of arrestees will induce some to provide truthful evidence of wrongdoing, including evidence that may allow the prevention of violent attacks. But these "successes" must be balanced against the wasted resources consumed by fruitless random searches and generalized monitoring of groups or movements, the mistakes caused by reliance on faulty coerced confessions, and, most importantly, the tremendous loss of trust in government (and the consequent shutting off of voluntary cooperation) generated by unfocused investigations and the harassment of communities on the basis of stereotypes. On balance, even measured only in terms of effectiveness, there is little evidence that curtailing civil liberties will do more good than harm. [2]

IMPLICATIONS OF A NEW, MORE DANGEROUS TERRORISM

In every age, dangers can be cited that make limitations on intelligence operations seem imprudent — threats of such an urgent and unique nature that it seems necessary to expand government powers, at least long enough to turn back the new threat. Today's proponents of expanding government power to fight terrorism argue that the terrorist threat now is qualitatively different than in the past. September 11 certainly gave these arguments added weight.

But the heightened risk of terrorism simply means that the consequences of failing to adopt a sound antiterrorism policy are more serious than ever before. It does not tell us what policy to adopt.

Indeed, aspects of the new threat of terrorism point in quite different directions. Before adopting measures that curtail personal freedom, it might be more effective to address the highly destructive products that pose such serious risk to life. The U.S. and its allies have not done nearly enough to gain control of the nuclear materials of the former Soviet Union, a project that probably would mean far more to national security than curtailing civil liberties. Lethal biological and chemical materials are widely produced and are subject to inadequate controls. A program of stringent federal regulation of anthrax would have no civil liberties implications, but could meaningfully restrict access to such products by both the malevolent and the merely careless.

It is also clear that not nearly enough was done with investigative and protective authorities that existed before the 1996 and 2001 Acts and that had little to do with intrusions on political freedoms. For example, prior to September 11 there were repeated warnings about poor airport security. Documents disclosed by the New York Times in January 1999 showed that explosives and guns avoided detection in government tests of airline security, due largely to lax practices on the part of screening personnel.[3] Similarly, it became clear following the embassy bombings in Africa that Washington officials were largely unresponsive to the intense, well-founded and forcefully expressed concerns of the American ambassador to Kenya, who warned repeatedly that the embassy was insufficiently protected against terrorist attack. Indeed, the CIA repeatedly told the State Department that there was an active terrorist group in Kenya connected to Osama bin Laden, since accused of masterminding the bombings there and in Tanzania.[4]

Despite the wartime rhetoric of stamping out terrorism everywhere, the terrorist threat will never be eliminated. We must develop sound responses. But in doing so, we should be careful not to sacrifice the fundamental principles that characterize our democratic identity. The better course is to adhere to our liberal principles, to use the criminal laws to punish those who plan or carry out violent acts and to invite critics of our government into the practice of democracy and tolerance.

REFORMING FBI COUNTERTERRORISM ACTIVITIES

The principles guiding FBI counterterrorism activities were laid down over 50 years ago, before World War II, and were last revised over 25 years ago, while the Cold War was still underway. At that time, the main national security threat was the Soviet Union, which was understood to be conducting a worldwide campaign against the United States through clandestine means and covert proxies.

At the beginning of the Cold War, the criminal law was thought to be of little relevance to this struggle. The foreign agents conducting or directing hostile actions against the U.S. were often operating under diplomatic immunity. It was assumed that criminal prosecution would reveal too much classified information, compromising continued counterintelligence efforts. Even with respect to U.S. citizens suspected of spying in the United States, the presumption was against criminal prosecution. Clandestine disruptive actions and double agent operations were justified as the best means of preventing damage to U.S. interests, on the ground that the criminal law was not available.

Major changes over the last two decades have upset many of the assumptions on which FBI national security activities were founded. The Soviet Union has disintegrated. Human rights protection has emerged as a leading principle of U.S. foreign policy (at least in theory). International law has undergone revolutionary change, to the point where the United States now has at its disposal a range of international sanctions to punish state sponsors of terrorism.

Most importantly, criminal law has assumed a primacy in national security policy. It is now routine to arrest and prosecute suspected spies, through trials in which all of the government's evidence is presented publicly and subject to cross-examination. The Classified Information Procedures Act makes such public prosecutions less risky to ongoing operations, while preserving defendants' rights to confront the evidence against them. U.S. criminal law has been given wide extraterritorial effect, reaching almost any attack anywhere in the world against an American citizen, U.S. government property or property owned by U.S. corporations. International cooperation in the field of criminal law makes it more likely than ever that terrorism can be dealt with through arrest and prosecution in U.S. courts.

A revised view of intelligence is also demanded by another change: The United States, always a diverse society, has become even more so. Consider just religious diversity. There are 3000 religious denominations and sects in the U.S. today. Not only are there more Muslims than Episcopalians in the United States, but there is a diversity within this diversity that defies common assumptions. For example, contrary to popular perception, most Muslims in the U.S. are not of Arab origin and most persons of Arab descent in the U.S. are not Muslims.

In the face of such diversity, principles of pluralism, tolerance of dissent, and individual rather than group culpability should guide the development of national security, intelligence, and counter-terrorism policy. The alternative is a stereotyping that can ossify or mislead the investigative focus: While the FBI was conducting an intensive investigation of the PLO-affiliated PFLP in the 1980s and 1990s, the U.S. government was promoting the signing of an Israeli-PLO peace accord, and the focus of terrorism concern in the Middle East shifted to anti-PLO Muslim fundamentalists. As soon as the FBI launched a massive campaign against Muslim fundamentalists in the wake of the World Trade Center bombing, the Murrah building in Oklahoma City was blown up by white, native born ex-GIs. And while the FBI and the INS pursued innocent Arab and Muslim political activists, terrorists careful to avoid any showing of religious or political orientation planned and carried out the September 11 attacks.

INTELLIGENCE IN A DEMOCRATIC SOCIETY

Improving "intelligence" is obviously a critical factor in preventing future terrorist attacks. Some advocate the clandestine collection, without the particular suspicion of wrongdoing, of large quantities of information, the immediate relevance of which may not be clear, in order to piece together a mosaic that might help policymakers anticipate actions of potential adversaries. The tools of this type of intelligence include black bag jobs and wiretaps under the Foreign Intelligence Surveillance Act, information sharing relationships with foreign intelligence services, and the sifting of vast databases of information on innocuous transactions. Much of this information is unreliable; rarely is it ever subjected to the testing of the adversarial process; and all too often it intrudes on protected political activity.

We favor another vision of intelligence, one rooted in the concepts of the criminal law. "Intelligence" in this context means the collection and analysis of information about a criminal enterprise that goes beyond what is necessary to solve a particular crime. Intelligence of this type is intended to aid law enforcement agencies in drawing a fuller picture of the enterprise. It allows the government to identify the silent partners, those who provide money for violent attacks or issue the commands. Intelligence allows investigators to link seemingly disparate crimes into a pattern. At its best, intelligence allows the government to anticipate and prevent a group's next dangerous crime, thereby saving lives.

The FBI routinely conducts "intelligence" operations of this second type against organized crime families and drug cartels. It does so subject to the ordinary rules of criminal procedure. The goal of such investigations is to arrest the leaders and to put them on trial for specific crimes. And one of the most important constraints on such criminal intelligence is the public trial — everything done in the name of criminal intelligence must ultimately bear scrutiny in a court of law.

The concept of criminal intelligence can be fully compatible with the Constitution. The First Amendment does not require the FBI to be deaf when someone advocates violence. The Constitution does not require the government to wait until a bomb goes off or even to wait until a bomb factory is brought to its attention — it does, however, require the FBI to focus its investigations on the interdiction of violence, and other criminal conduct. Too often, the FBI has not limited itself to uncovering evidence of a crime, but instead has conducted lengthy investigations that consist of routine monitoring and disrupting of lawful political activities.

We live in a world of political, ethnic and religious violence. There will undoubtedly be more acts of terrorism both here and overseas against U.S. targets. It is incumbent on those who criticize current counterterrorism policies to answer how they would go about addressing the threat of terrorism. We believe that an effective counterterrorism policy can be implemented in this country based on traditional criminal procedures directed at crimes of violence, including intelligence gathering aimed at preventing terrorist acts before they occur.

The FBI is at its best when it does criminal investigations. It is at its worst when it acts in a counterintelligence, monitoring mode, secretly pursuing an ideologically-defined target without the constraints and focus of the criminal code and without the expectation that its actions will be subjected to scrutiny in the adversarial context of a public criminal trial.

Counterterrorism investigations should investigate terrorist acts as crimes, regardless of their political motivation. Murder, kidnapping, or bank robbery by terrorists, even murder on a mass scale, is most effectively investigated using the same techniques that are applied to murder, kidnapping and bank robbery by non-terrorists. By and large, this was the FBI's focus under the Levi domestic security guidelines. The focus on criminal activity was also for some years a central feature of U.S. policy against terrorism abroad. In the 1980s, a major component of the policy was the extension of extraterritorial jurisdiction over crimes of violence committed by terrorists against Americans abroad, so that terrorists could be extradited to the U.S. to be tried here.

Indeed, the United States has continued to pursue this approach, in tandem with the broader monitoring approach reflected in the 1996 and 2001 antiterrorism laws. Federal prosecutors in New York sucessfully prosecuted al Qaeda members who carried out the African embassy bombings. The Justice Department is pursuing criminal charges in connection with September 11. If a criminal trial is possible against the hierarchy of entire organized crime families, it is also possible against those members of terrorist organizations who are engaged in carrying out or directly supporting violent activities, at least in situations short of war. In the case of a group having both legitimate and illegitimate activities, the focus should be on identifying and prosecuting all those responsible for the illegal activities, not penalizing innocent support of lawful conduct.

To reform FBI counterterrorism policies and avoid repetitions of CISPES-type cases, it is necessary to redraw the lines between criminal investigations and foreign counterintelligence investigations. Overbroad intelligence monitoring is a diversion from the harder work of identifying real terrorists. The CISPES case at the time it occurred was seen inside and outside the FBI as a waste of resources. Counterintelligence monitoring displaced the search for evidence of crimes. Even though the FBI had an allegation that CISPES was planning terrorist attacks in Dallas, the investigation never actually had as its goal a resolution of that allegation. In the few instances in which the FBI received information concerning other possible violent activity by specific CISPES chapters, agents failed to pursue those allegations. Instead, agents devoted their efforts to identifying all CISPES chapters throughout the U.S. and monitoring clearly legal activities. If members of CISPES had actually been planning terrorist activity, the investigation conducted by the FBI was not likely to have uncovered it. In the case of those convicted of the first World Trade Center bombing, some of whom were the subject of a counterintelligence investigation prior to the bombing, a similar adherence to the monitoring approach may have contributed to the FBI's failure to pursue the case to an earlier resolution, which could have prevented the 1993 attack.

All antiterrorism investigations in the United States, whether of foreign or domestic groups, should be conducted pursuant to criminal rules, with the goal of arresting people planning, supporting or carrying out violent activities and convicting them in a court of law. Law enforcement must stop framing terrorism investigations in political, religious or ethnic terms. The FBI still classifies its investigations as "environmental terrorism" ("eco-terrorism") or "Islamic fundamentalist terrorism" or "Puerto Rican terrorism." This only reinforces the notion that the Bureau's role is to monitor politics rather than to investigate crime. Instead, once a politically-motivated group advocating violence is identified, the goal of the investigation should be to identify those engaged in the criminal enterprise, not to identify those who share the ideology.

Such a counterterrorism program would, in may respects, be the exact opposite of what was reflected in the Antiterrorism Act of 1996 and the PATRIOT Act of 2001. Where those Acts empowered the FBI to investigate a new, broadly-defined offense of "support for terrorism," we would propose express legislative limits on the FBI's discretion to investigate First Amendment activities. Where those Acts expanded the concept of support for terrorism to include support for the political and humanitarian activities of groups that also engage in violence, we advocate limiting the crime of support for terrorism, like any crime of aiding and abetting, to support for activities that are themselves crimes. Where those Acts endorsed the unfocused approach of guilt by association, we would require the FBI to focus its investigations on collecting evidence of individual culpability. Where those Acts allowed the use of secret evidence, we maintain that the government should subject its evidence to the test of cross-examination. And where those Acts adopted a political approach to terrorism, we insist that the FBI must get out of the business of monitoring political activity and associations, foreign and domestic, and instead dedicate itself to the urgent task of identifying those planning violent activities. Only such a transformation can successfully meet the threat of terrorism without sacrificing our political freedoms.

APPENDIX

LAW PROFESSORS'
PETITION TO CONGRESS

*"... to enact legislation that will prevent the FBI
and other federal law enforcement agencies from undertaking investigations that threaten the exercise of First Amendment rights ..."*

Sponsored by the Constitutional Law Advisors to the
National Committee Against Repressive Legislation (NCARL).
Founded in 1960 as the National Committee to Abolish HUAC
(House Committee on Un-American Activities):

Thomas I. Emerson (1907-1991)
Professor Emeritus,
Yale Law School

Vern Countryman (1917-1999)
Professor Emeritus,
Harvard Law School

Carole Goldberg
Professor of Law,
UCLA School of Law

WHEREAS: The undersigned, for the reasons set forth below, respectfully petition the United States Congress to enact legislation that will prevent the FBI and other federal law enforcement agencies from undertaking investigations that threaten the exercise of First Amendment rights, and

WHEREAS: Our fears that the FBI will stray beyond legitimate law enforcement into the realm of protected speech and association are grounded in recent experience. Although the operation of investigative agencies are normally concealed from public view, the Senate's hearings on the Watergate break-in initiated a period of unprecedented and unsettling disclosures. In 1976, the report of the Senate Select Committee to Study Governmental Operations with respect to Intelligence, chaired by the late Senator Frank Church, revealed the scope of the FBI's neutralization program of the 1960's and 1970's, code-named "COINTELPRO." According to that report, the FBI had approved several thousand separate covert actions designed to disrupt groups, to "neutralize individuals deemed to be threats to national security and to prevent the propagation of dangerous ideas." Numerous civil liberties, civil rights, peace, labor, and social action groups were subjected to infiltration and harassment. Armed with knowledge acquired through blanket wiretaps, mail openings, and breaking and entering, the FBI initiated counter-demonstrations, disrupted tours and meetings, sent anonymous "poison pen" letters to discredit leaders and stimulate factional disputes, intimidated contributors, and even destroyed marriages, and

WHEREAS: Many political and civic organizations did not survive FBI "neutralization"; many were seriously weakened. Unquestionably free expression of ideas was inhibited, public perceptions were distorted, the nature of public debate was changed, and the course of national policies was influenced. Because they know what the FBI is capable of doing, today's groups challenging foreign policy in Central America, treatment of Central American refugees, nuclear arms proliferation, investment in South Africa and other controversial government policies are frightened and inhibited by the possibility of intrusive government surveillance. In fact, testimony before the House Judiciary Subcommittee on Civil and Constitutional Rights and documents recently disclosed under the FOIA have revealed that, during the 1980's, informants conducted intensive surveillance on individuals and organizations opposed to U.S. policies in Central America, and

WHEREAS: Sometimes other federal agencies also take aim at these dissenters. But this petition is focused on the FBI because, as the most significant federal criminal law enforcement agency, it sets an example when it establishes the range of acceptable investigative activities, and is often enlisted by other agencies to coordinate politically motivated investigations, and

WHEREAS: Notwithstanding the Senate Select Committee's disclosures, there still is no federal legislation specifically authorizing and limiting the investigative activities of the FBI. Since 1976, guidelines issued by the Attorney General have set forth standards and procedures for that agency's domestic intelligence gathering. In 1983, these guidelines were relaxed, enabling the FBI to reinstate some of the very practices the Church Committee condemned, and

WHEREAS: The guidelines permit "preliminary inquiries" into the activities of individuals or organizations, including physical surveillance, collection of newspaper clippings and other publicly available documents, and recruitment and placement of informants and infiltrators, where there is merely an allegation of possible future criminal activity. A fuller investigation, including mail openings and phone taps in addition to undercover operations, may be initiated whenever there is a "reasonable indication" that persons are "engaged in an enterprise for the purpose of furthering political or social goals wholly or in part" through criminal conduct. As the guidelines themselves concede, this "reasonable indication" standard is substantially lower than "probable cause" to believe a crime is about to be committed, the standard set for searches and arrests under the FourthAmendment to the Constitution. This weak standard is particularly troubling because federal statutes punishing speech such as the Smith and McCarran/Walter Acts, though substantially repudiated by the United States Supreme Court, have not been repealed by Congress, and hence serve as a convenient springboard for FBI investigations, and

WHEREAS: The guidelines provide that investigations are permissible when an individual has merely advocated criminal activity. There need not be an imminent likelihood of criminal conduct occurring, even though current court decisions render such an immediate danger necessary before speech can lose its constitutional protection. Once an organization is under investigation based on the speech of one of its members, the guidelines allow the FBI to collect information about all members who participate in its demonstrations, about the structure of the organization as well as the relationship of the members, and even about other organizations that cooperate with it. Even after an organization has become inactive or no longer presents an "immediate threat of harm," it maybe subjected to continued surveillance and infiltration, and

WHEREAS: Separate, secret guidelines set forth standards for FBI foreign counterintelligence investigations. Such investigations have several extraordinary features: the standard for initiating an investigation is itself classified; warrantless physical searches are permitted; a secret court considers all electronic surveillance requests; special exemptions exist protecting records from disclosure under FOIA; special access is available to telephone toll records and financial records. The focus of these investigations is the collection of intelligence and not necessarily the prosecution of crimes. Yet the definition of foreign intelligence agent is so broad that it can include peaceful domestic groups, and

WHEREAS: We believe that rights of free speech and association are invariably compromised by such broad investigative power. When secret informants are introduced into political organizations, they not only hear organization discussion and strategy, they learn about organization members and contributors who may wish to remain anonymous. If these infiltrators rise to leadership positions, as they may be encouraged to do, they may significantly affect the organization's positions, even to the point of becoming full-fledged agents provocateurs, and

WHEREAS: By rendering law-abiding groups vulnerable to such infiltration, the current FBI guidelines cannot help but make citizens reluctant to join controversial causes or to speak up at organizational gatherings. The emphasis on investigating organizations and not just individuals will also inhibit the formation of political coalitions and large-scale demonstrations. Indeed, by requiring FBI headquarters approval for infiltration that may influence the exercise of First Amendment rights, the guidelines acknowledge and approve just such intrusions into protected speech and association, and

WHEREAS: This nation's democratic institutions must have the opportunity to function as they are meant to, with new and unorthodox ideas welcomed but subject to full and free discussion. The existence of federal investigative agencies free to restrict this process betrays an ultimate lack of faith in a democratic society.

THEREFORE, BE IT RESOLVED:

Having witnessed the inadequacy of internal guidelines to restrain the FBI's excesses, we conclude that federal legislation is needed to ensure that the FBI (and, through its example, other federal law enforcement agencies) not use its investigatory powers to intrude upon political activities protected by the Constitution. This legislation should include the following:

1. provisions limiting FBI investigations to situations where there are specific and articulable facts giving reason to believe that the person has committed, is committing, or is about to commit a specific act that violates federal law, and also limiting such investigations to obtaining evidence of criminal activity;

2. provisions specifically prohibiting investigations of groups because of their members' exercise of First Amendment rights;

3. provisions specifically prohibiting preventive or covert action by the FBI designed to disrupt or discredit organizations engaged in lawful political activity;

4. repeal of federal speech and association crimes, including the Seditious Conspiracy statute, the Smith Act, the Voorhis Act, the Peacetime Military Sedition Act, the McCarran-Walter Act, and the extension of the Wartime Military Sedition Act;

5. provisions limiting how information acquired during investigations is disseminated to other agencies of the government, to the media, and to non-governmental organizations;

6. the requirement of a warrant before the FBI may engage in the most intrusive investigative techniques, including wiretapping and bugging, use of informers and infiltrators, searches of private records (held by banks, employers, health insurers, etc.), mail openings and mail covers;

7. provisions designed to ensure that the FBI will not exceed its lawful authority, including a requirement that sensitive investigations be approved, in writing, at a high level; establishment of regular Congressional oversight; protection for employees who disclose illegal or improper activities; creation of an independent office with responsibility for auditing FBI investigations and, if necessary, prosecuting those who violate the law in connection with such investigations; a requirement that all records of illegal investigative practices be segregated from the FBI's operational files and that the victims of such illegal investigative practices be notified of such segregation of records, allowed to inspect such records, and be given the option of having these records either destroyed or archived for historical purposes; and establishment of a private cause of action for individuals injured by unlawful investigative activity. AND,

BE IT FURTHER RESOLVED:

We petition the United States 102nd Congress to enact legislation that will achieve these ends.*

University of Akron	*American University -*
Carro, J. Dean	*Washington College of Law*
Jordan, William S. III	Brooks, Justin P.
Rich, William Douglas	Milstein, Elliot S. - Dean
	Paul, Joel Richard
University of Alabama	Schwartz, Herman
James, Frank S. III	WECHSLER, BURTON D.
Morgan, Martha I.	Williams, Joan Chalmers
Murphy, J. Wesley	
	Amherst College
Albany Law School - Union Univ.	COMMAGER, HENRY STEELE
Bloom, Ira Mark	
Gottlieb, Stephen E.	
Katz, Katheryn D.	

---

*   *In most cases, professors are listed at the law schools where they were teaching at the time they signed the petition. Names in CAPITAL LETTERS are the original initiators.*

University of Arizona
Ares, Charles E.
Ascher, Mark L.
Atwood, Barbara Ann
Feinberg, Joel
Silverman, Andrew
Spece, Roy G., Jr.
Williams, Robert A., Jr.

Arizona State University
BENDER, PAUL
CALLEROS, CHARLES RICHARD
Matheson, Alan A.
Spritzer, Ralph S.

Univ. of Arkansas - Fayetteville
Carnes, Charles N.
Strickman, Leonard P. - Dean

Boston College
Ansaldi, Michael
Baron, Charles Hillel
Berney, Arthur L.
Berry, Robert C.
Bloom, Robert M.
Brodin, Mark S.
Davenport, David S.
Donovan, Peter A.
Espinoza, Leslie B.
Fox, Sanford Jacob
Goldfarb, Phyllis
HEINS, MARJORIE
Houghteling, James L.
Kanstroom, Daniel
Landers, Rene
McEwen, Jean E.
Plater, Zygmunt J. B.
Rogers, James Steven
Smith, Robert H.
Spiegel, Mark
Tremblay, Paul R.

Boston University
Bone, Robert G.
Fisher, Stanley Z.
Harvey, William Burnett
LAHAV, PNINA
Partan, Daniel G.
Rossman, David
Simons, Kenneth W.
SOIFER, AVIAM

University of Bridgeport
Filler, Stuart
Krauss, Stanton D.
Margulies, Martin B.

Brooklyn Law School
Eyster, Mary Jo
Fink, Nancy H.
Garrison, Marsha
Herman, Susan N.
Kuklin, Bailey H. (see PEN)
SCHNEIDER, ELIZABETH M.

Univ. of Calif- Berkeley
Buxbaum, Richard M
FLETCHER, WILLIAM A.
Kuttner, Stephan
Rubin, Edward L.
Samuelson, Pamela

Univ. of California - Davis
Bartosic, Florian
Delgado, Richard
Dykstra, Daniel J.
GLENNON, MICHAEL J.
Oakley, John Bilyen
Perschbacher, Rex R.

Univ. of Calif - Hastings
Bird, Gail Boreman
Cohen, Marsha N.
Faigman, David L.
Grodin, Joseph R.
Levine, David E.
Massey, Calvin R.
Wingate, C. Keith

*Univ. of California
at Los Angeles (UCLA)*
AARON, BENJAMIN
Abel, Richard L.
ARENELLA, PETER
Bergman, Paul Bruce
Binder, David A.
Blumberg, Grace Ganz
Gillig, Susan Cordell
GOLDBERG, CAROLE
Handler, Joel F.
Jones, Edgar Allan, Jr.
Letwin, Leon
LOPEZ, GERALDO P.
LOWENSTEIN, DANIEL RAYS

Menkel-Meadow, Carrie J.
Moore, Albert J.
VARAT, JONATHAN D.

University of Southern
California Law Center
Arlen, Jennifer
Burton, Riley Paul - Emeritus
CHEMERINSKY, ERWIN
Franklin, Carolyn Crain
Jones, Francis E. Jr. - Emeritus

Cal Western School of Law
Belknap, Michal R.
Bohrer, Robert A.
Ehrlich, Scott B.
Leahy, James E.

Capital University
Distelhorst, Michael
Looper-Friedman, Susan E.

Campbell University
Beci, Donald L.

Case Western Reserve
Durchslag, Melvin R.
Joy, Peter

Catholic University
Bloomfield, Maxwell H.
Clark, Leroy D.
Kaplin, William A.
Sanchez, Samantha - Dean

University of Chicago
ALSCHULER, ALBERT
Becker, Mary E.
Herman, Mark J.
Palm, Gary W.
Schulhofer, Stephen J.
STONE, GEOFFREY R. - Dean
Strauss, David A.
Wood, Diane P.

Cleveland State University
Baker, Joan E.
Buckley, Thomas D.
Davis, Michael Henry
Henderson, Lynne M.
Snyder, Lloyd B.

University of Colorado
Deloria, Vine, Jr.
Getches, David Harding
Hill, David S.
Magraw, Daniel Barstow, Jr.
NICHOL, GENE R., JR. - Dean
Schlag, Pierre

Columbia University
Moglen, Eben
Strauss, Peter

Commonwealth School of Law
Massachusetts
Greer, Edward

University of Connecticut
BECKER, LOFTUS E., JR.
BRITTAIN, JOHN
Fernow, Todd D.
Macgill, H.C. - Dean
Moraveti, Thomas H.
MORAWETZ, THOMAS H.
SCHATZKI, GEORGE
Utz, Steven G.

Cooley Law School - Michigan
Koenig, Dorean M.

Cornell University
Alexander, Gregory S.
Kent, Robert B.
LoPucki, Lynn M.
Lyons, David
SHIFFRIN, STEVEN H.

Creighton Univ. Sch of Law
White, Michaela M.

Cumberland School of Law
Langum, David

University of Dayton
Saphire, Richard B.
Sultan, Allen

University of Denver
Pepper, Stephen L.

DePaul Univ. Col of Law
Bandes, Susan
EVENSON, DEBRA
Foster, Teree - Dean
Gaskell, Judith A.
Luecke, Mary Rita

APPENDIX

Nicholson, Marlene Arnold
Rutherford, Jane
Shaman, Jeffrey M.
Torrey, N. Morrison

Detroit College of Law
Kennedy, Kevin
Norris, Harold
Saltzman, Alan

University of Detroit
Keenan, Patrick A.
Kyser, Nickolas J.

Dickinson School of Law
Feldman, Harvey - Assoc Dean

Drake University Sch of Law
Anderson, Jerry L. - Assoc. Dean
INGBER, STANLEY
McCord, David
Ryman, Arthur, Jr.

Duke University
Bartlett, Katharine T.
Rowe, Thomas D., Jr.
SCHROEDER, CHRISTOPHER
Van Alstyne, William W.

Emory University
Alexander, Frank S.
Mills, Robin K.
Ordover, Abraham P.

University of Florida
Spitzer, Anne L.
Twitchell, Mary

Florida State University
Nerman, Anthony
Stempel, Jeffery
Van Doren, John W.

George Washinaton Univ. (DC)
Dienes, C. Thomas
Tremper, Charles

Georgetown
Birnbaum, Norman
Byrne, J. Peter
Chused, Richard
COHN, SHERMAN L.
Drinan, Robert F., S.J.
Ernst, Daniel R.
Eskridge, William N., Jr.

KRATTENMAKER, THOMAS G.
LAWRENCE, CHARLES
MATSUDA, MARI J.
NORTON, ELEANOR HOLMES
Roe, Richard
ROSS, SUSAN DELLER
SEIDMAN, LOUIS MICHAEL
TAGUE, PETER W.
TUSHNET, MARK V.
Wales, Heathcote W.

University of Georgia
Ball, Milner S.
Kurtz, Paul M.

Golden Gate Law Sch.
Calhoun, Robert K., Jr.
DeVito, Michael D.

Hamline University
Allen, Richard C.
Daly, Joseph L.
Swanson, Steven R.
Vogel, Howard J.
Weeks, John E.

Hampshire College
Risech, Flavio

Harvard University
BARTHOLET, ELIZABETH
BELL, DERRICK A.
Brudney, Victor - Emeritus
COUNTRYMAN, VERN - Emeritus (Dec.)
Donahue, Charles
Edley, Christopher
FIELD, MARTHA A.
Halperin, Daniel
Kennedy, Duncan
MICHELMAN, FRANK I.
MINOW, MARTHA
PARKER, RICHARD DAVIES
White, Lucie Evelyn
Wolfman, Bernard

University of Hawaii
Yamamoto, Eric K.

Hofstra Law School
FREEDMAN, MONROE H.
Kubitachek, Carolyn A.
Levine, Alan

195

Houston
Oldham, J.Thomas
Olivas, Michael
Paust, Jordan J.
Rosenberg, Irene Merker

Howard University
Bullock, Alice G. - Assoc Dean

University of Idaho
Gallant, Kenneth S.
Lewis, D. Craig
Macdonald, Jim
Seeger, Leinaala R.

Univ. of Illinois Col of Law
Kinports, Kit
Stone, Victor J.
Weiss, Samuel

Illinois Inst. of Technology
Chicago Kent Col.of Law
Deutsch, Stuart
Gerber, David J.
Matasar, Richard - Dean
Nahmod, Sheldon
Nance, Dale A.
Rudstein, David
Steinman, Joan
Stewart, Margaret

Northern Illinois University
Parnass, Jeffrey A.
Swift, Joel H. - Assoc. Dean

Southern Illinois University
Gross, Leonard

Indiana Univ. - Bloomington
Dau-Schmidt, Kenneth
Henderson, Lynne N.
Williams, Susan Hoffman

Indiana Univ.- Indianapolis
Galanti, Paul J.
Marsh, William E.
Stake, Jeff

University of Iowa
BUSS, WILLIAM G.
Cain, Patricia
CLINTON, ROBERT N.
Fellows, Mary Louise
Green, Michael

Knight, W.H. Jr.
Reitz, John C.
Wing, Adrien K.

John Marshall Law Sch.
LEWIS, MELVIN B.
Seng, Michael P.

University of Kansas
Schanck, Peter C.

University of Kentucky
Batt, John
Goldman, Alvin L.

Northern Kentucky Univ.
Krauss, Gene

Louisiana State Univ.
Blakesley, Christopher L.
Dakin, Melvin G. - Emeritus

Univ. of Louisville
Knowles, Laurence W.
Stenger, Robert

Loyola Univ. of Chicago
Amaker, Norman C.
Curtin, James S.
Geraghty, Diane

Loyola Law Sch. - Los Angeles
Bellson, Robert
Garbesi, Curt
Leonard, David P.
Manhein, Karl
May, Christopher W.
Michel, Vicki
Stewart, Daniel
Strauss, Marcy

Loyola Univ. - New Orleans
Rosen, Dan

University of Maine
Brett, Tybe Ann

University of Maryland
Colbert, Douglas L.
Herr, Stanley S.
Quint, Peter E.

U. Mass/Amherst
d'Errico, Peter

McGeorge School of Law,
Univ. of the Pacific
Davies, Julie A.
DRESSLER, JOSHUA
Gerwitz, Franklin
Levine, Lawrence C.
Sims, John Carey

Mercer University
Cole, John O.
Dantzler, Deryl D.
Posnak, Bruce
Sammons, Jack L.

University of Miami
Casebeer, Kenneth
Coombs, Mary 1.
Daniels, Wes
Diamond, Stephen
Fischl, Richard Michael
Sowle, Kathryn D.
Stotzky, Irwin P.

University of Michigan
Allen, Layman E.
CHAMBERS, DAVID L.
D'Aunne, Lisa
Ellsworth, Phoebe C.
Gewez, Martin
GROSS, SAMUEL R.
Lehman, Jeffrey S.
Lempert, Richard
Pildes, Richard
Reingold, Paul
ST. ANTOINE, THEODORE
Sandalow, Terrance
WHITMAN, CHRISTINA B.

University of Minnesota
Chomsky, Carol
Frase, Richard S.
Kilbourn, Wm. Douglas, Jr.
Kramer, Victor H.
Morris, C. Robert
SHERRY, SUZANNA

Wm. Mitchell Coll. Of Law
Davies, Jack

University of Mississippi
Bush, Larry S.

Univ. of Missouri - Kans. City
Kisthardt, Mary Kay
Linder, Douglas O.
Popper, Robert - Dean
Warner, G. Ray

University of Montana
Elison, Larry M.
Huff, Tom
Stone, Albert W.

University of Nebraska
Snowden, John Rockwell
Striman, Brian

University of New Mexico
Desiderio, Robert J.
Fink, Myron
Hart, Frederick M.
Kelly, Suedeen
Scales, Ann C.

City University of New York
Queens College
BURNS, HAYWOOD - Dean (Dec.)
Carpenter, Suzan A.
Copelon, Rhonda
Hyman-Browne, Ellen

New York University
AMSTERDAM, ANTHONY G.
Chase, Oscar G. - Assoc Dean
CHEVIGNY, PAUL G.
DORSEN, NORMAN
Galowitz, Paula
SEXTON, JOHN EDWARD - Dean
Shaviro, Daniel N.
Vincent-Daviss, Diana

New York Law School
Peritz, Rudolph
STROSSEN, NADINE

State Univ. of New York - Buffalo
Albert, Lee A. - Assoc Dean
Szczygiel, Anthony
Thuronyi, Victor

Univ. of North Carolina
Bennett, Walter H, Jr.
Daye, Charles E.
Pollitt, Daniel H.
Rosen, Richard A.

Northeastern - MA
Baker, Brook K.
Berman, Nathaniel
Brown, Judith Olans
Dalton, Clare
Hall, David
Klare, Karl
Meltsner, Michael
Schaffer, Daniel
Subrin, Stephen N.

Northwestern - University
D'Amato, Anthony
PERRY, MICHAEL JOHN

Notre Dame - Indiana
Kellenberg, Conrad

Nova University
Burns, Michael M.
Chase, Anthony
Coleman, Phyllis
Rohr, Marc
Sanchez, John

Ohio Northern
Avellone, Frank
French, Bruce Comly
Veltri, Stephen

Ohio State
Federle, Katherine Hunt
ERICKSON, NANCY S.
Goldberger, David
Holoch, Alan
Johnson, Bruce
Laughlin, Stanley K. Jr.
Merritt, Deborah Jones
QUIGLEY, JOHN B., JR.
Wilson, Charles E.

University of Oklahoma
Anderson, Jerry L.
Forman, Jonathan Barry

University of Oregon
Clark, Chapin D.
Forell, Caroline Anne
O'FALLON, JAMES M.
Schuman, David

Pace Law School
Cummings, Richard
Fentiman, Linda C.

Gershman, Bennett L.
Merton, Vanessa
Mushlin, Michael B.
O'Neil, Paul
Ottinger, Hon. Richard
Stein, Ralph Michael
Triffin, Nicholas
Westerman, Gayl

Univ. of Pennsylvania
BAKER, C. EDWIN
LESNICK, HOWARD
RUDOVSKY, DAVID
SUMMERS, CLYDE

Pepperdine
James, Bernard
Kavarre, Mark John

University of Pittsburgh
Burkoff, John M.
Cooley, Thomas, II - Dean Emer.
Flechtner, Harry M.
Frolik, Lawrence A.
Lobel, Jules
Luneburg, William V.
Seeburger, Richard H.
Shane, Peter
Wasserman, Rhonda

Quinnipiae College
Krauss, Stanton D.

Richmond
Kestin, Nina R. (Dec.)
Shepherd, Robert E., Jr.

*Rutgers Law School -
Camden and Newark*
ASKIN, FRANK - Newark
Clark, Roger S. - Camden
Feinman, Jay M. - Camden
FREEDMAN, ANNE E. - Camden
Franciona, Gary - Newark
Hull, N.E.H. - Camden
Hyman, Jonathan M. - Newark
KINOY, ARTHUR - Newark
Leubsdorf, John - Newark
NEISSER, ERIC - Newark
Paul, James C. N. - Newark
TAUB, NADINE - Newark

San Diego
ALEXANDER, LAWRENCE ALAN
Player, Theresa J.
Wiggins, Charles B.

Univ. of San Francisco
Denvir, John
Donovan, Dolores A.
Folberg, H. Jay - Dean
Garvey, Jack I.
Mounts, Suzanne E.
PEMBERTON, JOHN DEJ, JR.
Putz, C. Delos
Reiley, Eldon H.
Wildman, Stephanie M.

Santa Clara Univ.
Alexander, George J.
Anawalt, Howard C.
Steinman, Edward
Uelmen, Gerald F. - Dean
Wright, Eric W.

Seattle University
Strait, John

St. John's University
Lyndon, Mary Loring

St. Louis University
Goldman, Roger
Goldner, Jesse A.
Howard, Alan J.
Tuchler, Dennis J.

St. Mary's Univ.
ALDAVE, BARBARA BADER - Dean
Anderson, Joe E.
Cochran, Mark W.
Dittfurth, David - Assoc Dean
Haddock, Douglas R.
Mather, Victoria M.
Reamey, Gerald S.

South Carolina School of Law
Burke, W. Lewis
Crystal, Nathan M. - Assoc Dean
Flynn, Patrick J.
McAnineh, William Shepard
Smalls, O'Neal

South Dakota School of Law
Davidson, John H.

Southern Methodist Univ.
Bridge, William J.
Moss, Frederick C.
Reed, Roark M.
Winship, Peter

Southwestern University
Schmitt, Michael A.
Smith, L. Marshall
Solomon, Richard C.

Stanford University
BABCOCK, BARBARA ALLEN
COHEN, WILLIAM
Fried, Barbara
Friedman, Lawrence M.
Mendez, Miguel Angel
Radin, Margaret Jane
Rhode, Deborah L.
ROSENHAN, DAVID L.
WEISBERG, ROBERT

Stetson University
Batey, Robert
Brown, Mark
Gershon, I. Richard

Suffolk University
Ashe, Marie
Blumenson, Eric
Clark, Gerard J.
Murphy, Russell G.

Syracuse University
Bell, Peter A.
Bender, Leslie
Reuben-Cooke, Wilhelmina M. - Assoc. Dean

Temple University
Caine, Burton
Ohlbaum, Edward D.

Univ. of Tennessee - Knoxville
Gray, Grayfred B.
Lacey, Forrest W. - Emeritus
Overton, Elvin E. - Emeritus

University of Texas
LAYCOCK, DOUGLAS
Powe, Scott
Robertson, David W.
Sturley, Michael F.
TIGAR, MICHAEL E.

Texas Tech Univ. - Lubbock
Schoen, Rodric B.

Touro Law School
Silver, Marjorie A.

Tulane University
STICK, JOHN J.
Werhan, Keith

Univ. of Tulsa
Bires, Dennis E.
Blair, Chris
Ducey, Richard E.
Lacey, Linda J.

University of Utah
Martinez, John

Valparaiso Univ.
Hiller, Jack A.
Levinson, Rosalie B.

Vanderbilt Univ.
Johnston, Jason Scott

Vermont Law School
Cole, Liz Ryan
Dycus, Stephen
Firestone, David

Villanova University
Dowd, Donald
Rothman, Frederick P.

University of Virginia
Henderson, Stanley D.
Hetherington, John A. C.

Wake Forest Univ.
Foy, H. Miles III - Assoc. Dean
Parker, J. Wilson
Shores, David F.

Washington Univ. (St. Louis)
Greenfield, Michael M.
Jones, William C.
Swihart, R. Dale

Univ. of Washington (Seattle)
Aronson, Robert H. - Assoc. Dean
Burke, William T.
Hazelton, Penny A.
Jay, Stewart
Johnson, Ralph W.
Peck, Cornelius J.
Vaughn, Lea B.

Washington & Lee (VA)
Sundby, Scott E.

Wayne State University (MI)
Littlejohn, Edward J.
Sedler, Robert A.

West Virginia Univ. (Morgantown)
Ashdown, Gerald G.
Bastress, Robert M.
DiSalvo, Charles R.
Lewin, Jeff L.

Western New England Coll.
(Springfield MA)
Dunn, Donald J.
Goldstein, Anne B.
Leavens, Arthur
Levin, Stephanie A.
Miller, Bruce K.

Whittier Coll.
Brod, Gail Frommer
Gale, Mary Ellen

Widener Univ. Law Sch.
Gelfand, Gregory
Lipkin, Robert Justin

Willamette Univ.
Breen, Richard F., Jr.,
Burton, Claudia

Coll. of William and Mary
Gerhardt, Michael J.
Levy, John M.
NICHOL, GENE, JR.

Univ. of Wisconsin
Finman, Ted
Galanter, Marc
Longert, Jack
Thome, Joseph R.
Weisberger, June

University of Wyoming
Blackstone, M.
Squillace, Mark
Stevens, Ann B.

Yale University
BURT, ROBERT A.
Curtis, Dennis Edward
EMERSON, THOMAS I. (Dec.)
Goldstein, Joseph
Resnik, Judith
Rose-Ackerman, Susan

Yeshiva University
Clark, Elizabeth B.
de Grazia, Edward
Vogelman, Lawrence A.

NOTES

NOTES TO CHAPTER 1
INTRODUCTION

1. United States v. United States District Court, 407 U.S. 297, 314 (1972).

2. United States v. Robel, 389 U.S. 258, 264 (1967).

3. The FBI is not the only federal agency involved in counterterrorism. The Immigration and Naturalization Service, for example, enforces laws excluding and removing aliens for engaging in terrorist activity. The Bureau of Alcohol, Tobacco and Firearms has used its jurisdiction over firearms offenses to target radical domestic groups, and was responsible for launching the disastrous raid on a religious compound at Waco, Texas in 1993. The State Department denies visas to persons seeking to enter the U.S. to engage in terrorism. The Central Intelligence Agency has made collection of foreign intelligence on terrorism one of its priorities.

4. Antiterrorism and Effective Death Penalty Act of 1996, Pub. L. 104-132, 110 Stat. 1214.

5. Reno v. American-Arab Anti-Discrimination Comm., 1999 U.S. Lexis 1514 (U.S. Feb. 23, 1999).

6. For an account in Frank Wilkinson's own words, see GRIFFIN FARIELLO, RED SCARE: MEMORIES OF THE AMERICAN INQUISITION 530-36 (W. W. Norton, 1995).

7. Wilkinson v. United States, 365 U.S. 399 (1961).

8. DAVID HELVARG, THE WAR AGAINST THE GREENS 393 (Sierra Club Books, 1997).

9. *Id.* at 392.

10. *Id.* at 393-94.

11. The official name of the Church Committee was the "Select Committee to Study Governmental Operations with respect to Intelligence Activities." Its final report was published in six volumes, accompanied by seven volumes of hearings and supporting documents. INTELLIGENCE ACTIVITIES AND THE RIGHTS OF AMERICANS, FINAL REPORT OF THE SENATE SELECT COMMITTEE TO STUDY GOVERNMENTAL OPERATIONS WITH RESPECT TO INTELLIGENCE ACTIVITIES, 94th Cong., 2d Sess. (1976).

The initial evidence about the breadth and depth of FBI spying on dissenters became public not through Congressional oversight but as a result of a burglary at an FBI satellite office in Media, Pennsylvania in March 1971. Domestic counterintelligence documents were stolen, then released to the press and published widely.

12. *See* FBI OVERSIGHT: HEARINGS BEFORE THE SUBCOMM. ON CIVIL AND CONSTITUTIONAL RIGHTS OF THE HOUSE COMM. ON THE JUDICIARY, PART 2, 94th Cong., 2, 12 (1975) (testimony of Elmer B. Staats, Comptroller General, reporting on GAO review of FBI domestic intelligence operations.)

13. FBI AUTHORIZATION REQUEST FOR FISCAL YEAR 1986: HEARINGS BEFORE THE SUBCOMM. ON CIVIL AND CONSTITUTIONAL RIGHTS OF THE HOUSE COMM. ON THE JUDICIARY, 99th Cong., 1st Sess. 15 (1985).

14. *Id.* at 29.

15. SENATE SELECT COMM. ON INTELLIGENCE, THE FBI AND CISPES, 101st Cong., 1st Sess. 2 (1989) [hereinafter "SENATE INTELLIGENCE REPORT"]. Other agencies participated in the intelligence gathering. Customs agents questioned travelers returning from Nicaragua about their activities, seizing and copying from people's luggage personal written materials and turning them over to the FBI. Heidy v. U.S. Customs Service, 681 F. Supp. 1445 (C.D. CA 1988). *See generally*, BREAK-INS AT SANCTUARY CHURCHES AND ORGANIZATIONS OPPOSED TO ADMINISTRATION POLICY IN CENTRAL AMERICA, HEARINGS BEFORE THE SUBCOMM. ON CIVIL AND CONSTITUTIONAL RIGHTS OF THE HOUSE COMM. ON THE JUDICIARY, 100th Cong., 1st Sess. 200-204 (1987) (testimony of the Center for Constitutional Rights).

16. *See* Frank Tejo, *Lives on Hold: Palestinians accused of terrorism fight to stay in US*, DALLAS MORNING NEWS, Dec. 29, 1992 at 1A. For the legal history of the case, *see* Reno v. American-Arab Anti-Discrimination Comm., 1999 U.S. Lexis 1514 (U.S. Feb. 23, 1999), *vacating and remanding* 119 F.3d 1367 (9th Cir. 1997); American-Arab Anti-Discrimination Comm. v. Reno, 70 F.3d 1045 (9th Cir. 1995); American-Arab Anti-Discrimination Comm. v. Meese, 714 F. Supp. 1060 (C.D. Cal. 1989), *aff'd in part, rev'd in part*, American-Arab Anti-Discrimination Comm. v. Thornburgh, 970 F.2d 501 (9th Cir. 1991).

17. *See* Socialist Workers' Party v. Attorney Gen., 642 F. Supp. 1357, 1389 (S.D.N.Y. 1986) (quoting FBI memorandum).

18. Janine Anderson, *War: probes and profits; FBI questions OC residents from Mideast*, ORANGE COUNTY REGISTER, Feb. 8, 1991, at A5.

19. Kenneth Reich, *Arab-Americans upset over questioning by FBI*, L.A.TIMES, Jan. 12, 1991, at A1.

20. Emerson, *National Security and Civil Liberties*, 9 YALE J.WORLD PUB. ORDER 83, 99 (1982). *See also* THOMAS I. EMERSON, THE SYSTEM OF FREEDOM OF EXPRESSION (Random House, 1970).

21. Emerson, *National Security and Civil Liberties*, supra note 20, at 98.

22. *See, e.g.*, Neil A. Lewis, *Terror in Oklahoma*, N.Y.TIMES, Apr. 25, 1995, at 19 (quoting a former senior official as saying, "The problem is that these rules require we have a criminal predicate before we investigate. ...That means we have to wait until you have blood on the street before the bureau can act.").

23. *E.g.*, Deutch, *Terrorism*, FOREIGN POLICY (Fall 1997) at 10, 18-19 (arguing that "some loss of civil liberty inevitably accompanies measures to combat terrorism").

NOTES TO CHAPTER 2
THE FBI's INVESTIGATION OF CENTRAL AMERICAN ACTIVISTS

1. FBI CISPES document, 199-8848-128x1 (Nov. 10, 1983), *reprinted in* CISPES AND FBI COUNTERTERRORISM INVESTIGATIONS: HEARINGS BEFORE THE SUBCOMM. ON CIVIL AND CONSTITUTIONAL RIGHTS OF THE HOUSE COMM. ON THE JUDICIARY, 100th Cong. 230-31 (1988) [hereinafter "CISPES HEARINGS"].

2. FBI CISPES document, 199-8848-1 (Mar. 30, 1983), *reprinted in* CISPES HEARINGS, supra note 1, at 203.

3. SENATE SELECT COMM. ON INTELLIGENCE, THE FBI AND CISPES, 101st Cong., 1st Sess. 12, 20-22, 88-89 (1989) [hereinafter "SENATE INTELLIGENCE REPORT"]; CISPES HEARINGS, *supra* note 1, at 129 (testimony of FBI Director William S. Sessions). The Foreign Agents Registration Act is at 22 U.S.C. §§ 611 *et seq.*

4. BREAK-INS AT SANCTUARY CHURCHES AND ORGANIZATIONS OPPOSED TO ADMINISTRATION POLICY IN CENTRAL AMERICA: HEARINGS BEFORE THE SUBCOMM. ON CIVIL AND CONSTITUTIONAL RIGHTS OF THE HOUSE COMM. ON THE JUDICIARY, 100th Cong. 435-442 (1987) (testimony of Frank Varelli); SENATE INTELLIGENCE REPORT, *supra* note 3, at 58-59; ROSS GELBSPAN, BREAK-INS, DEATH THREATS AND THE FBI: THE COVERT WAR AGAINST THE CENTRAL AMERICA MOVEMENT (South End Press, 1991).

5. CISPES HEARINGS, *supra* note 1, at 117, 139 (statement of William Sessions, Director, FBI).

6. SENATE INTELLIGENCE REPORT, *supra* note 3, at 28.

7. FBI CISPES document, 199-8848-24 (May 23, 1983), *reprinted in* CISPES HEARINGS, *supra* note 1, at 207.

8. FBI CISPES document, 199-8848-103 (Oct. 7, 1983), *reprinted in* CISPES HEARINGS, *supra* note 1, at 218-19.

9. SENATE INTELLIGENCE REPORT, *supra* note 3, at 36.

10. *Id.* at 2.

11. *Id.* at 5-7, 81-85.

12. In April 1985, when the case was still open and its existence and scope were not yet publicly known, FBI Director Webster appeared before Edwards' subcommittee. Webster was asked about reports of FBI interviews of CISPES members. Characterizing the interviews as scattered and claiming that each had an independent counterintelligence purpose, he testified, "We are not keeping track of the membership of CISPES as such." FBI AUTHORIZATION REQUEST FOR FISCAL YEAR 1986: HEARINGS BEFORE THE SUBCOMM. ON CIVIL AND CONSTITUTIONAL RIGHTS OF THE HOUSE COMM. ON THE JUDICIARY, 99th Cong. 29 (1985) [hereinafter "FBI AUTHORIZATION HEARINGS"].

13. "[T]he scope widened substantively to include surveillance and reporting of political activities and to encompass rank-and-file members as well as leaders...." SENATE INTELLIGENCE REPORT, *supra* note 3 at 96. *See also id.* at 80.

14. FBI CISPES document, 199-8848-162 (Jan. 11, 1984), *reprinted in* CISPES HEARINGS, *supra* note 1, at 271.

15. FBI CISPES document, 199-8848-300X (Apr. 2, 1984), *reprinted in* CISPES HEARINGS, *supra* note 1, at 355-61.

16. *See* Statement of Rep. Don Edwards, Cong. Rec. H707 (March 3, 1988 daily edition), *quoted in* Gary M. Stern, *The FBI's Misguided Probe of CISPES*, CNSS Rep. No. 111 (Jun. 1988), *reprinted in* CISPES HEARINGS, *supra* note 1, at 23-24.

17. "Some have questioned whether the FBI may properly investigate an individual or group in the absence of a specific federal criminal violation. It is important to understand that the FBI docs have such authority in the international terrorism field." SENATE INTELLIGENCE REPORT, *supra* note 3, at 91.

18. FBI CISPES document, 199-8848-128 (Nov. 8, 1983), *reprinted in* CISPES HEARINGS, *supra* note 1, at 226-29.

19. FBI CISPES document, 199-8848-146 (Jan. 5, 1984), *reprinted in* CISPES HEARINGS, *supra* note 1, at 258 - 59.

20. FBI CISPES document 199-8848-[not recorded] (Jan. 16, 1984), *reprinted in* CISPES HEARINGS, *supra* note 1, at 247.

21. FBI CISPES document, 199-8848-166 (Feb. 2, 1984), *reprinted in* CISPES HEARINGS, *supra* note 1, at 313, 317.

22. FBI CISPES document, 199-8848-378 (May 11, 1984), *reprinted in* CISPES HEARINGS, *supra* note 1, at 374.

23. FBI CISPES document, 199-8848-436 (Jul. 26, 1984), *reprinted in* CISPES HEARINGS, *supra* note 1, at 396-404.

24. FBI CISPES document, 199-8848-483 (Aug. 8, 1984), *reprinted in* CISPES HEARINGS, *supra* note 1, at 406.

25. Gary M. Stern, *The FBI's Misguided Probe of CISPES*, CNSS Rep. No. 111 (Jun. 1988), *reprinted in* CISPES HEARINGS, *supra* note 1, at 32 (quoting FBI CISPES document 199-8848-482 (Aug. 10, 1983)).

26. FBI CISPES document, 199-8848-492 (Aug. 29, 1984), *reprinted in* CISPES HEARINGS, *supra* note 1, at 411-13.

27. FBI CISPES document, 199-8848-492 (Aug. 29, 1984), *reprinted in* CISPES HEARINGS, *supra* note 1, at 410-13.

28. FBI CISPES document, 199-8848 [not recorded] (Jun. 4, 1985), *reprinted in* CISPES HEARINGS, *supra* note 1, at 430.

29. *See* LEGISLATIVE INITIATIVES TO CURB DOMESTIC AND INTERNATIONAL TERRORISM: HEARINGS BEFORE THE SUBCOMM. ON SECURITY AND TERRORISM OF THE SENATE COMM. ON THE JUDICIARY, 98th Cong. (1984).

30. *See* SENATE INTELLIGENCE REPORT, *supra* note 3, at 42, 71.

31. Immediately after learning of the scope of the CISPES investigation in early 1988, Rep. Edwards asked the General Accounting Office ("GAO") to audit the FBI's international terrorism program. This was the first independent examination ever of the Bureau's international terrorism investigations. Edwards wanted to know whether the CISPES case was an aberration, as the FBI claimed, or whether it reflected broader issues in the FBI's approach to international terrorism. *See* GENERAL ACCOUNTING OFFICE, INTERNATIONAL TERRORISM: FBI INVESTIGATES DOMESTIC ACTIVITIES TO IDENTIFY TERRORISTS (1989) [hereinafter "GAO Report"], *reprinted in* FBI INVESTIGATION OF FIRST AMENDMENT ACTIVITIES: HEARINGS BEFORE THE SUBCOMM. ON CIVIL AND CONSTITUTIONAL RIGHTS OF THE HOUSE COMM. ON THE JUDICIARY, 101st Cong. 112-57 (1989).

 The GAO found that, between January 1982 and June 1988, the FBI opened and closed about 19,500 international terrorism cases. In 99 percent of the closed cases, the investigative record filled only one or two file folders, indicating that the investigation was not extensive. But the existence of 19,500 cases over a six and one-half year period, even if most were limited to one or two folders of information, means that the FBI collected as many as 30,000 folders of data on groups and individuals in the name of investigating international counterterrorism.

 During the same time period of 1982 through 1988, there were twenty-five international terrorist incidents in the U.S., all of them in 1982 and 1983. From 1984 through 1988, there were no international terrorist incidents in the United States.

 Nearly 68 percent of the FBI's international terrorism cases studied by the GAO were closed because no evidence was uncovered linking the subject to international terrorism or terrorist acts. *Id.* at 115. This further reinforces the finding that most of the FBI's cases do not involve the investigation of actual terrorists, but rather the pursuit of allegations or suspicions later found to be unsubstantiated. In another 22 percent, the cases "were closed because the subject moved or could not be located." *Id.* at 117.

32. *Id.* at 131.

33. *See, e.g., id.* at 133-35 (discussing five cases where basis for investigation was atten-

dance at meeting, participation in religious service, or being listed in foreign newspaper article).

34. *Id.* at 132-33.

35. Doyle, *Fresno Group Probed by FBI*, FRESNO BEE, Jan. 29, 1990, at A1.

36. SENATE INTELLIGENCE REPORT, *supra* note 3, at 80-86.

37. CISPES HEARINGS, *supra* note 1, at 188.

NOTES TO CHAPTER 3
THE INVESTIGATION AND ATTEMPTED DEPORTATION
OF THE LOS ANGELES 8

1. FBI, "Popular Front for the Liberation of Palestine (PFLP)" (1986), (report in four volumes), *reprinted in part in* American-Arab Anti-Discrimination Committee v. Reno, No. 96-55929 (9th Cir. 1996), Supplemental Excerpts of Record (vol. 2), at 354.

2. William Overend & Ronald L. Soble, *7 Tied to PLO Terrorist Wing Seized by INS*, LOS ANGELES TIMES, Jan. 27, 1987, at 1.

3. Reno v. American-Arab Anti-Discrimination Comm., 1999 U.S. Lexis 1514, (U.S. Feb. 23, 1999), *vacating and remanding* 119 F.3d 1367 (9th Cir. 1997); American-Arab Anti-Discrimination Comm. v. Reno, 70 F.3d 1045 (9th Cir. 1995); American-Arab Anti-Discrimination Comm. v. Meese, 714 F. Supp. 1060 (C.D. CA. 1989), *aff'd in part, rev'd in part*, American-Arab Anti-Discrimination Comm. v. Thornburgh, 970 F.2d 501 (9th Cir. 1991).

4. HEARINGS BEFORE THE SENATE SELECT COMMITTEE ON INTELLIGENCE ON NOMINATION OF WILLIAM H. WEBSTER TO BE DIRECTOR OF CENTRAL INTELLIGENCE, 100th Cong. 94-95 (1987).

5. *See* American-Arab Anti-Discrimination Comm. v. Reno, 70 F.3d 1045, 1053 (9th Cir. 1995).

6. FBI, "Popular Front for the Liberation of Palestine (PFLP)" (1986), *supra*, note 1.

7. *See* American-Arab Anti-Discrimination Committee v. Reno, No. 96-55929 (9th Cir. 1996) Supplemental Excerpts of Record (vol. 2), at 336.

8. *Id.* at 306-7.

9. Memorandum from Investigations Division, INS, *Alien Border Control Committee (ABC) Group IV - Contingency Plans* (Nov. 18, 1986), with attachments, on file with James X. Dempsey.

10. Memorandum from Deputy Attorney General D. Lowell Jensen to INS Commissioner Alan C. Nelson, *Formation of the Alien Border Control Committee* (June 27, 1986), on file with James X. Dempsey

11. FBI, "Popular Front for the Liberation of Palestine (PFLP)" (1986), (report in four vol-

umes), *reprinted in* American-Arab Anti-Discrimination Committee v. Reno, No. 96-55929 (9th Cir. 1996), Supplemental Excerpts of Record (vol. 2), at 354.

12. Thousands of Americans regularly attended such "haflis" across the United States, and contributed money to support humanitarian aid for those "back home." The events, like everything else in Palestinian culture at that time, were generally associated with one or more of the PLO factions, because most Palestinians identified the PLO as their legitimate political representative. The dinners were attended by large numbers of children, the elderly, and many non-Palestinians. Donations were solicited for humanitarian purposes only, and were directed to U.S. OMEN, an IRS-certified charitable organization that provided humanitarian aid to Palestinians in Lebanon, the West Bank, and Gaza. U.S. OMEN sent the money to various charitable institutions in the Middle East, such as the Ghassan Kanafani Foundation, which operates kindergartens and day-care centers in Lebanon.

13. American-Arab Anti-Discrimination Comm. v. Reno, No. 87-02107 (Memorandum opinion, C.D. Cal. 1986), *reprinted in* Reno v. American-Arab Anti-Discrimination Comm., No. 97-1252 (S. Ct.), Joint Appendix.

14. *See* American-Arab Anti-Discrimination Comm. v. Meese, 714 F. Supp. 1060 (C.D. Cal. 1989), *aff'd in part, rev'd in part,* American-Arab Anti-Discrimination Comm. v. Thornburgh, 970 F.2d 501 (9th Cir. 1991).

15. American-Arab Anti-Discrimination Comm. v. Reno, 70 F.3d 1045, 1064 (9th Cir. 1995).

16. American-Arab Anti-Discrimination Comm. v. Reno, 119 F.3d 1367 (9th Cir. 1997), *vacated and remanded,* 1999 U.S. Lexis 1514 (U.S. Feb. 23, 1999).

17. Reno v. American-Arab Anti-Discrimination Comm., 1999 U.S. Lexis 1514 (U.S. Feb. 23, 1999).

18. The Court's analysis leaves open the question whether the INS may deport an alien *solely* for engaging in First Amendment-protected political activity. Its decision addressed only whether an alien who faces deportation for some other ground has an affirmative defense where he has been selectively targeted for constitutionally impermissible reasons. The Court held that he does not, thereby unleashing the INS to use its immigration powers selectively to punish politically unpopular ideas.

19. Lisa Belkin, *For Many Arab-Americans, FBI Scrutiny Renews Fears,* N.Y. TIMES, Jan. 12, 1991, at 1A; Sharon LaFraniere, *FBI Starts Interviewing Arab-American Leaders,* WASH. POST, Jan. 9, 1991, at A14.

20. Emily Sachar, *FBI Grills NY Arab-Americans,* NEWSDAY, Jan. 29, 1991, at 6.

21. Belkin, *supra* note 18.

22. Sachar, *supra* note 19.

23. *FBI questions Arab-Americans in New Castle, Ohio,* UPI, Jan. 10, 1991.

24. *State Police, FBI Questioning Arabs,* ARKANSAS DEMOCRAT-GAZETTE, Jan. 16, 1991.

25. Jim Doyle, *Federal Agents Balancing Rights, Terror Concerns,* SAN FRANCISCO CHRONICLE, Feb. 19, 1991, at A7.

26. Jane Friedman, *In the Aftermath of Gulf War, Arab-Americans Assess Standing*, CHRISTIAN SCIENCE MONITOR, Mar. 13, 1991, at 9.

27. These documents are now at the not-for-profit National Security Archives in Washington, DC.

Notes to Chapter 4
Intelligence Investigations from
Amnesty International to Earth First!

1. FBI INVESTIGATION OF FIRST AMENDMENT ACTIVITIES: HEARINGS BEFORE THE SUBCOMM. ON CIVIL AND CONSTITUTIONAL RIGHTS OF THE HOUSE COMM. ON THE JUDICIARY, 101st Cong. 35-36 (1989) [hereinafter "FIRST AMENDMENT HEARINGS"].

2. *Id.* at 112.

3. *Id.* at 9-15.

4. Patterson v. FBI, 705 F. Supp. 1033 (D. N.J. 1989), *aff'd*, 893 F.2d 595 (3d Cir. 1990), *cert. denied*, 498 U.S. 812 (1990).

5. FIRST AMENDMENT HEARINGS, *supra* note 1, at 31-32.

6. *See* FBI COUNTERINTELLIGENCE VISITS TO LIBRARIES: HEARINGS BEFORE THE SUBCOMM. ON CIVIL AND CONSTITUTIONAL RIGHTS OF THE HOUSE COMM. ON THE JUDICIARY, 100th Cong. (1988) [hereinafter "FBI LIBRARY VISITS"]. *See also* Robert D. McFadden, *FBI in New York Asks Librarians' Aid in Reporting on Spies*, N.Y. TIMES, Sept. 18, 1987, at 1A.

7. FBI LIBRARY VISITS, *supra* note 6, at 332-33.

8. The federal Court of Appeals for the District of Columbia allowed the FBI to maintain the file and keep it secret, notwithstanding the Privacy Act's prohibition against the maintenance of records on First Amendment activities not pertinent to a legitimate law enforcement activity. J. Roderick MacArthur Foundation v. FBI, 102 F.3d 600 (D.C. Cir. 1996), *cert. denied*, 118 S.Ct. 296 (1997).

9. Susan Page, *AIDS Protest Held Near Bush's Home*, NEWSDAY, Sept. 2, 1991, at 13.

10. In response to the Freedom of Information Act request filed by the Center for Constitutional Rights, the FBI released just 22 pages of a file containing 451 documents from 16 FBI field offices, dating from February 1988 to October 1993. Greg B. Smith, N.Y. DAILY NEWS, June 21, 1995, at 21.

11. David W. Dunlap, *FBI Kept Watch on AIDS Group During Protest Years*, N.Y. TIMES, May 16, 1995, at B3.

12. Local police sometimes responded to ACT-UP demonstrations with excessive force. On September 12, 1991, a large group of ACT-UP activists greeted George Bush as he entered the Bellevue Hotel in Philadelphia for a fundraising event. The ACT-UP pro-

testers held up signs criticizing Bush's neglect of the AIDS issue. They blew whistles and yelled "shame." Other demonstrators, including some from NOW and groups representing the homeless and elderly, voiced their own criticisms of the Bush Administration in a demonstration of 7,500 in all. The ACT-UP contingent formed the largest and noisiest of the protesters. The Philadelphia police descended upon the ACT-UP members with nightsticks, violently throwing demonstrators into a paddy wagon. *See Panel: Cops Were Afraid*, NEWSDAY, Mar. 21, 1992, at 9.

13. Greg B. Smith, *FBI to Probe Itself on AIDS Group File*, N.Y. DAILY NEWS, May 18, 1995, at 5.

14. SENATE INTELLIGENCE REPORT, *supra* note 3 to chapter 2, at 5, 102.

15. Michael Taylor, *2 Earth First! Members Hurt By Bomb in Car; Radicals Reportedly Suspected in Oakland Blast*, SAN FRANCISCO CHRONICLE, May 25, 1990, at A1.

16. Rep. Edwards tried to answer Bari's question through the oversight process. In 1991, in response to Edwards' questioning, the FBI responded that it had not had an investigation of Earth First!, Cherney, Bari, or Redwood Summer before the bombing. In 1996, after six years of litigation, Bari's lawyer obtained a complete copy of the form 302 that was written by the FBI agent who responded to the scene of the bombing, in which the agent stated that, at the scene of the bombing, he was advised by the field office that Bari and Cherney "were the subjects of an FBI investigation in the terrorist field." In a teletype to headquarters the day after the bombing, the San Francisco field office noted that "Bari and Cherney were already considered potential suspects in 'Earth Night Action Groups; DS/T [Domestic Security/Terrorism] OO [Office of Origin]: San Francisco (SF File 100A-SF-80488), which involved the destruction of a Pacific Gas and Electric Power tower in Santa Cruz County." FBI teletype, 174-SF-90788-14 (5/25/90), on file with James X. Dempsey.

17. DAVID HELVARG, THE WAR AGAINST THE GREENS 334-35 (Sierra Club Books, 1997).

18. *Id.* at 397.

19. *Id.* at 396.

20. *Id.*

21. *Id.* at 400.

22. Information about the civil lawsuit can be found at http://www.monitor.net/~bari.

23. Earth First! was not the only domestic group classified as terrorist. In 1986, the FBI opened under the domestic security/terrorism category a preliminary investigation of eleven acts of vandalism at Chicago military recruiting offices. The perpetrators had left behind leaflets referring to the Veterans Fast for Life, and one of the suspects was identified with Silo Plowshares, another anti-war group. The Chicago field office of the FBI stated in a memo to headquarters that "it does not know the size or scope of this conspiracy although preliminary indications suggest that it is probably nationwide." The case was closed within 6 months.

24. CISPES HEARINGS, *supra* note 1 to chapter 2 (statement of William Sessions, Director, FBI).

25. Associated Press, *Georgia Professor Sues For Access to FBI File*, WASH. POST, Feb. 4, 1999 at A9 (FBI agents visited a Georgia State professor in 1994 a few weeks after he invited the secretary of the Office of Cuban Interests in Washington to a symposium).

NOTES TO CHAPTER 5
MECHANISMS FOR CONTROL OF THE FBI

1. Criminal offenses are defined mainly in Title 18 of the United States Code. Drug offenses are defined in Title 21. There are other criminal provisions scattered through other titles of the federal code.

2. 18 U.S.C. §§2510 - 2522.

3. 5 U.S.C. §552.

4. *See* Bivens v. Six Unknown Named Agents of Federal Bureau of Narcotics, 403 U.S. 388 (1971). The ability of citizens to recover damages against the government for law enforcement misconduct is a complex area, well beyond the scope of this work.

5. *E.g.,* 18 U.S.C. §2384 (seditious conspiracy) and §2385 (advocating overthrow of government). The Foreign Agents Registration Act, 22 U.S.C. §§611-21, widens the scope of the criminal law to reach activities that, in the absence of the Act's registration and disclosure requirements, would be entirely lawful. JOHN T. ELLIFF, THE REFORM OF FBI INTELLIGENCE OPERATIONS 33 (Princeton Univ. Press, 1979) (hereinafter "ELLIFF").

6. Between 1987 and 1997, only three law enforcement applications to conduct wiretaps were denied by judges at the federal, state or local level; 8594 requests were granted. ADMINISTRATIVE OFFICE OF THE U.S. COURTS, 1997 WIRETAP REPORT (Washington, D.C. 1998) at p. 30, available online at http://www.uscourts.gov/wiretap/table7.pdf. For a brief description of the erosion of the protections in the wiretap laws, see James X. Dempsey, *Communications Privacy in the Digital Age: Revitalizing the Federal Wiretap Laws to Enhance Privacy*, 8 ALBANY L. J. SCI. & TECH. 65, 75-8 (1997).

7. The best source for practical information on the FOIA is ALLAN ROBERT ADLER (ED.), LITIGATION UNDER THE FEDERAL OPEN GOVERNMENT LAWS (ACLU Foundation, 1997), in its 20th edition at this time and periodically updated. The Department of Justice Office of Information and Privacy publishes a detailed volume entitled "Freedom of Information Act Guide & Privacy Act Overview" and an exhaustive "Freedom of Information Case List," both available from the Government Printing Office. The document "A Citizen's Guide to Using the Freedom of Information Act and the Privacy Act of 1974 to Request Government Records," published by the House Committee on Government Reform and Oversight, 105th Cong., is available online at http://www.fas.org/irp/congress/1997_rpt/foia.html. For case studies of how the FOIA has worked at the FBI, CIA and other agencies, *see* ATHAN THEOHARIS (ED.), A CULTURE OF SECRECY: THE GOVERNMENT VERSUS THE PEOPLE'S RIGHT TO KNOW (Univ. Press of Kansas, 1998).

8. *See generally* Chapter 7 *infra; see also* HAROLD HONGJU KOH, THE NATIONAL SECURITY CONSTITUTION (Yale Univ. Press 1990).

NOTES

9. FBI STATUTORY CHARTER: HEARINGS BEFORE THE SENATE COMM. ON THE JUDICIARY, 95th Cong. 4 (1978) (testimony of Attorney General Griffin B. Bell).

10. *See* 28 U.S.C. §§ 531 - 540A (1988). The notes accompanying these code sections contain a number of other uncodified laws governing specific details of a wide range of FBI activities, but none constitutes a significant limitation on those activities.

11. 28 U.S.C. § 533 (1988) (Attorney General may appoint investigative officials).

12. 28 U.S.C. § 534 (Attorney General shall acquire crime identification and other records).

13. 42 U.S.C. § 3744 (1988) (FBI director authorized to establish training programs).

14. 18 U.S.C. §3052.

15. Pub. L. 90-351, Title VI, §1101, 82 Stat. 236, June 19, 1968, as amended by Pub. L. 94-503, Title II, §203, 90 Stat. 2427, Oct. 15, 1976.

16. ELLIFF, *supra* note 5, at 30-32.

17. 18 U.S.C. § 2385 (advocating overthrow of government — Smith Act); 18 U.S.C. § 2386 (Voorhis Act) (1988); 50 U.S.C. §§ 781-789 (1988) (Internal Security Act of 1960 and Communist Control Act of 1964). While these laws remain on the books, their constitutionality is highly questionable, and they have not been used in many years. *See* Scales v. United States, 367 U.S. 203, 224-30 (1961) (membership clause of Smith Act which makes it felony to belong to organization which advocates overthrow of government held not to violate First or Fifth Amendments when construed to apply only to members with specific intent to further illegal ends); Yates v. United States, 354 U.S. 298, 303-11 (1957), *overruled on other grounds*, Burks v. United States, 437 U.S. 1 (1978) (convictions for conspiring to organize group advocating overthrow of government reversed — word "organize" should be strictly construed); Dennis v. United States, 341 U.S. 494, 516 (1951) (sections of Smith Act which make it crime to advocate overthrow of government do not violate First or Fifth Amendment as applied to leaders of the Communist Party).

18. 18 U.S.C. § 2384.

19. United States v. Rodriguez, 803 F.2d 318 (7th Cir. 1986), *cert. denied*, 480 U.S. 908 (1987).

20. John Mintz and Michael Grunwald, *FBI Terror Probes Focus on U.S. Muslims; Expanded Investigations, New Tactics Stir Allegations of Persecution*, WASH. POST, Oct. 31, 1998, at A1.

21. *See* 18 U.S.C. §§ 791-798 (1988) (espionage sections making it unlawful, inter alia, to harbor spies, gather defense information, and photograph defense installations).

22. "[I]f credible information comes to the FBI's attention that a group or entity is acting under the direction and control of a hostile foreign power, the FBI may initiate a counterintelligence investigation. Such an investigation could be initiated even though the activities of the group or entity do not, on their face, violate a criminal statute. ... A foreign power can be a faction or entity or other similar foreign-directed group, which definition is in [the] unclassified portion of the AG Guidelines and which is the same

as that used in the Foreign Intelligence Surveillance Act." Letter from Acting FBI Director John E. Otto to Rep. Don Edwards, June 22, 1987, *reprinted in* BREAK-INS AT SANCTUARY CHURCHES AND ORGANIZATIONS OPPOSED TO ADMINISTRATION POLICY IN CENTRAL AMERICA: HEARINGS BEFORE THE SUBCOMM. ON CIVIL AND CONSTITUTIONAL RIGHTS OF THE HOUSE JUDICIARY COMM., 104th Cong., 1st Sess. Serial No. 42 (1987) at 545. *See also supra*, chapter 2, note 17.

NOTES TO CHAPTER 6
SEVENTY-FIVE YEARS OF REFORM AND RETRENCHMENT

1. This summary is based on the extensive expositions in the report of the Church Committee, INTELLIGENCE ACTIVITIES AND THE RIGHTS OF AMERICANS, BOOK II, FINAL REPORT OF THE SENATE SELECT COMMITTEE TO STUDY GOVERNMENTAL OPERATIONS WITH RESPECT TO INTELLIGENCE ACTIVITIES, 94th Cong. (1976) (hereinafter, "CHURCH COMM. REP. BOOK II"), and FRANK J. DONNER, THE AGE OF SURVEILLANCE (Knopf 1980) (hereinafter "DONNER").

2. *See* CHURCH COMM. REP. BOOK II, *supra* note 1, at 23-67; FBI OVERSIGHT, PART 2: HEARINGS BEFORE THE SUBCOMM. ON CIVIL AND CONSTITUTIONAL RIGHTS OF THE HOUSE COMM. ON THE JUDICIARY, 94th Cong., 1st and 2d Sess. 167-68 (1976) (citing General Accounting Office, FBI Domestic Intelligence Operations-Their Purpose And Scope: Issues That Need To Be Resolved); see also Socialist Workers' Party v. Attorney Gen., 642 F. Supp. 1357, 1375-77 (S.D.N.Y. 1986) (summary of history relating to FBI's investigation of SWP). *See generally* Comment, *Ideological Exclusion, Plenary Power, and the PLO*, 77 CALIF. L. REV. 831, 837-39 (1989) (discussing Palmer Raids).

3. CHURCH COMM. REP. BOOK II, *supra* note 1, at 23.

4. *Id.*

5. *Id.* at 23-24. The first of these authorizations was oral and was reflected only in then-secret memoranda written by Hoover. It was based on the ambiguous reference in the FBI's general authorities statute to investigations of "official matters" referred by the Secretary of State. In August 1936, at Hoover's urging, Roosevelt asked Secretary of State Cordell Hull to request the FBI to undertake an investigation of "subversive activities in the United States, particularly Fascism and Communism." Hull did so, and in the succeeding years Hoover parlayed this request into approval for a permanent domestic intelligence operation. DONNER, *supra* note 1, at 52 - 60.

6. CHURCH COMM. REP. BOOK II, *supra* note 1, at 24.

7. *Id.* at 32 - 33.

8. *Id.* at 38.

9. *Id.* at 45-46.

10. *Id.* at 38.

11. SUPPLEMENTARY DETAILED STAFF REPORTS ON INTELLIGENCE ACTIVITIES AND

THE RIGHTS OF AMERICANS, BOOK III, FINAL REPORT OF THE SENATE SELECT COMMITTEE TO STUDY GOVERNMENTAL OPERATIONS WITH RESPECT TO INTELLIGENCE ACTIVITIES, 94th Cong. (1976) at 15.

12. *Id.*

13. *See generally,* RICHARD CRILEY, THE FBI V. THE FIRST AMENDMENT (First Amendment Fdn. 1990).

14. For a full description of the FBI's COINTELPRO campaign against the SWP, *see* Socialist Workers' Party v. Attorney Gen., 642 F. Supp. 1357 (S.D.N.Y. 1986).

15. CHURCH COMM. REP. BOOK III, *supra* note 11, at 3.

16. Hampton and Clark were killed in a Chicago apartment on December 4, 1969. Police raided the house, supposedly looking for weapons. The police assertions that they fired into the apartment only after someone fired out seemed to be contradicted by the physical evidence, including the fact that Hampton was killed in his bed. It later emerged that Hampton's bodyguard and chief of security for the Chicago Panthers was an FBI informant, who provided the FBI a map of the apartment. The FBI gave the map first to one local police unit, which declined to raid the apartment, and then to the one that went forward with the raid that resulted in the deaths of Hampton and Clark. "It is fair to say that the FBI was shopping around for a law enforcement unit that was willing to conduct a raid that it, the Bureau, wanted to see carried out, but had no legal pretext for staging on its own.... Taken together, the indications were that the Bureau might have tacitly encouraged the unprovoked killing of the two Black Panthers at a time when there was no legal way of pursuing them otherwise." SANFORD J. UNGAR, FBI 466 (Atlantic - Little, Brown 1975). Ungar's descriptions of the culture and methodology of the Bureau remain highly relevant. The family of Hampton successfully sued the Chicago police and the FBI.

17. *See* Senate Resolution 400, 94th Congress (the charter of the Senate Select Committee on Intelligence) (1976) and House Rule XLVIII (the charter of the House Permanent Select Committee on Intelligence). These and many other documents on the intelligence oversight process are periodically collected in a booklet by the House Intelligence Committee entitled "Compilation of Intelligence Laws and Related Laws and Executive Orders of Interest to the National Intelligence Community," available from the committee or the Government Printing Office.

18. New York Times Co. v. United States, 403 U.S. 713 (1971).

19. United States v. United States District Court, 407 U.S. 297 (1972).

20. 50 U.S.C. §1801 *et seq.*

21. *See* FBI DOMESTIC SECURITY GUIDELINES: OVERSIGHT HEARINGS BEFORE THE SUBCOMM. ON CIVIL AND CONSTITUTIONAL RIGHTS OF THE HOUSE COMM. ON THE JUDICIARY, 98th Cong. 60-66 (Levi guidelines) (1983).

22. CURT GENTRY, J. EDGAR HOOVER: THE MAN AND THE SECRETS (Penguin Plume 1991) at 594 footnote.

23. *See generally* THEOHARIS, A CULTURE OF SECRECY, *supra* chapter 5, note 7.

24. The Clinton Administration, like the Bush Administration, has continued to operate under Executive Order 12333, issued by Ronald Reagan in 1981. E.O. 12333 was published in the Federal Register on December 4, 1981, 46 Fed Reg. 59941. It is also reprinted in "Compilation of Intelligence Laws and Related Laws and Executive Orders of Interest to the National Intelligence Community" 763 (July 1995).

25. Letter from Acting FBI Director John E. Otto to Rep. Don Edwards, June 22, 1987, *reprinted in* BREAK-INS AT SANCTUARY CHURCHES AND ORGANIZATIONS OPPOSED TO ADMINISTRATION POLICY IN CENTRAL AMERICA: HEARINGS BEFORE THE SUBCOMM. ON CIVIL AND CONSTITUTIONAL RIGHTS OF THE HOUSE JUDICIARY COMM., 104th Cong., 1st Sess. 545 (1987).

26. *See* FBI DOMESTIC SECURITY GUIDELINES: OVERSIGHT HEARINGS BEFORE THE SUBCOMM. ON CIVIL AND CONSTITUTIONAL RIGHTS OF THE HOUSE COMM. ON THE JUDICIARY, 98th Cong. 60-66 (Levi guidelines), 67-85 (Smith guidelines) (1983).

27. E.O. 12333, *supra* note 24.

28. *See generally* THEOHARIS, A CULTURE OF SECRECY, *supra* chapter 5 note 7.

29. Each year, the Attorney General submits to Congress a brief letter stating the number of applications made to the FISA court in the prior year and the number of orders granted. Steven Aftergood of the Federation of American Scientists has tracked these reports for many years. Aftergood's Project on Government Secrecy is an invaluable resource on issues of intelligence agency secrecy and accountability. http://www.fas.org/sgp/.

30. 50 U.S.C. §§1821-29, added by the Intelligence Authorization Act for FY 1995, Pub. L. 103-359, 108 Stat. 3443.

31. *See* ACTIVITIES OF FEDERAL LAW ENFORCEMENT AGENTS TOWARDS THE BRANCH DAVIDIANS: JOINT HEARINGS BEFORE THE SUBCOMM. ON CRIME OF THE HOUSE JUDICIARY COMMITTEE AND THE SUBCOMM. ON NATIONAL SECURITY OF THE HOUSE COMM. ON GOVERNMENT REFORM AND OVERSIGHT, 104th Cong. (1995), and THE FEDERAL RAID ON RUBY RIDGE IDAHO: HEARINGS BEFORE THE SUBCOMMITTEE ON TERRORISM OF THE SENATE JUDICIARY COMM. 104th Cong. (1995).

32. *See* FBI DOMESTIC SECURITY GUIDELINES: OVERSIGHT HEARINGS BEFORE THE SUBCOMM. ON CIVIL AND CONSTITUTIONAL RIGHTS OF THE HOUSE COMM. ON THE JUDICIARY, 98th Cong. 60-66 (Levi guidelines), 67-85 (Smith guidelines) (1983).

33. Attorney General Thornburgh made minor changes in 1989.

34. The Privacy Act would seem to prohibit this. The Act provides that a federal agency shall —

> maintain no record describing how any individual exercises rights guaranteed by the First Amendment unless expressly authorized by statute or by the individual about whom the record is maintained or unless pertinent to and within the scope of an authorized law enforcement activity.

5 U.S.C. 552a(e)(7). The courts, however, have declined to rule FBI intelligence gathering as illegal under this provision. In Jabara v. Webster, 691 F.2d 272 (6th Cir. 1982),

the appellate court held that intelligence investigations are "law enforcement" activities within the meaning of (e)(7) and that it is not necessary to show any relationship to a specific criminal act.

35. Of course, commercially available electronic databases of news stories, such as Nexis, obviate the need for the FBI to clip and index press reports of demonstrations and meetings.

36. COMBATING DOMESTIC TERRORISM: HEARING BEFORE THE SUBCOMM. ON CRIME OF THE HOUSE JUDICIARY COMM., 104th Cong., 1st Sess. 27 (May 3, 1995) (testimony of Louis J. Freeh).

37. Jim McGee, *The Rise of the FBI*, WASH. POST MAGAZINE 10, 25 (July 20, 1997).

38. Thus both the World Trade Center bombing and the destruction of Pan Am flight 103 over Lockerbie, Scotland are international terrorist incidents. The dividing lines between domestic and international terrorism are not always clear. For example, some Jewish extremist groups in the United States have been classified as domestic terrorist groups, despite ties in Israel, while Islamic, Palestinian and other Arab groups operating in the U.S. are classified as international terrorists, subject to investigation under the more expansive foreign counterintelligence guidelines. *See, e.g.*, FBI, *Terrorism in the United States 1987.*

39. *Attorney General Guidelines for FBI Foreign Intelligence Collection & Foreign Counterintelligence Investigations* (April 1983) (a heavily redacted copy of the guidelines has been released under the FOIA, and is on file with James X. Dempsey).

40. *See* Healy v. James, 408 U.S. 169, 187 (1972); Keyishian v. Board of Regents, 385 U.S. 589, 606-07 (1967). But in Palestine Information Office v. Schultz, 853 F.2d 932, 939-42 (D.C. Cir. 1988), the federal court of appeals held that the First Amendment was not implicated by an order shutting down an office funded solely by and representing only one foreign entity. This case, however, did not approve the investigation of groups receiving domestic funding and representing domestic members.

41. The LA 8 case offers the most well-documented recent example of this approach in action. The district court concluded there that the FBI never really devoted much attention to determining whether the individuals it was investigating actually intended to support any illegal activity. Rather, the FBI proceeded on the basis of guilt by association, assuming that it was enough to link the individuals to the PFLP and to show that the PFLP engaged in terrorist violence. The court concluded that the nefarious nature of the PFLP was "irrelevant" under the First Amendment absent specific intent on the part of individuals to further the group's illegal activities. American-Arab Anti-Discrimination Committee v. Reno C.A. No. 87-2107 (C.D. Cal. Apr. 29, 1996), *reprinted in* Reno v. American-Arab Anti-Discrimination Committee, No. 97-1252 (S.Ct.), Joint Appendix.

42. CISPES AND FBI COUNTERTERRORISM INVESTIGATIONS: HEARINGS BEFORE THE SUBCOMM. ON CIVIL AND CONSTITUTIONAL RIGHTS OF THE HOUSE JUDICIARY COMM.,100th Cong., 2nd Sess., Serial No. 122 (1988) at 135 (emphasis added).

43. John Kifner, *Roots of Terror: A special report — Alms and Arms: Tactics in a Holy War*, N.Y. TIMES, March 15, 1996 at A1.

44. Airtel memorandum from Director, FBI to All SACs, "Amendments to the Attorney

General Guidelines for FBI Foreign Counterintelligence Collection and Foreign Counterintelligence Investigations (FCIG)," dated October 13, 1989, on file with James X. Dempsey.

45. *See, e.g.*, Handschu v. Special Services Div., 605 F. Supp. 1384 (S.D.N.Y. 1985), 349 F.Supp. 766 (S.D.N.Y. 1972). *See generally*, Paul G. Chevigny, *Politics and Law in the Control of Local Surveillance*, 69 CORNELL L. REV. 735 (1984).

46. Seth Rosenfeld, *FBI wants S.F. cops to join spy squad*, SAN FRANCISCO EXAMINER, Jan. 12, 1997, p.A1.

47. *Lawyer Fears Daley May Be Opening Door To Red Squad's Return*, CHICAGO TRIBUNE, Nov. 17, 1998. See Plaintiffs' brief opposing City's motion to modify decree, http://www.concentric.net/~Gutmanpc/briefinopposition.prn.

48. *See* H.R. 50, 102nd Cong., 1st Sess., 137 Cong. Rec. E69 (1991) (Edwards' floor statement). *See also* H.R. 5369, 100th Cong., 2nd Sess., 134 Cong. Rec. H8140.

49. Pub. L. 103-322, 108 Stat. 2022-23 (1994).

50. Sec. 120005 of Pub. L. 103-322, 108 Stat. 2022, adding 18 U.S.C. §2339A.

NOTES TO CHAPTER 7
CONSTITUTIONAL LIMITS — THE ROLE OF THE JUDICIARY

1. 395 U.S. 444, 447 (1969). The case involved the violent rhetoric of the Ku Klux Klan.

   Earlier in the century, the Court had upheld convictions for anti-draft speeches and for advocating the overthrow of the government by force. *See* Schenck v. United States, 249 U.S. 47 (1919) (upholding convictions for anti-war, anti-draft speeches); Debs v. United States, 249 U.S. 211 (1919) (same); and Dennis v. United States, 341 U.S. 494 (1951) (upholding conviction under Smith Act of leaders of the Communist Party in the United States). But the deferential approach reflected in these cases gradually gave way with the waning of McCarthyism to a First Amendment theory that acknowledged the value of a much broader range of anti-government speech. *See generally*, SMOLLA & NIMMER, FREEDOM OF SPEECH (Matthew Bender 1994).

2. *See, e.g.*, NAACP v. Claiborne Hardware Co., 458 U.S. 886 (1982); R.A.V. v. City of St. Paul, 505 U.S. 377 (1992).

3. Beginning with a series of cases in the 1950s and 1960s in which it overturned states' attempts to curb the activities of the National Association for the Advancement of Colored People (NAACP), the Supreme Court recognized that "[e]ffective advocacy of both public and private points of view, particularly controversial ones, is undeniably enhanced by group association." NAACP v. Alabama ex rel. Patterson, 357 U.S. 449 (1958).

   The Court over the years rejected direct and indirect attempts at curbing associational activity. In 1958, the Court held that recruiting members for a group is protected under the right of association. Staub v. City of Baxley, 355 U.S. 313 (1958) (striking down restriction on solicitation of members for unions and other organizations as violation of First Amendment). *See also* City of Watseka v. Illinois Public Action Council, 796 F.2d 1547, 1558-59 (7th Cir. 1986) (upholding award of damages for First Amendment violation based in part on organization's "inability to recruit new members").

In 1981, it held that raising and contributing money to a group is a form of "collective expression" also fully protected by the First Amendment. Citizens Against Rent Control v. Berkeley, 454 U.S. 290, 295-96 (1981). *Accord*, Federal Election Comm. v. National Conservative Political Action Comm., 470 U.S. 480, 495 (1985); Roberts v. United States Jaycees, 468 U.S. 609, 626-27 (1984) (First Amendment protects Jaycees' "fund-raising"); Village of Schaumburg v. Citizens for a Better Environment, 444 U.S. 620, 632-33 (1980) (First Amendment protects charitable solicitation of funds).

Furthermore, the Court has held that politically active groups have a right to protect their membership from scrutiny: in one of the earliest NAACP cases, the Court held that groups cannot be compelled to disclose information about their membership. NAACP v. Alabama ex rel. Patterson, 357 U.S. 449 (1958). More recently, the Court has held that there is a right to engage in political speech anonymously. McIntyre v. Ohio, 514 U.S. 334 (1995).

4.   Healy v. James, 408 U.S. 169, 186 (1972). In 1961, the Supreme Court warned against the danger "that one in sympathy with the legitimate aims of . . . an organization, but not specifically intending to accomplish them by resort to violence, might be punished for his adherence to lawful and constitutionally protected purposes, because of other and unprotected purposes which he does not necessarily share." Noto v. United States, 364 U.S. 290, 299-300 (1961). Holding that this danger of curtailing association was more serious than the threat of illegal activity, the Court ruled that in order for the government to punish an individual's association with the group, it must prove that the individual specifically intended to further the unlawful ends of the group.

Under these principles, the Court has struck down statutes barring Communist Party members from public and private employment, Keyishian v. Board of Regents, 385 U.S. 589, 606-07 (1967); Elfbrandt v. Russell, 384 U.S. 11, 17 (1966); United States v. Robel, 389 U.S. 258 (1967); ballot access, Communist Party of Indiana v. Whitcomb, 414 U.S. 441, 448-49 (1974); the right to travel abroad, Aptheker v. Secretary of State, 378 U.S. 500 (1964); and the practice of law, Baird v. State Bar of Arizona, 401 U.S. 1 (1971); Schware v. Board of Bar Examiners, 353 U.S. 232 (1957).

5.   Another major development in First Amendment protections was the Pentagon Papers case, in which the Supreme Court refused to enjoin the New York Times from publishing classified national security information. The Court's opinion set a very high presumption against prior restraints and has served to ensure that information on matters of national security, once obtained by the press, can almost always be presented to the public. New York Times Co. v. United States, 403 U.S. 713 (1971).

However, government officials who publicly disclose information that they learned through their official duties and were supposed to keep secret may be punished administratively, including being fired. Employees of the CIA and others with access to intelligence information may also be required to sign agreements that they will submit any writings, even after they leave the government, for prepublication review to ensure that no classified information is disclosed. The Supreme Court has upheld the use of such agreements as essentially just another contractual agreement, and has held that the government is entitled to forfeiture of the profits of any writings not submitted for review. Snepp v. United States, 444 U.S. 507 (1980).

6. 1999 U.S. Lexis 1514 (U.S. Feb. 23, 1999).

7. Laird v. Tatum, 408 U.S. 1 (1972).

8. Donohoe v. Duling, 465 F.2d 196 (1972). Donohoe was decided approximately one month after *Tatum*.

9. Socialist Workers Party v. Attorney General, 510 F.2d 253 (2d Cir. 1974).

10. Philadelphia Yearly Meeting of the Religious Society of Friends v. Tate, 519 F.2d 1335 (3d Cir. 1975)(approving photographing and compilation of records, but not the sharing of the information with private employers or broadcaster). *See also* Fifth Avenue Peace Parade Comm. v. Gray, 480 F.2d 326 (2d Cir. 1973). In Rizzo v. Goode, 423 U.S. 362 (1976), the Supreme Court made it more difficult for courts to control police practices in general.

11. Philadelphia Yearly Meeting of the Religious Society of Friends v. Tate, 519 F.2d at 1338-39. In a more recent case, a group of Arizona churches brought suit against the United States for conducting an undercover investigation of the sanctuary movement. Presbyterian Church v. United States, 807 F.2d 518 (9th Cir. 1989). The agents involved infiltrated four churches wearing recording devices, and recorded prayers, hymns and Bible readings while attending worship services and Bible study classes. The churches contended that the infiltration and recording of religious services violated their First Amendment rights to the free exercise of religion and association. The churches claimed concrete injury was suffered as a result, since "INS surveillance . . . chilled individual congregants from attending worship services," and that this in turn adversely affected the ability of the church to carry out its religious mission. The trial court agreed and let the case go forward.

12. Halkin v. Helms, 690 F.2d 977 (D.C. Cir. 1982).

13. Socialist Workers Party v. Attorney General, 642 F. Supp. 1357 (S.D.N.Y. 1986). The court awarded a total of $264,000 in damages and placed restrictions on the use of records illegally compiled by the FBI in the course of the investigation. With one exception, the court denied the SWP's requests for declaratory and injunctive relief because there was no prosecution or threatened activity against the SWP.

14. Similarly, in 1984, the federal court of appeals for the District of Columbia also held that the FBI's COINTELPRO campaign violated the First Amendment. The court stated:

> Government action taken with the intent to disrupt or destroy lawful organizations, or to deter membership in those groups, is absolutely unconstitutional. The Government could not constitutionally make such participation unlawful; consequently, it may not surreptitiously undertake to do what it cannot do publicly.

Hobson v. Wilson, 737 F.2d 1 (D.C. Cir. 1984), *cert. denied sub nom.* Brennan v. Hobson, 470 U.S. 1084 (1985).

15. The Alliance to End Repression is a Chicago coalition of civil liberties, civil rights and community action groups. The Chicago Committee to Defend the Bill of Rights is the Chicago affiliate of NCARL and a member of the Alliance.

16. Alliance to End Repression v. City of Chicago, 91 F.R.D. 182 (N.D. Ill. 1981).

17. Alliance to End Repression v. City of Chicago, 742 F.2d 1007 (7th Cir. 1984).

18. Alliance to End Repression v. City of Chicago, 119 F.3d 472 (7th Cir. 1997).

19. Despite the limiting interpretations imposed by the court of appeals, the settlement has remained in place and was invoked again in 1991 when the FBI undertook its interviews of Arab-Americans in Chicago near the time of the Persian Gulf war. Alliance to End Repression v. City of Chicago, 1994 U.S. Dist. LEXIS 17052 (N.D. Ill. 1994).

20. Socialist Workers Party v. Attorney General, 642 F. Supp. at 1416.

21. United States v. United States District Court, 407 U.S. 297, 320 (1972).

22. United States v. Ehrlichman, 376 F. Supp. 29 (1974), aff'd, 546 F.2d 910 (D.C. Cir. 1976), cert. denied, 429 U.S. 1120 (1977).

23. They relied on United States v. Butenko, 494 F.2d 593 (3rd Cir. 1974), cert. denied sub nom. Ivanov v. United States, 419 U.S. 881 (1974), and Zweibon v. Mitchell, 363 F. Supp. 936 (D.D.C. 1973) (both cases involving wiretapping).

24. 376 F. Supp. at 33-34.

25. Halperin v. Kissinger, 807 F.2d 180, 194 (D.C. Cir. 1986).

26. In balancing the government's interest in "self-defense" against the defendants' interest in privacy pursuant to the Fourth Amendment's guarantee of freedom from warrantless searches, the court found not only that no Fourth Amendment rights were encroached, but also that the transcripts of the alleged conversations need not be revealed to the defendants to allow them to prepare their defense. United States v. Butenko, 494 F.2d 593, 608 (3d Cir. 1974)(en banc), cert. denied sub nom. Ivanov v. United States, 419 U.S. 881 (1974). A warrantless national security wiretap was also upheld in United States v. Brown, 484 F.2d 418 (5th Cir. 1973), cert. denied, 415 U.S. 960 (1974).

   However, in Zweibon v. Mitchell, 516 F. 2d 594 (D.C. Cir. 1975), cert. denied, 425 U.S. 944 (1976), the court of appeals, in a case involving a domestic organization, questioned whether any national security exception to the warrant requirement would be permissible, concluding that "an analysis of the policies implicated by foreign security surveillance indicates that, absent exigent circumstances, all warrantless electronic surveillance is unreasonable and therefore unconstitutional."

   With the adoption of the Foreign Intelligence Surveillance Act, and its amendment in 1994 to cover physical searches, Congress mooted many aspects of the debate over a national security exception to the Fourth Amendment's warrant clause; the Act requires judicial authorization but grants to a secret court the authority to issue orders for electronic surveillance and physical searches in national security cases.

27. United States v. Aguilar, 883 F.2d 662 (9th Cir. 1989).

28. Hoffa v. United States, 385 U.S. 293 (1966).

29. 18 U.S.C. App. 3.

30. Kwong Hai Chew v. Colding, 344 U.S. 590 (1953) (holding that INS could not subject returning permanent resident alien to "summary exclusion" procedure in which INS would rely on secret evidence).

31. The INS has long claimed the authority to use secret evidence to deny discretionary relief from deportation. Jay v. Boyd, 351 U.S. 345 (1956). According to an INS statement in February 1998, it had used classified evidence in approximately 50 cases since 1992. Letter dated February 3, 1998, from INS Acting General Counsel Lori Scialabba to Gregory T. Nojeim, on file with James X. Dempsey.

32. Rafeedie v. INS, 880 F.2d 506, 516 (D.C. Cir. 1989); Rafeedie v. INS, 795 F. Supp. 13 (D.D.C. 1992) (holding unconstitutional the INS's attempt to expel a permanent resident alien on the basis of undisclosed classified information).

33. American-Arab Anti-Discrimination Comm. v. Reno, 70 F.3d 1045, 1069 (9th Cir. 1995).

34. United States ex rel. Knauff v. Shaughnessy, 338 U.S. 537, 551 (1950).

35. NAACP v. Alabama ex rel. Patterson, 357 U.S. 449 (1958).

36. NAACP v. Button, 371 U.S. 415 (1963).

NOTES TO CHAPTER 8
PROLOGUE TO THE 1996 ANTITERRORISM ACT

1. Omnibus Counterterrorism Act of 1995, H.R. 896, 104th Cong. (1995); Omnibus Counterterrorism Act of 1995, S. 390, 104th Cong. (1995).

2. These last-mentioned provisions were dropped from the Antiterrorism Act, although the posse comitatus changes were enacted later in 1996 on another bill and the roving wiretap changes were adopted in 1998, as discussed below in chapter 10.

3. 18 U.S.C. §2339A, as added by Pub. L. 103-322, §120005, 108 Stat. 2022.

4. INTERNATIONAL TERRORISM: THREATS AND RESPONSES: HEARINGS BEFORE THE HOUSE COMM. ON THE JUDICIARY, 104th Cong., 1st Sess. (1995) (hereinafter "FULL COMMITTEE HEARINGS").

5. COMBATING DOMESTIC TERRORISM, HEARINGS BEFORE THE SUBCOMM. ON CRIME OF THE HOUSE COMM. ON THE JUDICIARY, 104th Cong., 1st Sess., Serial no. 52 (1995) (hereinafter "COMBATING TERRORISM HEARINGS").

6. *Id.* at 88.

7. *Id.* at 46.

8. FULL COMMITTEE HEARINGS, *supra* note 4, at 57-59.

9.   *Id.* at 65, 72-74, 475.

10.   COMBATING TERRORISM HEARINGS, *supra* note 5.

11.   On May 15, 1995, Rep. Richard A. Gephardt introduced H.R. 1635, embodying the Clinton Administration's reaction to the Oklahoma City bombing. On May 25, Judiciary Committee Chairman Henry J. Hyde introduced his own bill, H.R. 1710, which narrowed the scope of Clinton's proposal in some areas while widening it in others.

NOTES TO CHAPTER 9
THE ANTITERRORISM ACT'S CENTRAL PROVISIONS

1.   Pub. L. No. 104-132, 110 Stat. 1214.

2.   18 U.S.C. §2339B (Supp. II 1996), as added by Section 303 of the Antiterrorism Act, 110 Stat. 1250.

3.   Section 411(1) of the Act, amending 8 U.S.C. §1182(a)(3)(B) (Supp. II 1996) to add a new subclause, "is a member of a foreign terrorist organization, as designated by the Secretary ... ."

4.   Grounds for exclusion or inadmissibility are codified at 8 U.S.C. §1182 (1994 & Supp. II 1996). Grounds for deportation or removal are codified at 8 U.S.C. §1227 (Supp. II 1996). The two are interrelated, for a person is deportable (subject to removal) if she was inadmissible at the time of her entry to the United States. 8 U.S.C. §1227 (a)(1)(A) (Supp. II 1996).

Subsequent to the enactment of the 1996 Antiterrorism Act, Congress passed the Illegal Immigration Reform and Immigrant Responsibility Act ("IIRIRA"), Pub. L. No. 104-208, 110 Stat. 3009, which substantially rewrote the immigration laws. IIRIRA replaced the concept of "exclusion" with "inadmissibility," and the concept of "deportation" with "removal," but we use both the old and the new terms here. For a description of the IIRIRA and for more information about immigration law in general, *see* CHARLES GORDON, STANLEY MAILMAN, AND STEPHEN YALE-LOEHR, IMMIGRATION LAW AND PROCEDURE (Matthew Bender, rev. 1998).

5.   Section 401 of the Antiterrorism Act, adding a new Title V to the Immigration and Nationality Act, 8 U.S.C. §1531 *et seq.* (Supp. II 1996).

6.   See footnote 27, infra.

7.   The effects and constitutionality of these habeas provisions are beyond the scope of this treatment. The Supreme Court has begun to sort out their statutory and constitutional implications. *See, e.g.,* Stewart v. Martinez-Villareal, 118 S.Ct. 1618 (1998) (Antiterrorism Act habeas provisions did not bar review of prisoner's claim that he could not be executed because he was insane); Williams v. Taylor, 163 F.3d 860 (4th Cir, 1998), *cert. granted,* No. 98-8384 (April 5, 1999).

8.   The Act's other immigration law changes are not even nominally related to terrorism. Most notable is a provision that severely curtails the ability to claim political asylum,

by requiring an undocumented alien entering the U.S. to be immediately sent back to the country he is fleeing unless he can prove, at the border inspection point, a credible fear of political persecution. 8 U.S.C. §1225 (Supp. II 1996), as amended by Sec. 421 of the Antiterrorism Act.

The Act also changed immigration law by making aliens who enter the U.S. without inspection (e.g., aliens who did not enter at border crossings) subject to removal by exclusion rather than deportation. 8 U.S.C. §1251 (Supp. II 1996), as amended by Sec. 414 of the Act. In the past, aliens once in the U.S. were entitled to greater procedural protections. Under the changes brought about by the Act, aliens who enter without inspection are treated as if they never entered at all: they are treated like other applicants for admission, even if they have been in the U.S. for many years.

The Act's effect on habeas challenges to deportation proceedings has been the subject of several appellate opinions. *See* Sandoval v. Reno, 1999 U.S. App. Lexis 989 (3rd Cir. 1999), and cases cited therein.

9. Written testimony of Mary A. Ryan, Assistant Sec. for Consular Affairs, Dept. of State, before the Subcomm. on International Law, Immigration and Refugees of the House Judiciary Comm., Feb. 23, 1994, at 7. *See also* written testimony of Chris Sale, INS, *id.*, at 9.

10. Designation of Foreign Terrorist Organizations, 62 Fed. Reg. 52650 (Oct. 8, 1997), discussed below in chapter 10. *See also* Treasury Department regulations, 62 Fed. Reg. 67729 (Dec. 30, 1997), *codified at* 31 C.F.R. ch. V; Executive Order 13099, 63 Fed. Reg. 45167 (Aug. 25, 1998).

11. 18 U.S.C. §2339B (Supp. II 1996), as added by Section 303 of the Antiterrorism Act, 110 Stat. 1250.

12. 8 U.S.C. §1182(a)(3)(B)(i)(V), as added by Section 411 of the Antiterrorism Act, 110 Stat. 1268.

13. 8 U.S.C. §1189(b), as added by Section 302 of the Antiterrorism Act.

14. 8 U.S.C. §1189(a)(8), as added by Section 302 of the Antiterrorism Act.

15. 18 U.S.C. §2339B, as added by Section 303 of the Antiterrorism Act, provides:

Whoever, within the United States or subject to the jurisdiction of the United States, knowingly provides material support or resources to a foreign terrorist organization, or attempts or conspires to do so, shall be fined under this title or imprisoned not more than 10 years, or both.

16. 18 U.S.C. §2339A (Supp. II 1996).

17. 18 U.S.C. §2339A(c) (1994) (repealed 1996), as added by Pub. L. 103-322, §120005, 108 Stat. 2022.

18. Elfbrandt v. Russell, 384 U.S. 11 (1966).

19. In 1987, Congress adopted a temporary provision limiting exclusion and deportation based solely on political activities. The new provision stated that no alien could be denied a visa, excluded from the United States or deported because of past, current or expected beliefs, statements or associations which would be protected by the

Constitution if engaged in by a U.S. citizen in the U.S. Foreign Relations Authorization Act for Fiscal Years 1988 and 1989, Pub. L. No. 100-204, §901, 101 Stat. 1331; Foreign Operations, Export Financing, and Related Programs Act, 1989, Pub. L. No. 100-461, §555, 102 Stat. 2268.

At the same time, the courts, recognizing the adverse impact of ideological exclusions on the First Amendment rights of U.S. citizens who wanted to hear the views of controversial speakers, had begun to question the constitutionality of ideological exclusions. *See* Allende v. Schultz, 845 F.2d 1111 (1st Cir. 1988); Abourezk v. Reagan, 785 F.2d 1043 (D.C. Cir. 1986), *aff'd by an equally divided Court*, 484 U.S. 1 (1987).

Later in 1996, the exclusion provisions were further expanded by Pub. L. 104-208, §342(a)(2), 110 Stat. 3009, which added a new subsection (a)(3)(B)(i)(III) to 18 U.S.C. §1182, making inadmissible any alien who has, "under circumstances indicating an intention to cause death or serious bodily harm, incited terrorist activity."

20. 8 U.S.C. §1182(a)(3)(B)(i)(IV), as amended by Section 411 of the Antiterrorism Act.

21. *See* Title IV of the Antiterrorism Act, adding a new title V to the Immigration and Nationality Act, codified at 8 U.S.C. §1531 (Supp. II 1996) *et seq.*

22. The definition is convoluted, at best, and is not directly linked to the Secretary of State's designation of "foreign terrorist organizations." The definition of alien terrorist in the removal provision, 8 U.S.C. §1531(1), refers to 8 U.S.C. §1227(a)(4)(B), which in turn refers to 8 U.S.C. §1182(a)(3)(B)(iii). That latter section states that "engage in terrorist activity" means "to commit ... an act of terrorist activity or an act which the actor knows, or reasonably should know, affords material support to any individual, organization, or government in conducting a terrorist activity." The INS, however, has taken the position that this definition encompasses any providing of material support to an organization that has engaged in terrorism, even if the support is intended to be used, and is in fact used, only for lawful humanitarian or political ends.

23. 8 U.S.C. §1534(e)(3), as added by Sec. 401 of the Antiterrorism Act, 110 Stat. 1262.

24. Compare this standard with the one under Sec. 6(c) of the Classified Information Procedures Act, which permits the substitution of a summary for classified evidence only if the summary "provide[s] the defendant with substantially the same ability to make his defense as would disclosure of the specific classified information." 18 U.S.C. App. 3 (1994).

25. 8 U.S.C. §1534(e)(1), as added by Sec. 401 of the Antiterrorism Act, 110 Stat. 1262. The Foreign Intelligence Surveillance Act has a set of procedures intended to balance the rights of individuals against the national security. Those procedures include a requirement that the government give a defendant notice when it intends to use information from a FISA wiretap and allow the defendant to move to suppress the evidence if it was obtained illegally. The Antiterrorism Act makes such provisions, which have been followed in the most serious criminal espionage cases, inapplicable in deportation cases against "alien terrorists."

26. 8 U.S.C. §1536, as added by Sec. 401 of the Antiterrorism Act, 110 Stat. 1265. Once the court has ruled that an alien is deportable, the Attorney General, if she finds it appropriate in view of the foreign policy of the United States, may send the alien to any country willing to receive him or her, including a country where the alien may

face torture or death. If no country is willing to receive a noncitizen ordered deported under the new provisions, the Act states that "the Attorney General may, notwithstanding any other provision of law, retain the alien in custody." Any alien in custody pursuant to this provision "shall be released from custody solely at the discretion of the Attorney General."

27. Kwong Hai Chew v. Colding, 344 U.S. 590 (1953); Rafeedie v. INS, 880 F.2d 506 (D.C.Cir. 1989), *later proceeding*, 795 F. Supp. 13 (D.D.C. 1992); American-Arab Anti-Discrimination Comm. v. Reno, 70 F.3d 1045 (9th Cir. 1995); Al Najjar v. Reno, 97 F. Supp. 2d 1329 (S.D. Fla. 2000), *vacated as moot*, 2001 U.S.App. LEXIS 25304 (11th Cir. 2001); Kiareldeen v. Reno, 71 F. Supp. 2d 402 (D.N.J. 1999).

NOTES TO CHAPTER 10
THE IMPACT OF THE ACT AND ITS CORE CONCEPTS

1. *See generally* David Cole, *Secrecy, Guilt by Association, and the Terrorist Profile*, 15 JOURNAL OF LAW AND RELIGION 267 (2001); John Mintz and Michael Grunwald, *FBI Terror Probes Focus on U.S. Muslims*, WASH. POST, Oct. 31, 1998, at A1; Ronald Smothers, *Secret Data and Hidden Accusers Used Against Some Immigrants*, N.Y.TIMES, Aug. 15, 1998, at A1.

2. *2nd Presidential Debate Between Gov. Bush and Vice President Gore* (Tr. of Oct. 11, 2000 Presidential Debate), N.Y.TIMES, Oct. 12, 2000, at A23.

3. See William Glaberson, *U.S.Asks to Use Secret Evidence in Many Cases of Deportation*, N.Y.TIMES, Dec. 9, 2001, at B1.

4. It is not entirely clear why the government has failed to use the removal procedures of the 1996 Act. One reason may be that the 1996 Act's procedures require the government to provide to the alien facing deportation at least a summary of the evidence against him, and the government has sought to avoid even that limited concession to due process.

Second, alien terrorist removal proceedings under the Antiterrorism Act would take place before a federal judge who would have the authority to rule immediately on a constitutional challenge to the use of secret evidence. By invoking other provisions of the Immigration and Nationality Act, the government instead has brought its cases before immigration judges who could not declare the procedures unconstitutional. In this way, the INS was able to avoid for years constitutional review of its secret evidence theories.

A third reason may arise from the fact that the secret evidence procedures under the 1996 Act apply only to someone who is an "alien terrorist," which the law defines as someone who "has engaged, is engaged, or at any time after admission engages in any terrorist activity." (The definitions section of the removal provision, 8 U.S.C. §1531(1) (Supp. II 1996), refers to 8 U.S.C. §1227(a)(4)(B) (Supp. II 1996), which in turn refers to 8 U.S.C. §1182(a)(3)(B)(iii) (Supp. II 1996).) The definitions of "engage in" and "terrorist activity" do not encompass mere membership, and before the 2001 USA PATRIOT Act, they clearly did not include fundraising for peaceful political and humanitarian activities.

Therefore, ironically, the secret evidence procedures Congress adopted in 1996 did not cover many of the aliens against whom the government sought to use secret evidence, for the cases generally involved mere membership and/or fundraising for peaceful activities.

5. Immigration law has recognized a distinction between the use of secret evidence as the basis for deportation, and the use of secret evidence to oppose discretionary relief such as suspension of deportation, adjustment of status, or asylum, which are forms of relief from deportation normally available to aliens. Prior to the enactment of the "alien terrorist removal" provisions in the 1996 Antiterrorism Act, there was no statutory authority to use secret evidence in deportation proceedings. However, even prior to the Act, the government claimed the authority to use secret evidence to deny certain relief to aliens it was seeking to deport on the basis of technical violations. In those cases, the secret evidence was used not to support the deportation itself, but to deny relief that would otherwise block the deportation, like asylum. The law has further drawn a distinction between "discretionary" relief, such as asylum, adjustment of status or suspension of deportation, and "mandatory" relief, such as withholding of deportation and amnesty. The Supreme Court has allowed the use of secret evidence to deny discretionary relief, although it has never squarely ruled on its constitutionality. It has never accepted the use of secret evidence to deny mandatory relief, and the only lower court to address that issue has barred the use of secret evidence. American-Arab Anti-Discrimination Comm. v. Reno, 70 F.3d 1045 (9th Cir. 1995). See also testimony of Walter D. Cadman, INS, before the Subcomm. on Technology, Terrorism and Government Information of the Senate Judiciary Comm., Feb. 24, 1998, and letter from INS Acting General Counsel Lois Scialabba to Greg Nojeim of the ACLU, Feb. 3, 1998, on file with James X. Dempsey. In another 1996 statute, the Illegal Immigration Reform and Immigrant Responsibility Act, Congress for the first time expressly authorized use of secret evidence to oppose discretionary "relief from removal." See 8 U.S.C. 1229 a (b) (4) (B).

6. Mintz and Grunwald, *supra* note 1.

7. William Branigin, *Secret U.S. Evidence Entangles Immigrants; Rarely Used Law Now Falls Most Heavily on Arabs*, WASH. POST, Oct. 19, 1997, at A1.

8. Matter of Al Najjar, No. A-26-599-077 (U.S. Imm. Ct. Oct. 27, 2000) (Decision of Immigration Judge) All of the quotes in the following two paragraphs are from this decision.

9. Ronald Smothers, *Secret Data and Hidden Accusers Used Against Some Immigrants*, N.Y. TIMES, Aug. 15, 1998, at A1.

10. Matter of Kiareldeen, A77-025-332, slip op. 15 (U.S. Immgr. Ct. Apr. 2, 1999) (Dec. of Immgr. J.).

11. Matter of Kiareldeen, No. A77-025-332, slip dissent 1 (BIA June 29, 1999) (Moscato, J., dissenting to Dec. Denying Request to Lift Stay of Release Order).

12. *Id.* at 1-2. The other two judges on this panel declined to lift the stay of Kiareldeen's release order pending appeal, but did not dispute Judge Moscato's characterization of the evidence.

13. Tim Weiner, *6 Iraqis Who Aided C.I.A. Are Ordered Deported From U.S.*, N.Y. TIMES, Mar. 11, 1998, at A1.

14. R. James Woolsey, *Iraqi Dissidents Railroaded By U.S.*, WALL STREET JOURNAL, June 10, 1998, at A18.

15. Id.

16. James Risen, *Evidence to Deny 6 Iraqis Asylum May Be Weak, Files Show*, N.Y. TIMES, Oct. 13, 1998, at A9; Patrick J. McDonnell, *New Files Cast Doubt on Case Against 6 Iraqis*, L.A. TIMES, Aug. 10, 1998, at B1; Vernon Loeb, *Iraqis Detained on Flawed Data, Lawyers Say*, WASH. POST, July 19, 1998, at A16.

17. Vernon Loeb, *Iraqi Dissidents' American Dream — and Nightmare*, WASH. POST, Dec. 28, 2000 at A1; Dan Weikel, INS Judge Frees Iraqi Dissident Held for 4 Years, L.A. TIMES, Aug. 19, 2000.

18. The first list of 30 "foreign terrorist organizations" was issued by the Secretary of State in October 1997. 62 Fed. Reg. 52650. It included old and new groups, some nearly defunct, others that enjoy major support. Eight of the groups are based in the Middle East and support Palestinian and/or Islamic causes. Four in Algeria, Egypt and Iran support Islamic causes. Two in Israel are radical Zionist groups. The remaining sixteen are spread throughout the world. Dozens, if not hundreds, of groups who have engaged in violent activity in recent years as part of a political movement were not on the list.

19. The delay in issuing the list angered advocates of the Antiterrorism Act, who harshly criticized the government for dragging its feet in the fight against terrorism. "We are bitterly disappointed that … the administration has failed to designate a single foreign terrorist organization — even the most obvious and deadly ones," said an official of the Anti-Defamation League of B'nai B'rith. Benjamin Wittes, *Anti-Terrorism Act: Rhetoric vs. Reality*, LEGAL TIMES, Jun. 2, 1997, at 1.

Under a separate, earlier law, the State Department is required to report annually on terrorism groups. In 1998, when it issued its report on terrorism, following the designation of the first 30 groups, the State Department included additional groups, but these additional groups were not designated for purposes of the Antiterrorism Act. The State Department report is available at http://www.state.gov/www/global/terrorism/1997Report/1997index.html

Under separate authority, the President has designated by Executive Order certain foreign terrorist organizations with whom it is illegal to have financial transactions. The designation came in the form of a declaration of a state of emergency initially issued in January 1995, and renewed each year since, in the name of dealing with the threat that terrorism poses to the Middle East peace process. 63 Fed. Reg. 3445 (Jan. 22, 1998), continuing Executive Order 12947 (Jan. 23, 1995). In August 1998, the President issued Executive Order 13099, amending E.O. 12947 to add Osama bin Laden and his Islamic Army. 63 Fed. Reg. 45167 (Aug. 25, 1998). The list issued by the Secretary of State and that issued by the President are combined in the regulations of the Treasury Department's Office of Foreign Assets Control, Appendix A to 31 C.F.R. Chapter V. The Executive Order freezes the assets of designated foreign terrorists and organizations, if such assets are in the United States or under the control of U.S. persons in the U.S. or abroad. It additionally bans dealings or transactions in the property of such terrorists by U.S. persons.

20. The plaintiffs also challenged the Act on other grounds, arguing that it invited view-

point discrimination by the Secretary of State because it provided her with unrestricted discretion to designate an organization as terrorist. This open-ended standard allows the Secretary to target supporters of politically disfavored groups. In addition, the plaintiffs contended the Act was impermissibly vague by failing to define "material support or resources" and "national security," such that citizens will not understand what conduct is prohibited, and government officials are free to enforce the Act in an arbitrary and discriminatory manner. Memorandum of Points and Authorities in Support of Plaintiffs' Motion for Preliminary Injunction (May 11, 1998) in Humanitarian Law Project v. Reno (C.A. No. 98-1971) (C.D.Cal.).

21. Humanitarian Law Project v. Reno, No. 98-56062 (9th Cir. March 3, 2000).

22. Trial Transcript, Feb. 18, 1998, in Nasher Ltd. v. Crestar Bank, Civil Action No. 98-227-A (hereinafter "Nasher Ltd."), p. 9.

23. Preliminary Injunction, Feb. 27, 1998, in Nasher Ltd., *supra* note 19.

24. Trial Transcript, Nasher Ltd. supra note 19, at 15; Government's Brief in Opposition to Plaintiff's Motion for Preliminary Injunction), Feb. 26, 1998, p. 4 ("At no time has OFAC instructed Crestar Bank to block the account pursuant to the Act ... [or] made an affirmative demand for a report").

25. Trial Transcript, Nasher Ltd., *supra* note 19, at 15-16.

26. Mintz and Grunwald, *supra* note 1.

27. 10 U.S.C. §382, added by Sec. 1416 of Pub. L. 104-201.

28. Sec. 604 of Pub. L. 105-272, 112 Stat. 2396, 2413, amending 18 U.S.C. §2518(11)(b).

29. Sec. 601-602 of Pub. L. 105-272, 112 Stat. 2396, 2404, amending the Foreign Intelligence Surveillance Act to add a new Title IV (pen registers and trap and trace devices) and a new Title V (access to certain business records). A pen register is a device that records the dialed numbers identifying outgoing calls on a surveilled line; a trap and trace device identifies the number of origin of incoming calls on a surveilled line.

30. FOREIGN TERRORISTS IN AMERICA: FIVE YEARS AFTER THE WORLD TRADE CENTER BOMBING, HEARING BEFORE THE SENATE JUDICIARY SUBCOMMITTEE ON TERRORISM, TECHNOLOGY AND GOVERNMENT INFORMATION, 105th Cong., 2d Sess. (1998).

NOTES TO CHAPTER II
FIGHTING A WAR AGAINST TERRORISM,
AT HOME AND ABROAD

1. Pub. L. No. 107-56.

2. NAACP v. Claiborne Hardware Co., 458 U.S. 886 (1982).

3. PATRIOT Act, Section 411. The Act defines as a deportable offense the solicitation

of members or funds for, or the provision of material support to, any group designated as terrorist. There is no defense available for those who can show that their support had no connection to furthering terrorism. The government is free to designate any organization that uses or threatens to use violence as terrorist. In addition, the law makes aliens who support even nondesignated groups deportable if the group has engaged in violence, unless the alien can show that he neither knew nor reasonably should have known that his support would further the group's violent activity.

4. *See, e.g.*, Scales v. United States, 367 U.S. 203 (1961); United States v. Robel, 389 U.S. 258, 262 (1967); Keyishian v. Board of Regents, 385 U.S. 589, 606 (1967).

5. PATRIOT Act, Section 412.

6. United States v. Salerno, 481 U.S. 739, 746-47 (1987).

7. The Supreme Court recently held that even aliens who have been finally ordered deported have a constitutionally protected liberty interest in remaining free, and that the INS's authority to detain them is therefore limited. Zadvydas v. Davis, 121 S. Ct. 2491 (2001).

8. County of Riverside v. McLaughlin, 500 U.S. 44 (1991).

9. United States v. Salerno, 481 U.S. 739.

10. PATRIOT Act, Section 411.

11. PATRIOT Act, Section 218, amending 50 U.S.C. §§ 1804(a)(7)(B) and 1823(a)(7)(B).

12. 50 U.S.C. §1801 et seq.

13. PATRIOT Act, Section 213, amending 18 U.S.C. §3103a.

14. A copy of this manual is available at http://www.cdt.org/security/011030doj.

15. The prohibition is now codified in 50 U.S.C. §403-3(d)(1).

16. Fed. R. Crim. P. 6(e).

17. PATRIOT Act, Section 203.

18. PATRIOT Act, Section 203(a), incorporates by reference the definition of "foreign intelligence" contained in 50 U.S.C. §401a.

19. PATRIOT Act, Section 215, amending 50 U.S.C. §§1862 and 1863.

20. Stuart Taylor, *Never Say Never*, LEGAL TIMES, Sept. 24, 2001 at 70.

21. Craig v. Boren, 429 U.S. 190 (1976).

22. Malcolm Gladwell, writing in The New Yorker shortly after September 11, argued that it is cognitively impossible to remain alert in reviewing metal detectors at airports, because the fact that the vast majority of luggage will pose no threat inevitably causes the security personnel to let their guard down.

23. Whitney v. California, 274 U.S. 357, 375 (1927).

NOTES TO CHAPTER 12
CONCLUSION

1. INTELLIGENCE ACTIVITIES AND THE RIGHTS OF AMERICANS, BOOK II, FINAL REPORT OF THE SENATE SELECT COMMITTEE TO STUDY GOVERNMENTAL OPERATIONS WITH RESPECT TO INTELLIGENCE ACTIVITIES 289 (1976).

2. A useful discussion of this and many other issues involving terrorism and civil liberties can be found in PHILIP B. HEYMANN, TERRORISM AND AMERICA (MIT Press, 1998). This sensitive book serves as a commendable response to the calls of many for substantial curtailment of civil liberties in the name of fighting terrorism. Heymann argues that the current counterintelligence approach of the FBI, properly managed, would produce no intolerable limitations on the First Amendment.

3. Matthew L. Wald, *Tests Show Holes in Airline Security*, N.Y. TIMES, Jan. 11, 1999, at A1.

4. James Risen and Benjamin Weiser, *Before Bombings, Omens and Fears*, N.Y. TIMES, Jan. 9, 1999, at A1.